Y0-BVN-663

Paradox—The Next Strategic Dimension

Paradox—The Next Strategic Dimension

USING CONFLICT TO RE-ENERGIZE YOUR BUSINESS

Jane McKenzie

McGRAW-HILL BOOK COMPANY

London · New York · St Louis · San Francisco · Auckland
Bogotá · Caracas · Lisbon · Madrid · Mexico
Milan · Montreal · New Delhi · Panama · Paris · San Juan
São Paulo · Singapore · Sydney · Tokyo · Toronto

Published by
McGRAW-HILL Book Company Europe
Shoppenhangers Road, Maidenhead, Berkshire SL6 2QL, England
Telephone 01628 23432
Fax 01628 770224

British Library Cataloguing in Publication Data
McKenzie, Jane
    Paradox: Next Strategic Dimension — Using
    Conflict to Re-energize Your Business
    I. Title
    658.402

    ISBN 0-07-709165-5

Library of Congress Cataloging-in-Publication Data
McKenzie, Jane.
    Paradox–the next strategic dimension : using conflict to re-
    energize your business / Jane McKenzie.
        p.   cm.
    Includes bibliographical references and index.
    ISBN 0-07-709165-5 (hardback : alk. paper)
    1. Reengineering (Management)   2. Organizational change-
    -Management.   I. Title.
    HD58.87.M38   1996
    658.4'063–dc20   95-43633
                                                                              CIP

McGraw-Hill
A Division of The McGraw-Hill Companies

12345 BL 9876

Typeset by Keyword Typesetting Services Ltd
and printed and bound in Great Britain by Biddles Ltd, Guildford, Surrey

Printed on permanent paper in compliance with ISO Standard 9706.

Contents

Introduction

This book was written for revolutionaries. People, like me, who have become dissatisfied with the limitations of conventional management techniques that never seem quite adequate for the complexity of real life situations. Revolutions usually start with someone challenging some pretty fundamental assumptions about the way things are; there follows a period of conflict and tension, designed to generate the sort of disruption that will lead eventually to a new regime and better conditions for everyone. This is precisely what this book sets out to do in the context of business management.

It starts with an unequivocal challenge to some of the most basic 'givens' of the Western business world—capitalism, strategy and profit. Each has serious limitations. Together, they are a recipe for disaster for three reasons; they encourage tunnel vision, they are too simplistic and too exclusive. Radical statements indeed, but bear with me for a moment. Just try to stick with the tension that such statements may have already stirred up. This book is about the creative use of conflict to re-energize your outlook on business management. I encourage you, whenever you find something that you don't agree with in this book, to use the tension that provocation creates, constructively. Use it as a stimulus to look beyond the narrow confines of a comfortable business philosophy. Don't reject, re-evaluate. Ask yourself, how can both opinions exist simultaneously and be correct. I am not saying that capitalism, strategy or profit are bad *per se*. In fact, I know that they make a valuable contribution to the way we all live. These drivers are not wrong, just incomplete. My point is simply that there are always two sides to every argument. The problem is that people naturally feel more comfortable with one idea, and so see only the bad side of the alternative that does not fit their mental picture.

Unfortunately, it is human nature to want a peaceful life, so we often try to avoid conflicts of interests, whether they be interpersonal or just in the mind. People prefer the comfort of the known, so they hide behind prejudice, predetermined rules and functional barriers to protect themselves from the complexity of ever-changing reality. The trouble is that the differences of opinion don't go away, they just go underground and eventually subvert the effectiveness of our original choice. Unfortunately, when so many organizations are boldly setting out into the unknown, along the road to Re-engineering and business transformation, it is likely to be a rough ride if we try to hold on tightly to our business preconceptions and prejudices.

There is no denying, radical change is a frightening and painful prospect, without some framework against which to orient oneself. This book uses conflict as the central focus of such an orientation process. Having challenged the status quo, it then explores some of the most frequently occurring conflicts in business management—is strategy top down direction or a collection of successful bottom up initiatives? Is successful competition a function of forward planning or random opportunism? Can we plan for the unknown? Should we take decisions that optimize added value for the whole company or satisfy the requirements of various local constituencies? How does the organization fit into society, and how does society influence the way businesses can organize themselves? Finally how can we as managers provide stability, and yet be at the forefront of change? These are basic dilemmas that managers face every day, and they are implicit in almost every decision. Of course there is no one magic answer to these questions, but there are some simple guiding principles that will help managers resolve their dilemma in their own unique fashion. In fact, when companies reconcile their most important conflicts, transformation will occur spontaneously. Dilemma resolution offers an alternative regime to guide change management.

In total there are 15 important paradoxes covered in this book. Five top level dilemmas, that control the main strategic business drivers and 10 underlying frictions, which if left unmanaged will slow the repetitive cycles of change. Three years of research have shown that these dilemmas apply to decision making on many levels, and to a wide variety of industries. The dilemmas have been turned into the diagnostic questionnaire contained in Appendix A. This will allow you to profile the personality of your company, business unit, department or team along the paradoxical dimensions. Further research has shown that bottom line performance is intimately linked to how well a business scores in reconciling these dilemmas. The evidence is presented in the second section of the book.

Why should paradox management be effective? Two reasons. It brings the most fundamental prejudices out in the open, and so attacks one of the key change inhibitors and benefit degraders that often remain hidden and unmanaged. Then it puts the arguments into a framework designed to stimulate creativity and learning, both of which are necessary to drive the revolution forward. Dilemmas are a way to encapsulate and manage the ever-present value differences in our business world. Conflict resolution harnesses the energy inherent in differences of opinion.

Business is a dynamic interactive system, that cannot be divorced from a larger societal system; both face similar management challenges; both exhibit many of the symptoms of natural Chaos in the way they operate—conflict, turbulence, unpredictability and large scale upheaval following on from apparently small events. These are the conditions that any new management process must address. They are also the common denominators of Chaos. Mother Nature has spent a millennia perfecting a method for managing Chaos. Scientists have named this the Fractal Order.

In the process of developing this work, I have drawn on Nature's template for Chaos management to help develop a framework that emulates the effectiveness of fractals. As such, the paradoxical technique is designed to allow infinite variety in finite form, but still provide a quantifiable order to the disorderly process of transformational change.

To counteract the tunnel visioned, simplistic and exclusive aspects of conventional management ideas, the model described in this book is far-reaching, complex and multi-faceted. It can be used in many ways, to:

- Identify which strategic drivers need most attention at the outset of a change programme, by profiling the organizational character.
- Stimulate creative thinking on how to change, through the use of associated analogies and metaphors, to resolve each paradox.
- Encourage the development of the appropriate corporate qualities essential to the new organizational design.
- Provide guidance as to the sort of manual and electronic tools and techniques that can help develop a more balanced corporate character profile.
- Monitor and measure progress along the most important strategic dimensions, during the change process, through the use of a derivative diagnostic.
- Give a finite structure to the decision making process across all levels of the organization, without inhibiting variety.
- Help maintain the momentum of change initiatives, by feedback loops that encourage learning.
- Provide a forward looking indicator that has a demonstrable and tangible association with ultimate bottom line performance.

But the success of all of these opportunities depends on input from you, the reader. My hope is that the ideas in this book will show you a different angle on the management process and help you think more creatively and more comprehensively about the alternatives before you.

Part 1
THE CONCEPT OF
PARADOXICAL
MANAGEMENT

Challenging management by grand design

As strategy has blossomed, the competitiveness
of Western companies has withered.
This may be coincidence, but we think not.
Hamel and Prahalad, 1989[1]

1.1 Introduction

It is an onerous job being a manager. Managing is a complex process and it is getting more complicated by the year. There was a time when it was sufficient to have a vision of excellence, supported by a rational strategy for survival and growth over the next five to ten years. Businesses were encouraged to follow some Grand Design—a strategic prescription for the best fit between environmental, cultural and physical resources. Unfortunately, that approach no longer works. A bold statement, but perhaps not unjustifiable. Think how difficult it is to collect accurate and reliable input for a long term plan. In these days of partnering, outsourcing and globalization, key information is widely dispersed among many independent players. Once you get the data, even playing the percentages, the number of variables involved and the uncertainty surrounding each one makes accurate prediction impossible. Add to that the relentless pace of change, both social and technological, and it is almost guaranteed that the analysis will be out of date before the plan is committed to paper.

Rapid change, uncertainty and complexity have become a way of life in the 1990s. This is reflected in three new management themes of this decade. The application of Chaos theory to business; the idea of IT-enabled transformation or Re-engineering; and the concept of the learning organization. Each of them focuses on a different aspect of change, but ultimately they all contain the same basic message. Traditional management philosophies of the 1970s and 1980s can no longer solve the problems of today's business world; we need to be radically rethinking our approach to management.

This chapter will take a look at both the old and the new, to see whether they are mutually exclusive or whether they *all* have an important contribution to make. Is it time to abandon conventional management principles? Considering some of the spectacular failures they have produced, it might seem desirable, but first we should stop and ask why they failed. Are the new ideologies any better? If so which one should we choose? From experience we know that there is no universal panacea.

Every one of the remedies will have some unpleasant side effects. So what is the solution? In the following pages we will review the most popular electives to focus on—capitalism, profit, strategy, Re-engineering and learning are all recommended solutions. Unfortunately, we shall find them all wanting, *in isolation*. Yet, the final section of this chapter suggests one possible answer; don't choose, synthesize. A moderate dose of each nostrum might be the best way to get fit enough to cope with the hazards of the current business environment.

1.2   The business climate—a legacy of failed processes?

> How products are made and designed must, in the end, depend on how the social systems creating those products are made and designed. Lonely, ugly and adversarial relationships will result in badly fitting assemblies of junk that shake apart when used—not a bad description of certain American and British automobiles in the recent period of decline.
>
> Hampden Turner, 1990[2]

Organizations and their management cannot be examined in isolation. Their activities and results are intimately connected with the state of society as a whole, both through the people who work in the organizations and through the customers who ultimately desire their products. To understand the business climate then, it must be set in the wider context of society's idiosyncrasies.

Capitalism and communism

Apart from the odd flirtation with truly socialist ideals, the major Western economies have largely embraced capitalist philosophies. Up until relatively recently, former Eastern bloc countries favoured a communist approach. As an extreme form of socialism, communism represents an almost polar opposite to capitalist principles. Throughout the 1960s, 1970s and 1980s this polarity spawned a cold war that seemed to spiral ever downwards towards the possibility of nuclear holocaust. Eastern bloc countries characterized the West as corrupt and decadent; Westerners saw communist regimes as oppressive and restrictive. So long as both sides were investing so much in defending their position, neither needed to expend much effort in questioning the success of their own values. But there are always two sides to every coin. The failures of communism are now well documented. The underlying principles may have value, but the implementation was poor. Centralized long-range planning on such a grand scale does not produce effective coordination; instead it produces oppression, inefficiency, stagnation and corruption.

Perversely, although it kills overt entrepreneurial activity, the spirit survives, driven underground into a black market economy that bears all the marks of pure capitalism.

Yet how successful has pure capitalism been? Capitalism may offer everyone an opportunity to better themselves through private enterprise in deregulated markets, but taken to the extreme it is cut-throat and uncompassionate. Uncontrolled competition in world trade and finance has produced societies increasingly polarized into the 'haves' and the 'have nots', with the growing number of 'have nots' resorting to crime and violence to rectify the inequality. Taken to the extreme, free enterprise societies disenfranchise the weak and the underprivileged. It is ironic that freedom in America gives adults the right to carry a gun, but not the right to medical care when they are sick. All across the so-called civilized world, an overemphasis on the pursuit of individual success is destroying basic societal values such as sharing and community. Everyone is looking out for their own skin. Self-fulfilment is important but when it takes priority over self-sacrifice and obedience, moral standards decline. For example, the negative aspects of self-fulfilment distort even basic structures such as the legal system. The primary objective of the law is to hold people responsible for antisocial actions. However, when personal gain becomes the most important measure of success, the legal system is easily perverted to the point where it encourages abdication of personal responsibility. In the US, the legal system offers numerous examples of a litigious society gone mad. Individuals happily sue their *friend* if they are injured playing sport on the friend's property. Couples sue the sheriff who arrests them at an illegal Sunday cock fight, because the experience of seeing their parents arrested traumatized the children. There was an even more bizarre case. A homeless couple sued a metropolitan railway authority, because a train came along while they were making love on a mattress on the line, and they incurred injuries! The defence case rested on the grounds that even homeless people have a right to be intimate somewhere. Such incidents would be humorous if they were not true. They may seem far-removed from business issues, but like ripples from a stone dropped in a pond, the turbulence spreads out to affect far more than those in the immediate vicinity. Organizations suffer from the knock-on effects of such behaviour because they are ripe targets for litigation. Take the insurance industry for example. Escalating insurance premiums and massive claim settlements take money out of productive circulation, concentrating it in the hands of a few, with no added value for society as a whole. The medical claims budget in Great Britain rose over 800 per cent in 1994. Is it likely that doctors have reduced their standards of care by a similar proportion? If not, then sadly the result of compensating a few is more suffering for the many, because the settlement money is lost to the cause of patient care. The precedents created by each case open the door to greater and greater litigation, and people become more focused on protecting their backs than being productive. We have only to look at the disclaimers and let out clauses that have become *de rigueur* for every auditor, consultant or practising professional to see how far the situation has gone. Eventually, the system itself will fail under the stress, and everyone will be hurt in a crisis of major proportions.

So, pure capitalism has no claim to outstanding success either. Unfortunately, the weaknesses in the philosophy of Western society have been further aggravated by the logical choice of control criteria in business.

Strategy and profit

Much of today's management theory has its roots in the so-called 'scientific paradigm'. This mind set assumes cause and effect relationships; depends on logical analysis and strategic planning. Best practice is defined by what worked in the past—experience that has been analysed, pigeon-holed and categorized to fit into a logical rationale. But, reasoning by linear processes simply channels thinking along comfortable tracks in an attempt to reduce complex situations to manageable proportions. Logic alone is destructive, creativity and innovation require intuitive leaps of understanding to break out of well-worn channels and connect apparently unrelated events. Strategic planning alone may have been valuable in the 1970s and 1980s (although, as you can see from the opening quote of this chapter, some would even dispute that) but these were decades of relative stability and reasonable predictability. Managers could select a strategic lever and pull, reasonably certain of a cause and effect result. Will these methods work in an unpredictable future? Probably not. Conditions in the 1990s are different. The trouble is that no-one wants to abandon all that reassuring knowledge. So, the question is 'can tools derived from the known become adequate to manage the unknown, in the globally interconnected 1990s?' The answer of this book is 'yes', but only if they do not remain unidimensional choices.

The whole body of learning on strategy is but a reflection of the important functional disciplines necessary to organizational operation (Fig. 1.1).

Working together, these disciplines make a complete and balanced team. However, because most of the advice in each box comes from analysing historical success stories, each theory places differential emphasis on certain aspects of the whole genre. Some gurus say that strategy should be directed from the top, others believe that it will emerge from various initiatives at the bottom. Some emphasize structure and documented processes, others focus on visions, cultures and shared norms. Who is correct? The answer is all of them and none of them. Used in isolation, each of these accepted points of control have only limited success. A quick review of the business press reveals equal amounts of

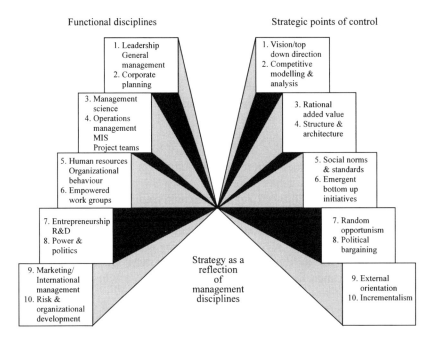

Fig. 1.1   Strategy as a reflection of management disciplines

failure for each approach. Indeed, many organizations are beginning to question the value of expensive strategic planning exercises because they have not seen any substantial benefits from the process. This may be another example of a good idea, poorly implemented.

The problem is that when strategic planners extrapolate from the known, they dismiss the elements that seem inappropriate now. But, over time, these factors come into play, but remain unmanaged. The components of business stay the same, but the dynamics keep changing. Certainly that has been the case in recent years. No doubt, many business people look back wistfully to simpler times, when the problems to be managed were on a smaller scale. Time and distance placed natural limits on complexity by isolating organizations into localized pockets. Successful predators from outside an industry were once few and far between. Nowadays even the giants are vulnerable to the small fry— Ted Turner challenged CBS, Michael Dell challenged Compaq, and Richard Branson's Virgin Airlines successfully took on giants of the industry such as British Airways. The barriers to entry are no longer insurmountable. Affordable air travel and powerful electronic communications link markets across time zones and geographical distance, thereby surmounting the natural 'containment walls'. This has brought faster change, greater complexity and massive unpredictability. Organizations are stepping even further into the unknown, once they get interested in the idea of transformational change. Corporate transformation is not simple re-organizing, it is about changing the most fundamental nature of the organization. It is a trail blazing adventure across new frontiers—frontiers of the mind as well as physical borders. There are few predictable results in this domain and new skills will be required to manage the uncertainty that reigns in open space. In this brave new world is the strategy process doomed to failure also? Must we abandon all our old management aids?

Perhaps, but perhaps not. The answer will be 'almost certainly' if the final emphasis continues to rest predominantly on quantitative methods and hard numbers as it has done for the past 30 years. Control against plan is often distilled into one key managemen measurement—profit. The fact is that focusing solely on bottom line targets, however attractive they may be, is a blinkered approach that leads inexorably to destruction; concern with profit as an overriding priority ignores too many other interacting values in the environment. Ultimately, these values have greater significance for companies and society as a whole. In the end society exacts its retribution for such neglect.

Unless we re-evaluate our ideals, we may be hard put to avoid the kind of future pictured in the thought provoking front cover of *The Economist* magazine (Fig. 1.2).

The tarot cards predict a future that is the product of an incomplete and dated management approach.

When managers see their job as maximizing profits they inevitably take too much out of a business system, without replenishing its lifegiving resources (Fig. 1.2a). Only the Grim Reaper wins in the end. We have all watched as organizations cut back on training when times get tough, then bemoan the fact that the available labour pool is increasingly ill adapted to the information age. In the end it costs more in lost business, recruitment and high salaries for scarce talent, than the training would have done; but who measures that sort of data anyway?

In the name of maximizing profits, industries blithely kill off the land and the sea and pollute the air. What about accounting for the cost to society? Few have done it, until very recently. Instead, most companies only tackle the issue when their policies come home to roost in the guise of exhausted natural resources, or government intervention. The US power industry is currently burdened by this fate. They are paying dearly for enforced compliance with environmental protection laws. In the end, all society bears the long term burden of shortsighted profiteering.

Control by profits is about as effective as looking backwards while you walk off a cliff (Fig. 1.2b). Just because your earlier steps propelled you forward safely does not mean that the same steps will do the same in the future. As Charles Hampden Turner says, 'profits come too late to steer by'.[2] He cites General Motors as a warning. GM managers were so busy controlling by profits that they dismissed the Japanese activity undermin-

Your
financial
future

a XIII

DEATH

b

THE FOOL

c X

THE WHEEL OF FORTUNE

d XV

THE DERIVATIVE

Fig. 1.2   Your financial future (reproduced from *The Economist*)
(reproduced with permission)

ing their lofty position until collapse was imminent. Unfortunately, this
scenario was not an isolated incident. In various forms it has been played
out again and again across both the automotive and electronics industries. Profit only gives the illusion of control. In reality it is nothing more
than a simplistic, historical agglomeration of effects. Today's profits are
the result of decisions taken months or even years ago. In a dynamic
marketplace, where circumstances are changing all the time, decisions
taken months ago are no longer relevant control mechanisms for current
conditions. What is needed is a set of forward-looking indicators, a less
simplistic control mechanism that takes into account the complex set of
interacting values really affecting market position. Unfortunately, profit
as a measure of value often conflicts with forward-looking values such as
market share, quality, integrity and most of all knowledge accrual. Is it
not common practice conveniently to ignore quality, if it means one

more sale can be shipped in the quarter? How many companies forego market share on lower margin products for the sake of profit maximization? Who cares about integrity when quarterly results are the only yardstick?

Planners in today's unpredictable world probably empathize with the blindfolded figure spinning the wheel of fortune (Fig. 1.2c). Recurring cycles of boom and bust over the past 20 years suggest that the approaches to strategy developed during this period have not been as successful as one might have hoped. Of the 43 excellent companies identified by Peters and Waterman[3] in 1982 only 33 per cent of them remained excellent five years later. Nineteen per cent were in serious trouble and a further twenty six per cent were in a substantially weakened position; no doubt why many organizations are expressing serious dissatisfaction with current approaches to strategy. Indeed, if the competitiveness of Western companies has withered[1] this is a sad testimony to our ideals of rational planning and control. Part of this degeneration can be attributed to blind faith in the narrow parameter of profit as a value to steer by, but part must be laid at the door of an over-simplistic view of planning. We analyse situations, reduce them to the consistency of rubble and then expect the re-assembled fragments to be representative of reality. More generally, both failures are symptomatic of a human tendency to pursue singular objectives to the extreme, to the exclusion of all else. Dependence on one guiding principle alone is the shortest route to catastrophe. Take alcoholics. Most believe that only their willpower stands between them and the rapid slide back into inebriation. They pin all their hopes of sobriety on willpower alone. Inevitably something trips them up and they fail, only to pick themselves up and be even more determined to overcome the demon drink through sheer force of their will. And so they repeat this destructive behaviour until either death or some external saviour intervenes. This blind belief in one solution does not only apply to alcoholics; overstressed executives, organizations and societies all fall into the same trap—live by the same old formula and next time we'll get it right! When things go wrong, leaders often implement 'more of the same', rather than changing tack into uncharted waters. In the end, what were once valuable panaceas, just aggravate a vicious circle. The first chance of redemption comes when more balanced thinking takes over, disabling the vicious cycle by adopting a more holistic outlook. Think of the nuclear arms race, apartheid in South Africa, IBM's mainframe dependence, parenting a teenager—they are all different issues but the common link is that the problem only remits when the two sides concede the importance of each other and start working in harmony.

Hanson-type conglomerates are the ultimate destiny of businesses that revere profit above all else. Such enterprises are attractive to investors only so long as they can sustain the smokescreen of growth. However,

'The Derivative' (Fig. 1.2d) has no coordinating objective apart from monetary gain. Conglomerates are often weak in terms of real added value because they neglect internal health problems in the drive for expanded earnings year on year. Profit becomes a hungry Moloch that must be served at all costs. Unfortunately, when these companies asset strip and cherry pick, the cost is high in terms of job losses and depletion of the industrial base. Failure is sudden and catastrophic when the organization can no longer stay ahead of the market, but is consumed by its own driving motive. The consequence is a local economy that can no longer support the quality of life aspired to, or a country that has lost its ability to produce the necessary mix of inputs. Consider this. Financial services currently contribute a healthy offset to the UK balance of payments deficit, but if too much of the productive base is eroded, what will happen when growing third-world producers develop financial muscle? In unidimensional countries, balance of payments deficits grow and nations delude themselves that they are not bankrupt.

The extent of these failures is actually quite frightening when you consider that they occurred at a time when 'management, planning and control' were the watchwords of the era.

The cause of their failure

Having impugned both capitalism and communism, disparaged both strategy and profit, what are we left with. Actually we are left with a paradox.

Clearly, the profit motive is not all bad. Few would dispute the fact that societies in which profit has been a driving motive have a more comfortable lifestyle than less sophisticated societies where specialization is less, and self-betterment has little meaning. In modern societies people do what they are best at. Those with a talent for working with their hands contribute most by following their forte. Those who have an aptitude for the complexities of high finance are giving their best when they work in that field. Refinements of this nature are beneficial because they focus expertise and hone skills. Money is the most effective mechanism to mediate value differences between skills. In a well balanced society, money acts as an incentive to differentiate between opportunities for new development. After all no-one would invest and develop new products and services if they could not see some return for the risk being taken. Profit provides a reasonable measure for comparing the contribution of each new project .

Clearly, both capitalism and communism also have their good points. Communist principles centre upon admirable qualities such as sharing, caring and community. Capitalist principles develop the entrepreneurial spirit and self-dependency.

No-one disputes that each aspect of strategy has its own unique benefits (Fig. 1.3). Without any plan at all, there would be no coordination, no guidance or direction, no deepening of understanding through analysis. In any case, all the theory worked at some time, for some organizations. The problem is deciding which advice is most appropriate for *your* circumstances.

Theme Strategy as ...	Pros	Cons
Leadership, vision and control from the top	Gives guidance and coherence	Isolated from detail of reality
Structured competitive planning in advance	Ordered prediction based on known conditions	Limits vision in the face of the unexpected
Resources analysis as a route to optimize total added value	Theoretical profit optimization for whole organization	Ignores competing values in the various constituencies
Creating internal structural fit	Assimilates current environmental demands	Structure limits future strategic options
Establishing cultural norms and standards for stability	Unifies and gives comfort and stability to group members	Force for resistance to change
An emergent design based on grassroot initiatives	Tried and tested projects emerge from detailed practice at lower levels	Can lack coherence
An opportunistic approach to fortuitous circumstances	Flexible response to unexpected	Disordered and unpredictable use of resources
Political negotiation between local constituencies with conflicting values	Rationalizes difference by surfacing and addressing conflict	Disruptive; produces suboptimal solutions
Deliberately manipulating the external environment	Active intrusive open system	Hard to accommodate constantly changing demands
Logically incremental change	Moves organization steadily along culturally acceptable path	Constant change tears company apart

Fig. 1.3   Pros and Cons of the strategic themes

In fact, the principal cause of each process failure is the pursuit of one value system to the exclusion of its complementary opposite. It is not wrong to pursue profit, in fact it is essential. But when we ignore other equally important values, such as learning, co-operation, and societal obligations, the dark side of profit comes back to haunt us. All aspects of strategy are invaluable, but if one is pursued to the detriment of others then the system breaks down. Why? Because we are working with an incomplete tool box. Capitalism is admirable so long as it does not neglect the values of sharing and community. Even communism could work if it were not pursued to the extent of denying all personal freedom.

The legacy of these failed processes is evident everywhere. Former eastern bloc countries are struggling with terrible turbulence and conflict. Western societies have crumbling infrastructures, declining moral standards and more violent crime. The environment is polluted and there are holes in the ozone layer. Business faces greater uncertainty and radical surgery.

The paradox is this. We have sought control by consistently following a chosen set of predefined principles, but in so doing we have lost control and created Chaos.

1.3   Chaos—the future for business?

Where Chaos begins, classical science stops.

Gleik, 1987[4]

Is this all we have to look forward to? Business buffeted by increasingly more violent turbulence that it is powerless to control? The answer all depends on how we try to manage Chaos. If we carry on as before, with traditional formulae for control, the answer must be a resounding yes. But, if there were some way to correct the obvious deficiencies of biased approaches there could be a chance to regain some measure of control. However, before we break new ground with one possible approach to the paradox of 'Chaos Management', it is important to have a general understanding of what Chaos means in business terms.

Chaos has been described as a science for the real world and a theory that touches all disciplines.[5] It is the product of discoveries in many different branches of science that have come together to produce a higher-level understanding about the common order governing all of them. Chaos Theory focuses on the turbulence and unexplainable phenomena that were once written off by scientists as 'exceptions to the rule'. Paradoxically, it is now these exceptions that are defining the rules. Unorthodox thinking has caused a revolution in the scientific community, challenging some long-held assumptions about the way the world works. Since management theory was grounded in many of these assumptions, and industries, surrounded by turbulence, are looking for a way through the storm, it would perhaps be profitable to examine accepted management philosophy under the magnifying glass provided by natural Chaos.

There are three particularly illuminating concepts that lie at the heart of Chaos Theory. The first is the Butterfly Effect (Fig. 1.4), the second is the recurring beauty of fractal geometry (Fig. 1.5 on page 17) and the third is a common denominator linking the first two, namely the operation of Strange Attractors.

The Butterfly Effect

The Butterfly Effect was named after a paper presented by a meteorologist called Lorenz entitled 'Predictability; does the flap of a butterfly wing in Brazil cause a tornado in Texas?'[6] The paper described the pattern of deterministic, non-periodic air flows produced by iterating a simplified version of Saltzman's three equations for convection. Using the output of one round of calculations as the input of the next and plotting the result in three dimensions, Lorenz produced a pattern that bears a remarkable similarity to the wings of a butterfly (Fig. 1.4). In fact, it is an accurate simulation of the infinite complexity of the global weather system.

However, for the layman, the title of the paper is probably more meaningful than the contents. The answer to the question posed is 'yes'. A small event like a butterfly flapping its wings can be amplified several thousand miles away to produce a raging tornado. What connects the

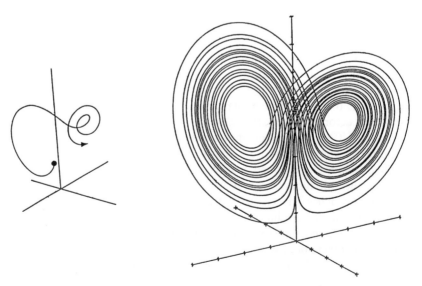

Fig. 1.4   Chaos in action (adapted from Gleick, 1987)[4] (reproduced with permission)

two events is a process governed by three simple but non-linear equations. The findings of Lorenz rang the death knell for the dream of accurate long-term weather forecasting. It probably also means the same for strategic planning as most companies practise it today.

The key to understanding this three-dimensional double spiral lies in degrees of accuracy. Lorenz found that minute changes in the interacting variables accumulate without demonstrable effect for a while, but suddenly a combination of them will create a violent divergence in the system. In general terms, the weather patterns would cycle for a period of time around what appeared to be a steady state, although conditions never exactly repeated themselves. Then, sensitive to subtle differences in initial conditions, the forces of nature would behave quite differently, shooting off on to a completely different trajectory, around which they would spiral for a further period. Doesn't this bear a remarkable similarity to business trends? Highs and lows in highly sensitive stockmarkets; overnight shifts in seemingly balanced exchange rates; sudden failure of what had up until now been a successful business strategy? Lorenz also realized that this pattern was universally applicable to any system that behaved non-periodically, so he started to look for other examples where the Butterfly Effect held true. He found that with the right equations, and by using the output of one iteration as the input of the next (i.e. a nonlinear equation) he could accurately describe a variety of phenomena, such as the disorderly rotation of waterwheels and the operation of electrical dynamos. Since then scientists in other disciplines, such as astronomy, biology, physics and mathematics, have found the same recurring patterns consistently describe events in their fields. Chaos is everywhere.

Society is a human system and business is a sub-system of that whole. The question is, will the same pattern hold true for the human system? This book will conclude that the answer is 'yes'. That may seem a depressing prospect, but once we understand and accept it, we can use the basic rules to design a new, more effective management process.

Fractal geometry

During the 1960s Bennoit Mandelbrot was exploring the phenomenon of disordered interactions from a different perspective—that of scaling. He discovered that what appeared to be aberrations on one level produced symmetry on another. Historically, mathematicians had linearized nonlinear equations by excluding the aberrations. This made the equations easier to solve, and solution had always been the primary objective. But that was, in fact, a form of self-censorship; by conveniently excluding the unexplainable, a theory becomes self-sustaining even in the presence of important anomalies. In other words, linear equations confine one to the micro scale—limited situations for which the rules hold true. This same criticism applies to the linear reasoning and logic that we apply to business. It is customary, yet dangerous, to assume that if $x + y = z$ in one company it will also do so in another.

The world, as Mandelbrot showed, is essentially non-linear. Non-linear systems exhibit relationships that are not consistently proportional. Nonetheless, Mandelbrot was able to show that there was a kind of geometric structure to the irregularities that occurred. This order held true, even in apparently unrelated issues such as 'word frequencies in linguistics, error bursts in the transmission of messages, turbulence, galaxy structures, fluctuations of the stockmarket and the level of the river Nile'.[7] The explanation was one of scale. The shape of 'reality' depended on your perspective. For example, if we look at the world from out in space it appears to be a three-dimensional round ball, if we look at it from an airplane, it looks like a one-dimensional flat surface. From the ground the hills and valleys look three-dimensional, but going deeper and deeper into the atomic structure of the earth, we find that solids break down into almost zero-dimensional particles, that have a three-dimensional internal structure. The most interesting factor about this phenomenon, is the recurrence of the same patterns as one goes down through the various levels.

Mandelbrot coined the word fractal to describe this idea.[8] Fig. 1.5 shows the most famous fractal image—the Mandelbrot set. Once again, the result comes from repetitively plotting iterations of a few simple equations and mapping the results to produce the characteristic gingerbread man shape that occurs repetitively at various levels of the complex pattern. However, viewed at ever-increasing depth, these gingerbread men form all sorts of other intricate patterns, such as sea horses' tails, and whirling jewel-like islands. The benefit of fractals is that they fit infinite surface area into a finite space or produce infinite variety in finite form. Is this not the goal of many organizations? A way to offer as many varieties as the customer wants but in a controlled fashion; a diverse portfolio of talents organized into a coherent structure.

Continuing research shows that this fractal geometry permeates nature. The human body is a working model of the value of fractals. The human lungs, packed into the tiny space of the chest cavity would, if spread out, cover more than the surface area of a tennis court. The huge area is the most efficient way to transfer oxygen quickly to the blood within a confined space. Literally miles of intestines fit into the abdominal cavity. Again, the fractal design provides the best way to extract the maximum amount of benefit from the food as it is passed through the gut. The protein surfaces of haemoglobin are fractal, so that enzymes can more easily stick to their rough surface. Computer simulations that apply the principles of fractals, can regenerate accurate replicas of mountain scenery, trees and moonscapes. Fractals are everywhere. So why not in business? As this book will try to show later, there is a very clear fractal dimension to business management. By using a simple formula

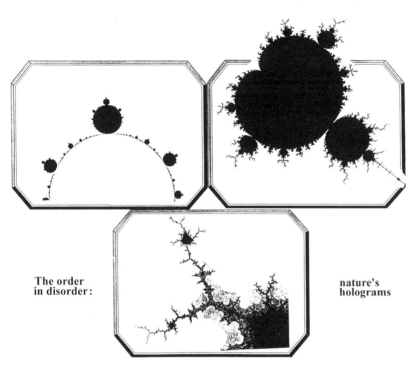

**The order
in disorder:**

**nature's
holograms**

Fig. 1.5   The order in disorder: nature's holograms (adapted from
Mandelbrot, 1977)[8]

that describes the repetitive variables in the management process we can
learn to create infinite variety within the finite organizational form. The
uniqueness this brings should be a distinct competitive edge.

Strange attractors

The common denominator between the Butterfly Effect and fractal geometry is what is called a strange attractor. In any system there are three
types of attractor: fixed points, which, as the name suggests, are static;
limit cycles which are periodic orbits that hold a system in a stable cycle;
and strange attractors, which cause the Chaos in the system.

> In rough terms the strange attractor is a lot of periodic orbits and aperiodic
> paths all rolled up into one big tangled mess.[9]

much like a bowl of spaghetti with sauce. It is the whole mass of stretched
and folded spaghetti that constitutes the attractor, not just one point in it.
The interesting part of a strange attractor is that the periodic orbits are
unstable so that, paradoxically, if we move off the orbit by just a fraction,

the attractor acts like a repeller, which is what drives the system to change.

Politics provide a real life example of how attractors work. The underlying dogma serves as the immovable fixed point for each particular party. Some people will promote its principles vehemently and serve the party unquestioningly. Interpretations of the dogma into social policy generally create limit cycles, in which voter loyalty remains in a stable pattern. Certain combinations of circumstances and social policy create strange attractors. If only a few voters are influenced to question and reject the dogma, the effect can be amplified by the system as they persuade others, until the outcome is a landslide victory for the opposition. That is why the polls are so often wrong. They only sample from a small area, and they can easily miss the small disturbances that build into unpredictable results.

Implications for management

There are some important parallels between the developments of Chaos Theory and the business context in the 1990s: re-engineering is also a new science that aggregates explorations and insights from many different disciplines. Business transformation could be described as a search for strange attractors, in so far as we are looking for the mix of change initiatives that will spark sudden radical improvements. Business history shows similar repetitive two-phase spirals of highs and lows, boom and bust, each cycle exhibiting a familiar pattern, but never exactly replicating the outcome. Finally, predicting the effect of interacting information flows upon the whole business climate has become about as inaccurate as the long-range weather forecast; short term accuracy is about all that is achievable.

Stacey's[10] graphical explanation of the consequences of multiplying decisions (Fig. 1.6), explains why long term prediction is an impossible objective.

Change decisions can be segregated into three different categories: 'closed', 'contained' and 'open-ended', but after the first decision is made, the outcomes of all future decisions are interactively affected. In the days when geographical distance insulated activities and international time zones limited the possibility of effective transnational coordination, both the number and impact of the interactions was less. Organizations were an isolated set of feudal markets. Under such conditions, five-year planning and control against preset quantitative measures was a viable proposition, because the effects of most business decisions were narrowly contained. The 5 per cent of unknowns could safely be written off as noise in the system, when we could accurately construe 95 per cent of our actions. Obviously such situations still exist, but less and less. Nonetheless, if the timeframe from action to reaction is predictably

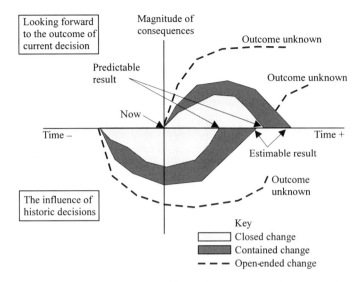

Fig. 1.6   The cumulative effect of interacting decisions (from Stacey, 1991)[10] (reproduced with permission)

short and the consequences narrowly defined we are dealing with what Stacey calls 'closed change'. When the timeframe is more medium term, we trade accuracy for extended duration and, although predictions become 'probable' and 'likely', they still lie within reasonable margins of error. This is 'contained change'. Conventional business theory is largely built on the assumption that we are handling one or other of these types of change. In those circumstances rational analysis, financial control and formal structure are adequate. These are what Stacey calls ordinary management tools.[11] However, in today's business climate, there are so many open-ended situations that the predictable percentage is at best 50 per cent, and the other 50 per cent uncertainty represents much more than noise in the system. Potentially it hides severe danger. This new type of situation, characterized by multiplexed interdependencies and tenuous connections between cause and effect, Stacey calls 'open-ended change'. It needs a new type of control that he calls 'extraordinary management'.

One cannot help but draw parallels here between the various types of attractor—fixed point, limit cycles and strange attractors—and Stacey's closed, contained and open-ended change, respectively. It is the combination of all three attractors that makes up the dynamic systems that contain disorder within orderly limits. Therefore it is reasonable to conclude that a combination of *both* ordinary and extraordinary management skills will be needed to handle the process of transformation. Clearly, the answer to one of the questions at the start of the chapter is 'no, we cannot abandon the old methods of management completely'.

What other lessons can we learn that might apply to business? Conventional business theories are like the linear equations favoured by mathematicians—neat formulae that produce a definitive answer by excluding the aberrations. Such models act as limit cycles within the business system, keeping plans and goals within self-sustaining limits on the micro scale. They are unlikely to help us achieve transformation, but they do give some stability to the system. The strange attractors in business are presently confined largely to unmanaged macro scale influences. However, if managers can step back and take a wider but less self-limiting perspective, they could find the strategic strange attractors that would enable the revolution to occur spontaneously. Hamel and Prahalad are effectively saying the same thing[12] when they say that senior managers should spend more time looking outward and forward and communicating with colleagues to build a commonly shared, but well tested fantasy for the future.

Radical change in chaotic systems is the result of many small accumulating variations, influenced by some stable and semi-stable flows, so, by implication, and guided by a consistent framework, corporate transformation should be the outcome of many open-ended changes accumulating and interacting within the more stable context to create radically different behaviour. Indeed, Pascale hinted at this when he stated that:

> True transformation of organizations requires a critical mass of change initiatives.
>
> Pascale, 1990[13]

Chaos principles call into question several aspects of business theory. Firstly, the quixotic ideal of equilibrium that underpins all economic theory. It is misleading to start from the assumption that price will reach an equilibrium point that balances supply and demand, when we know that the presence of strange attractors will make this impossible to achieve. Nonetheless, most business theory still starts out in pursuit of the impossible. The focus is all wrong. It is the far from equilibrium states that create the real interest in the system. That is where change can begin, because that is where there is tension in the system. So, rather than aiming for the limit cycle and writing off the aberrations as exceptions we should be concentrating on the anomalies and making them work for us. This means that static normative planning models that assume perfect equilibrium are out; dynamic frameworks that explore the tensions creating the interesting behaviour are in.

The assumptions of linearity in business reasoning would appear unrealistic in the light of the evidence of non-linearity in other systems. It is a question of scale. What seems a reasonable and logical interpretation from analysis at one level becomes an echo of its former intention at other levels, so what seems like a complete picture supporting a decision may only be a fragment of the knowledge needed to address a much larger and more complex picture. It is inevitable then that detailed prescriptions for strategy will be invalidated by unforeseen discrepancies in production or sudden market fluctuations. But, since fractals show that aberrations at one level may be the key to the underlying order at another, we should be homing in on these oddities and looking for the connections elsewhere in the system. Obviously it is easier to cope with definitive categorical models, but if the principles embedded in them are not consistently applicable on several scales they will not prove truly viable.

1.4   IT-enabled revolution—a storm in a tea cup or the way forward?

> Any serious restructure of business or government must directly attack the organization of knowledge and the entire system of power based on it. For the cubbyhole system is in crisis.
>
> Toffler, 1990[14]

In many ways the idea of Re-engineering is appropriate to notions of chaotic interconnectedness. Unfortunately, however, there is so much confusion surrounding the whole concept that some people are beginning to dismiss it as just the latest management fad. Even Hammer[15] admits that it needs fanaticism to outweigh the cynical response of employees. The usual reaction is 'keep a low profile and hope the current craze blows over'. Part of the problem is the scale of the proposed change. It is threatening when viewed as a whole. However, that is not the only qualification. Try asking the simple question 'What is Business Process Re-engineering (BPR)?' You will get almost as many definitions as responses. No-one really has a clear understanding of what is involved. Inevitably, with no clear objective, the number of programme failures is high. Nadler[16] estimates the waste of consultancy money to be between $5 and $20 million per annum. That may be conservative. So is this multi-million dollar industry a storm in a tea cup, or does it really shine a light on the way forward?

Perhaps we should start by eliminating what it is not. There are five myths about Re-engineering that need to be dispelled right from the start.

Myth 1 Re-engineering is synonymous with downsizing

Very often the current skill set is not the one that will be needed in the future. Unfortunately, until the organization has taken a few steps into its future, it is impossible to make that judgement accurately. Nonetheless, businesses anxious to show some rapid improvements from a

Re-engineering programme rashly attack the most attractive target first. Slashing heads before experience reveals the actual skills required in the transformed operations generally proves to be short-sighted and costly in terms of redundancy and subsequent rehiring costs, not to mention loss of the most valuable source of knowledge and new ideas. You don't motivate by downsizing either, so those who are left don't participate wholeheart-edly, because they are expending all their energy worrying where the axe will fall next. In the end, it may be that the same number of staff can handle more business or develop new skills. This is adding value, not cutting costs.

Myth 2 Re-engineering is a one-off programme that can be mapped out in detail by investing in an extensive consultancy exercise

However good they are, consultants cannot know as much as managers about the subtle nuances of the business. Yes, they can bring valuable input, based on their experiences in other organizations, but they should not be expected to provide *the* solution. People only buy into something that they have been involved in developing. For the ultimate solution to stick, it must come from motivated people within. Besides, transforma-tional change is a continuous process with no definitive end and consul-tants are too expensive to be a permanent fixture. Their strength lies in facilitating new insights, by questioning long-held assumptions and teaching people to open their eyes to unforeseen opportunities.

Myth 3 Re-engineering can be relegated to the IT domain

Certainly good Re-engineering programmes produce added value through the use of information and supporting technology. Yet, even though IT has a major part to play in the process of Re-engineering, associating a far-reaching strategic intent with a narrow focus such as IT is dangerous. Firstly, it ignores the cultural changes that are an integral part of Re-engineering. Secondly, there is a risk that changes will be reduced to mere Electronic Data Interchange (EDI). Thirdly, the range of the programme will immediately be limited by the sphere of influence of the specialist. This can be very narrow, as a result of the long history of dissension between information systems and technology (IS&T) specialists, and what is so unfortunately termed 'the rest of the business'. The shortage of *quantifiable* returns from burgeoning IT investment has become a source of serious concern in many industries. However, managers are wary of personally venturing too far into a domain that is shrouded in mystique and incomprehensible jargon, so they delegate authority for the entire information resource to a convenient functional specialism. In the end, responsibility for use of information still rests with operational managers. Thus, senior staff commit the ultimate sin of segregating responsibility and authority. The practical difficulties of such a set up are well known—scapegoating, unproductive arguments and schism. Operations managers accuse IS&T people of not knowing enough about business issues, whereas IS&T personnel bemoan the fact that others don't appreciate their problems. Many initiatives founder on the rock of internal resistance, and added value is lost amidst political storms.

Myth 4 Re-engineering is about restructuring operational processes

If this is how the programme is perceived then all the emphasis is placed on mapping data flows and re-ordering internal methods. Generally, the results of this outlook are little more radical than simple tinkering. Mapping existing data flows immediately imprisons our perspective in concrete blocks from which we cannot escape. Focusing on process improvements within the organizational boundaries is too introspective. What about the dynamics of the market place? What about extending business scope—fantasizing about what could be? The multi-million dollar study sponsored by an impressive group of international corporations* and conducted by the Massachusetts Institute of Technology (MIT)[17] identified three transformational levels of IT-induced reconfiguration: Process, Network and Scope Redesign. Unfortunately it seems that attaining each level has been interpreted as a process of climbing a ladder—in other words that internal process change is the stepping stone to network change and the pinnacle of business scope redefinition is only reached after the network has been redesigned. In fact, the change is better tackled in reverse. Envisioning a new business scope automatically points to a different set of relationships and business processes. In addition, the imagination is not immediately constrained by assumptions about industry givens. Far better to look outwards and forwards first.

Myth 5 Re-engineering is wiping the slate clean

Clearly this is impossible. An organization is made up of people. People need time to adjust. It is naive to imagine that they can simply erase ingrained attitudes, feelings and beliefs overnight. Shared values and social norms give definition to their lives. Indeed, culture is the glue that gives cohesion to a random assortment of people. Trying to eradicate all reference points at one go is likely to tear the organization apart. The change has to happen at a pace that is comfortable enough for people to accommodate; if not, they will go into a state of what Toffler calls 'Future

*The line up of organizations included American Express, British Petroleum (BP), Digital Equipment Corporation (DEC), Eastman Kodak, Ernst & Young, General Motors, International Computers Ltd (ICL), Bell South, MCI Communications, the US Internal Revenue Service (IRS), the CIGNA Corporation and the US Army.

Shock'.[18] Once that happens, individuals' productive involvement in any change programme will be minimal; they will be more concerned with stabilizing their own lives than contributing to more instability. Yet ironically, it is important to ensure that the culture is not so strong or change so slow that people fall back into old habits and thus obstruct the process of change.

Embarking on a Re-engineering programme from any one of these perspectives is guaranteed to produce disappointing results. If such myths are allowed to stand unchallenged for too long, the inevitable poor results will breed prejudice against what is potentially a sound theory. Then the verdict of history on Re-engineering will be a sorry 'thumbs down' for the fad of the early 1990s. Yet all of these myths are, in some way, part of the Re-engineering phenomenon. So how can they be turned around to shine a light on the path to the twenty-first century?

Perhaps if we define Re-engineering in broader terms (Fig. 1.7) this will help. If we go back to the MIT study, we find one simple theme—breaking down the barriers that currently limit business operations. The goal then is networking, sharing information and linking in new configurations inside and outside the company. The purpose is to extend the range of operations, but buying and selling companies is not the way to do it. This is a relationship exercise, not a restructuring. That implies keeping people, not replacing them by technology. Yes, IT is advocated as the

Fig. 1.7 Shedding a new light on the process of business Re-engineering

principle enabler, but that is very different from automation. It is interesting to note that when the experts drew the final version of their now famous MIT90s framework (Fig. 1.8), they omitted the *direct* link between technology and strategy, that was in the earlier version.[19]

All the other boxes link directly to each other. The first impression is one of technology divorced from strategy. On reflection, it could be interpreted as saying that structure, management processes, individuals and roles are, in fact, an obstruction preventing IT from taking its place as the linking function between corporate, business and strategic business unit (SBU) strategy—which is a basic recommendation of the study. In reality, the missing arrow is probably no more than an attempt to show that the power of technology only works *through* the three central domains. IT-enabled transformation is not confined to the electronic passage of information across physical boundaries; it requires an interactive partnership between people and technology—kind of bionic organization.

The purpose of crossing borders is to develop a web of new relationships, which will build into what Drucker calls a New Society of Organizations.[20] The natural consequence of community is greater *inter*dependence. For management this means satisfying the values of more and more interrelated parties, both inside and outside their power base. Multiplexing relationships inevitably aggravates Chaos. For this reason, Re-engineering falls squarely into the open-ended change category (Fig. 1.6). It is a deliberate move into uncharted territory, where participants will have little experience of the consequences of more than 50 per cent of their decisions. The idea of strategy and planning under such conditions is hard to imagine, but it is possible with a guiding framework that is based on paradoxical conflicts. The conflict re-energizes, while the framework gives order to the chaos.

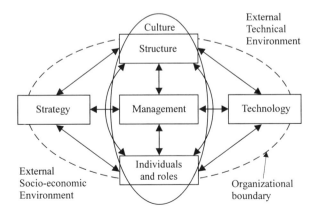

Fig. 1.8 A flaw in the academic theory? (from Scott Morton, 1991)[17] (reproduced with permission)

The sheer unpredictability of the process calls into question other accepted business norms, such as directorship, structure, politics, quality. Yet this is a good thing. As Drucker points out[21] revolutionary change cannot occur until managers are prepared to question the validity of existing business theories. After all, how meaningful can theories developed in the 1970s and 1980s be in a rapidly changing world? This is where we come up against cognitive barriers too. Being asked to abandon old viewpoints and change the ground rules for management is not an attractive prospect. We can find lots of excuses not to. However, it has been said that for real transformation to happen:

> a majority of individuals in an organization must change their behaviour.
>
> Blumenthal and Haspeslagh, 1994[22]

Behavioural change in any context requires that individuals challenge the mental patterns and fundamental assumptions that have always shaped their lives. In organizations these human biases actually limit the capacity to get benefit from change initiatives because they can adversely prejudice a participant's outlook. Transforming the organization is not, as most people think, a process of actively pushing through a change programme. Rather is should be a set of actions designed to remove the constraints upon change. Altering mind sets, removing blinkers and opening peoples eyes to new possibilities is the new task of management. For most industry leaders, any suggestion of removing the points of reference that gave the organization stability and recognizable form is a frightening prospect. How can they meet quarterly profit forecasts amidst so much disruption?

Unfortunately, it may be the only route to Chaos Management. Indeed, research shows that in many cases adding a deliberate dose of chaos to existing Chaos actually restores order. Perhaps it is better to be proactive, rather than merely responding to crisis after crisis. Isn't it better to start the revolution yourself than be a casualty of it? At least, you have some small forewarning if the Chaos is of your own creation.

Of course the worry with all the extremist talk surrounding revolution is that history tells us that revolutions are notoriously unstable. Overthrowing a regime, however unsuccessful, spreads insecurity and fear. People do not act rationally under such conditions. If a better life does not emerge fairly quickly then either new revolutionaries push for supremacy or the people, looking back through rose-coloured glasses, hanker after the old regime. The result is either anarchy or a steady slide back to the old ways, neither of which is ideal. In the search for an effective model for revolution, Mother Nature comes out on top. Her transformations evolve, but the end result is fairly radical. Steady change in a self-ordering pattern produces a solid foundation on which to build more change. What is needed is a pattern for evolutionary revolution in business, and a way to ensure that the process does not take several millennia! Evolving a revolution may sound paradoxical, but just as in the Butterfly Effect, a series of small changes with revolutionary intent are likely to be amplified in a chaotic system to produce sudden transformational change. The rest of this book is about developing such an approach. The first part of the book explains the basic procedure; Part 2 describes how this works in practice.

Clearly though, we need a driving objective that will sustain the momentum for change. This is where learning comes into play.

1.5   Creativity and learning—a force for revolution?

A learning organization is an organization skilled at creating, acquiring and transferring knowledge *and* at modifying its behaviour to reflect new knowledge and insights.

Garvin, 1993[23]

The nature of power

Alvin Toffler has spent the last 25 years as a prophet. He has travelled the world, talking to everyone from presidents to murderers, international business tycoons to South American squatters, collecting vast amounts of data about the way our society is changing. The pages of his books are full of valuable insights about how people cope with change,[18] where change is taking us[24] and perhaps, most importantly, how to control change in the future.[14]

His analysis spans many scales, but he identifies a clear pattern in the complex mass of interacting variables. The conclusion can be summed up in one sentence. *As we move into the twenty-first century, the nature of power is changing.* This has far-reaching consequences for the process of management.

There are only three basic sources of power: physical force, monetary influence and mental power. All forms of power are simultaneously available and usable at pretty much every level of social interaction. Wherever one person has a desire, another has a reciprocal source of potential power.

Throughout history, the most primitive source of power has always been violence. Animals fight for territorial supremacy, countries fight wars, overseers beat slaves, and parents spank their children. The limitation of brute force is that when the underdog gets his chance, he will fight back. It is a punitive tool that creates resentment and resistance.

As human systems grow more civilized, wealth becomes a more flexible alternative to physical force. Money can be used as an incentive as well as a coercive. For many years, money has been the predominant source of power in business and society, making and breaking lives and defining the status of countries and organizations.

Yet the dawn of the information age started a shift in the balance of power. Knowledge is taking over as the dominant means of control. Knowledge is fundamentally different from the other two sources of power. Principally it is more versatile: not only can it be used to punish, coerce and motivate, it can also be used to transform. Knowledge can amplify the power inherent in force and wealth—guided missiles and the Guinness scandal—or it can prevent them from being wasted—diplomacy and expert systems. Unlike money and physical force, knowledge is an infinite resource, accessible to those outside the realms of a privileged few, and not consumed with use. Indeed, the more it is used, the more it grows.

We should not forget that the word power has two meanings. The first, that has just been discussed, pertains to control. The second relates to energy. Information is also power. It is the energy flowing through the organizational circuits, and if it is to drive the business engine efficiently, it has to produce the sort of power that brings control—knowledge.

Efficient power usage—the importance of double loop learning

For an organization to be an efficient power user, there must be a mechanism to convert information into knowledge. This is the learning process. It might appear that this is a simple two-phase motor, involving creativity and application. The creativity phase finds new ways to link scraps of information together and the application phase puts the ideas into practice. However, at this stage the knowledge output is weak, low grade power, because it is localized and has not been put to any rigorous test. We can extend the range by asking whether the learning can be applied across a wider range of data? In other words, what further contribution can the knowledge make, as it stands? This helps to ensure that the learning is firmly embedded into everyday behaviour, which is important when old habits die hard and there is resistance in the circuit. However, the world does not stand still. To get full value out of knowledge it has to be challenged by asking what conditions cause the underlying assumptions to break down? In other words, what more can we learn from its *in*validity? This leads back to the creativity phase.

Learning is a cyclical process, with three important and repetitive phases. Challenge, change and crystallize and then challenge, change and crystallize again. It was Chris Argyris who first coined the term 'Double Loop Learning'[25] to describe this process. Unfortunately, many organizations fail to recognize this and so lose momentum in their change programmes. The second cycle should amplify the feedback from the initial change, thereby stimulating further change. However, when you have invested your reputation in the learning produced by the first loop it is hard to admit that there might be some weaknesses in the original logic, or that it may no longer be applicable. ITT's financial wizard, Harold Geneen, fell into this very trap. Geneen was an outstanding entrepreneurial accountant, who saw an opportunity to turn a motley collection of telecommunication businesses into a powerful conglomerate. Diversification, decentralization and careful surgery supported by strong information systems and tight financial control looked like an excellent formula for success. Tried and tested repeatedly, from the late 1960s to the mid 1970s, the formula produced staggering growth and made ITT the largest conglomerate in the world. In a little under a decade, Geneen and his management team brought 100 companies under the ITT umbrella, but ultimately the recipe went bad and the giant got sick. Managers had become addicted to acquisition and diversification, never questioning the wisdom of overindulgence. Institutionalized greed made financial targets unrealistic. In the enthusiasm for more of the same, operational health was neglected. Various divisions developed major problems with products that had become dated, and processes that were inefficient. However, detailed maintenance issues were obscured by the driving certainty that more growth was the only answer. No-one ever challenged the formula until a new incumbent took over the role of Chief Executive Officer (CEO). He was then faced with the painful task of slimming down the workforce by a massive 60 per cent and ruthlessly slashing an overweight portfolio of companies.

ITT is by no means unique. Digital Equipment Corporation (DEC) became so obsessed with quality engineering, they forgot that the customer cares about cost too. Procter & Gamble learned that product proliferation captures market share, but never questioned whether too much diversity might be hard to coordinate. Unfortunately, if we don't keep challenging what we consider to be knowledge, we fall into the trap of 'running learning loop repeatedly over static information models'.[26] In the end we get squashed flat!

Transformational change cannot happen without learning, but it is going to be important to make sure that the knowledge we gain does not end up strangling us at a later date. Clearly, the second part of the learning loop is very important to power maintenance. But it is also important to find a way to speed up revolutions of the learning cycle, because in the end:

the ability to learn faster than your competition may be the only sustainable competitive advantage.

De Geus, 1988[27]

1.6   Synthesis—a new strategic response?

One of the interesting lessons that emerges from this chapter is that there is a common denominator in all the examples of failure. Societal, business and individual philosophies all fail when an idea is taken too far. Why do humans do this? Generally, it is because we focus on the object of our interest and our enthusiasm temporarily blinds us to everything else. We become linear and predictable, rather than multi-dimensional characters with a range of responses. That is when we selectively dismiss the danger signs, characterizing them as anomalies and exceptions to the rule.

In one sense, each of the five debunked myths about Re-engineering is a truth to be followed, but at the same time as downsizing, the changes must expand the involvement of existing resources. Although it is necessary to work to some formal plan, it is also imperative that the organization develops instinctive and unplanned responses to random events; certainly IT has a major role to play, but IT services must be aligned with business added value. Undoubtedly, business processes need restructuring, but it should be in the cause of constructing industries of the future, and at a pace that people can accommodate and then assimilate. Then the important principles can be built into a stable learning culture that sustains the momentum for further change.

In reality, the message is an old one. More than 2000 years ago, a playwright called Plautus was exhorting his audience to 'Moderation in all things'. The motto still applies today.

Moderation implies restraint and temperance, taking judicious risks; it suggests striking a balance between opposing forces. But, it also has associations of modulation, and arbitration and has come to mean less than optimum in many people's minds. Certainly it is a different approach for those who have long aspired to decisiveness, directorship and optimization. But, we must not overlook the word 'all'. Moderation in *all* things brings more values into the equation, and factors in the reality that they are truly variable. This may mean compromise but in the end a more flexible approach is perhaps a safer bet than a definitive, but wrong choice—particularly when no-one knows which one of the variables will turn out to be the key to shaping the future.

Traditionally, management practices have been very exclusive, even down to the fundamentals such as competition, market position and knowledge. Competition implies a winner and a loser. The winner takes all, but the loser is out of the game. There are always more losers than winners, so this is a very single-minded approach. Why can't there be more than one winner? Win/win solutions make for a less divisive society. Michael Porter suggests squeezing the organization either into a top quality niche or a low cost box. What is wrong with being a premium quality operator at a cheaper price? It might stretch the ingenuity a bit, but it makes it harder for the competition, and it is feasible.

Historically managers devise strategy by some mysterious proprietary knowledge given only to management; the average worker does not participate in the process. What is it that gives management more or better knowledge than those at the sharp end of the business? IBM once fell foul of this arrogant assumption, doggedly sticking to their mainframe strategy way beyond the time that the market would tolerate. There were many lower down in the organization who saw the writing on the wall, and tried to get the message through, but in its complacency the giant of the computer industry shut its ears and paid the price. A more moderate response that gave credence to both visions of the future would have been more in keeping with market trends.

The introduction to this chapter posed several questions. Is it time to abandon old management principles? Although they have not always produced the desired results, there is little to suggest anything fundamentally wrong with any of the ordinary management techniques: objectives, strategy, reasoned problem-solving and financial control are a necessary part of everyday existence. The same disciplines are still needed to manage closed and contained change. The problem is that they do not shape the future.

Are the new techniques any better? Certainly, Chaos, Re-engineering and Learning provide stimulating new points of view. They can shape the future. It is clear that we need some extraordinary new management techniques to start the process of open-ended change that will eventually lead to transformation, but if we rush off blindly in pursuit of the new and neglect the present, then we stand every chance of committing the same sins of omission as before.

The sensible option would be to synthesize. To build the old into a product that satisfies the requirements of the new. Synthesis is the process of combining ideas into a more complex whole. For management this means consistently measuring decisions against a multi-dimensional checklist of criteria so as to avoid the linear response. Tackling the inter-related variables simultaneously rather than in sequence also provides an opportunity to shorten the timeframe for learning.

How will this work in practice? Simple; look for the solution that satisfies both your initial preference *and* that of that inconvenient dog in the manger opposite!

This is the essence of paradox. The next chapter will consider how and why paradox should become the next strategic dimension. Starting with a discussion of the benefits of a paradoxical approach, Chapter 2 will outline a framework for applying dilemmas to business decisions and then discuss why that framework is an appropriate way to revolutionize business management in a climate of Chaos and how it synthesizes knowledge into a more holistic approach.

Changing the basic approach

Change is not made without inconvenience,
even from worse to better.
Richard Hooker, 1554–1600

2.1 Introduction

This book comes with its own health warning. Radical change demands radical measures, and transforming an organization is a painful process. The road to recovery is at best uncomfortable, at worst positively disagreeable. As the chapters unfold, the reader will be asked to endure a variety of unpleasant treatments—heightened conflict, intensified political power brokering, some duplication of effort, more ambiguity and greater vulnerability. Indeed, at times, the therapy may seem worse than the illness. However, by the end of the book, it will become evident that conflict can be a potent source of creativity and that the other activities are highly productive attributes, so long as they are used in the right context.

Although conventional responses to business management may seem more palatable, they frequently aggravate the condition they are designed to cure. Extending conflict is generally viewed as something to be avoided. It appears to be time-consuming, negative and disruptive. Hence, in search of the stable equilibrium, most managers spend large proportions of their day smoothing out differences between departments: Marketing say the product must meet certain specifications; Manufacturing say that is impossible within the cost constraints, someone has to decide who is right; Finance are pushing for a level of income that sales people believe is untenable, someone has to agree to either cut costs or increase volume, so putting off the evil day, sales targets are often raised. Managers feel better, because they have made a decision that allows everyone to get on with their job with the minimum of fuss. Unfortunately, in the face of open-ended change, conflict avoidance, and quick decision making is little better than brushing the dust under the proverbial carpet.

Pushed underground, the problem foments as political resistance, only to resurface somewhere else in a more virulent form, which eventually requires bloodletting to cure—either the marketing manager leaves in disgust, because penny pinching eventually kills the viability of the product, or Manufacturing make expensive items that are never sufficiently profitable; the sales department does not meet its inflated targets, so heads roll. In both cases, the end result is bad for business. There is no marketable product, and the sales department is now smaller, so it is even more difficult to meet larger sales targets.

Every time these situations occur, an opportunity to re-energize the organization is lost. We excise the irritation, rather than using it as a spur to creativity. Dissonance is a sign of misalignment, of imbalance in the system, but that is where the interesting behaviour occurs. Generally, people do not see eye to eye, because they are each working within a different but perfectly reasonable set of constraints. Once we dispose of the belief that their arguments are excuses or unreasonable demands, and accept them as simply conflicting but equally necessary principles, it becomes possible to look dispassionately for a scenario that will accommodate both. Easier said than done, certainly. It may sound plausible to accept troublemakers as loyal and interested employees but how do you manage the disruption that they will inevitably create? This chapter develops the skeleton of a process designed to contain the major sources of disorder in any business environment within an ordered framework. By giving the conflict a consistent structure, it is possible to manage Chaos.

2.2 Paradox—the next strategic dimension

> Faced with the task of building multiple strategic capabilities in highly complex organizations, managers in almost every company . . . made the simplifying assumption that they were faced with a series of dichotomous choices. When the new competitive challenges emerged, however, such unidimensional biases become strategically limiting.
>
> Bartlett and Ghoshall, 1987[28]

F. Scott Fitzgerald once defined the test of a first-class mind as the ability to hold two opposing ideas simultaneously and still retain the ability to function. Sad to say, this is not one of the most notable attributes of either management theory or practice, even though it is clearly desirable in this era of complexity and radical change. In practice, managers usually maintain their ability to function through the time-honoured but simplistic mechanism of selection and choice. In the Information Age, managers need the power boost that a Scott Fitzgerald style intellect could contribute.

The dictionary defines a paradox or dilemma as a self-contradictory proposition. As the very embodiment of mental conflict, it would appear to have potential application in the current circumstances. A paradoxical framework could provide a convenient and accessible means of developing and exercising the desired intelligence muscles.

The idea has several benefits. Dilemmas conveniently encapsulate the ever-present value differences implicit in any system involving people. Dilemmas also encourage the user to acknowledge that each proposition acts as a natural brake on the excesses of its opposite. Psychologists have long recognized this requirement for balancing forces in the human system. Robert Johnson observed 'No aspect of the human psyche can live in a healthy state unless it is in tension with its opposite. Power without love becomes brutal; feeling without strength becomes sentimental'. The same need for balance is also appropriate to business strategy, except that it turns into a tension between hard and soft management techniques.

Handy has dubbed this 'The Age of Paradox',[29] but this is not to say that its power is new. The power of dilemmas has been known for many centuries. Socrates used them as a teaching aid 400 years before the birth of Christ. His teaching methods would seem strange to us today, because our expectations are that teachers impart knowledge directly. In that sense, Socrates never taught. His approach was to question his students continuously until he got them to admit to two beliefs that seemed to conflict. Carefully, he would point out the contradiction and then walk away, as if his job was done. Why did he get such a formidable reputation as a teacher? The power of his teaching lay in the tension he created in the minds of his students. Left to deal with the conflict between acknowledged beliefs, the students were forced to discover how they had lived with their own inconsistencies. This encouraged them to think more deeply until they found some acceptable synergy between the two ideas. In so doing, the students created a higher dimension which accommodated both beliefs. Accepting and recognizing inconsistencies in one's own thinking opens the mind to new possibilities. One is forced to challenge the assumptions implicit in one's current logic. The friction that this causes stimulates a deeper understanding of this complex world than ever could be gained from pat answers given straightaway.

It is for this very reason that religious truths are often presented in paradox. Christians are encouraged to give up all their worldly goods to be rich, be humble in order to be exalted and die so that they can live. Living according to such antithetical notions forces one to break out of narrow assumptions and explore more complex alternatives than one might otherwise do. Perhaps this is why Hammer is exhorting us not to automate but obliterate;[15] has the time come for businesses to die so that they might live?

There are many other examples of the educative value of paradox—the poetry of T S Eliot, in the works of Chaucer and Shakespeare and the pictures of M C Escher (Fig. 2.1). Creative people use paradox to set the scene for a broader frame of reference that helps their audience take a larger view.

Consider this picture by Escher and think about how the figure in the forefront cannot exist without the one in the background. Without evil

Fig. 2.1   A paradoxical encounter by M.C. Escher (reproduced with permission)

there can be no good; without sorrow there is no joy, and vice versa. Watch how the shapes interact, and the black and white figures reflect the action of their opposites in a constantly revolving loop. Creations of art such as this can be viewed as fundamental metaphors for our business processes. When we make business decisions, we tend to view propositions as black and white 'either/or' choices. We weigh the pro's and con's and choose the option with most pro's and *eliminate* the other. At least we think we can eliminate the other, but the alternative lurks in the background and often comes back to haunt us. Dismissing opposites and hiding behind convenient functional barriers produces unpredictable results, because the interactive complexity of the full picture is lost. Selection neglects the reality that alternatives are, in fact, mutually dependent. The benefits are complementary. The upside of one proposition offsets the downside of its opposite number. For example, most organizations choose either to centralize or decentralize. Centralizing brings benefits such as economies of scale and global coordination, but tends to underplay the need to be locally responsive to customers. Eventually, too much central control becomes unwieldy and unresponsive so the same company swings around to embrace total decentralization. In the process it loses the benefits of coordination and economies of scale. Most business people are all too familiar with this disruptive pendulum effect. Swinging back and forth between the two extremes achieves nothing except to make staff cynical about the proclaimed objectives of each move. The alternative is to reconcile the dilemma; to face the fact that both choices are equally valuable and find a way to get the benefits of both by becoming a 'centrally/decentralized'[30] organization. It is possible with a little creativity and a judicious dose of information technology. Some companies are doing it already. For example, organizations collect purchasing economies of scale by centralizing buying power, without taking away the ability of local units to satisfy customer requirements on delivery and quality. A common purchasing database is run by centralized buyers who negotiate with the suppliers, but updated by local people who have the choice as to quality, quantity and customer requirements. The partnership is mediated by on-line access to the database.

In the long term, synthesizing values is a more profitable exercise in the complex world we live in, although, in the short term, it may appear more costly in terms of time and effort. The more information and values we can reconcile into our business operations in creative combinations, the more difficult it is for the competition to copy our formula for success. But we have to look long term for the high returns. Goods and services that are high quality *and* low cost, technologically advanced *as well as* environmentally safe, functional but attractive take investment now, but, in the long run, they add more value than simple products which only fulfil an immediate need. Niche marketing is a dead-end street when circumstances change, whereas satisfying a range of customer values makes a product more durable and more flexible in a rapidly changing world. This is probably why the Japanese have concentrated their efforts on fundamental technologies that have multiple uses and a wide range of potential, even though, in the early stages, profitability may be low.

Interesting ideas, but how does the average manager put them into practice? Fortunately there is also a convenient way to operationalize the whole process.

Working with paradox

To make the task of managing paradox more graphic, more quantifiable and perhaps more appealing to the rational mind, Hampden Turner[2] defined a basic dilemma template in the form of a graph with an x and y axis (Fig. 2.2).

Each axis represents an opposing value. The weighting you attribute to *Value A* versus *Value B* creates a set of coordinates on the graph. The greater the distance from the top right-hand corner (point 10/10), the poorer the performance in reconciling the dilemma. Choice can make decisions top heavy, lopsided, compromised, adversarial or, at the most desirable point, synergized.

Let us put this into context by examining, as an example, two *extremes* of attitude towards employees today. *Value A* can be described as

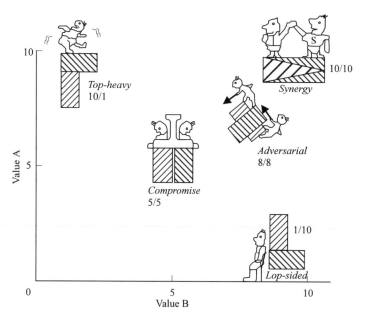

Fig. 2.2   The basic dilemma template (after Hampden Turner, 1990)[2] (reproduced with permission)

'Employees managed as machines' and *Value B* as 'Employees viewed as intelligent sensitive beings'. In simplistic terms, organizations that see people as machines, switch them on and off at will, expect perfect and consistent performance, irrespective of their personal circumstances, demand constant compliance and few holidays or ill health (Fig. 2.3).

Many American businesses fit into this top-heavy category. Power has indeed become brutal. Lopsided organizations, on the other hand, respect individuals, bend over backwards to keep them happy and contented in their jobs but impose insufficient pressures and controls to stimulate performance. Some Swedish companies have wrestled with the fact that feeling without strength becomes imbalanced sentimentality. Britain in the 1970s and early 1980s was typical of the adversarial positions. Unions fought fiercely on behalf of the masses against a management trained in the techniques of Taylor and others of his ilk. The battle raged back and forth with no victors. The mid- to late 1980s was a period of adjustment, when British companies often sat in the middle, having compromised on both counts. They looked back fondly to the days when people were no more than numbers and pieces of equipment, but were being pushed into a more democratic mode of operation by legislation. Britain's indifferent performance during that period is a sad testimonial to the effect of such a compromise, however there are hopeful signs that in the 1990s the nation is beginning to develop its own solution to the

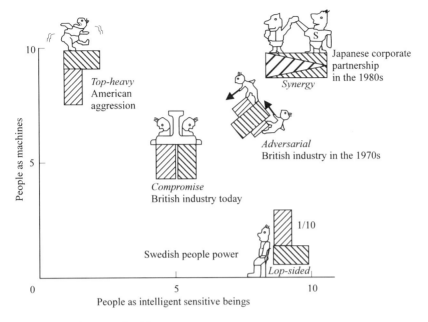

Fig. 2.3   The people dilemma

paradox. The philosophies of larger Japanese corporations used to provide a working example of synergy. The business committed itself to the
security and happiness of individuals and their families, but expected, in
return, total commitment and flexibility in the performance of the
employees' designated duties. Unfortunately, even this solution is beginning to show flaws, but that is an inevitable consequence of dynamic
paradox (see Fig. 2.4). There are, of course, scenarios other than the
Japanese that could fulfil the criteria of synergy. Handy's portfolio
career[31] is another possible alternative.

Hampden Turner has used this dilemma template to explain a variety
of thorny issues—why some capitalist cultures are more successful than
others,[32] why businesses in the same industry are more profitable than
others,[2] and why people[33] and corporate cultures[34] differ from one
another. As this chapter will explain, it is also possible to use it to
evaluate strategic performance potential by applying it to certain core
transformation paradoxes.

Handy says that 'paradox has become the cliché of our times'.[29] The
more turbulent the times, the more complex the world and the more
paradoxes there are. This highlights another important facet of dilemmas,
touched on earlier in the context of Japanese success. Even though we
may reconcile one tension, the solution inevitably creates another paradox, with which we have to cope (Fig. 2.4). Hence, the Japanese attitude
to employment is showing flaws. Their solution to the people dilemma is

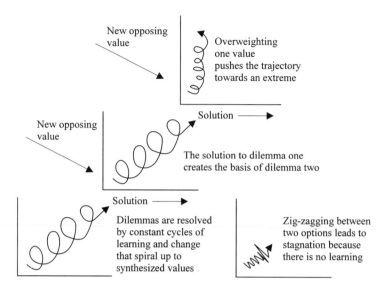

Fig. 2.4   Perpetual dilemma resolution

interacting with other economic and social parameters to create new turbulence to be stabilized, by a challenge to the accepted paradigm. Remember—challenge, change, crystallize, but then challenge, change and crystallize again.

Paradox is perpetual. Competitive alliances may be the current solution to the paradox between competing and cooperating, but it is not the final solution. If the alliance is between members of the industry, they immediately face the dilemma of monopolizing versus sustaining healthy competition. Resolve that through some form of regulation and they come up against some another imbalance in the dynamic marketplace.

What is the use of paradox to busy managers, if resolving one dilemma only creates another? Are we not just multiplying our problems? Well, in keeping with the theme of the book, the answer to that is 'yes and no'. Yes, there is a continuous stream of new problems to be managed, but their very novelty is a positive step forward. Creatively combining values generates more energy than it expends, which has to be better than constantly going round in circles managing the crises produced by long-unresolved conflicts in the system. Remember the Butterfly Effect? Lots of small inputs are amplified to produce radical results. The learning necessary to adapt continuously to new frames of reference amplifies the effect of each resolution, until transformation occurs spontaneously. New conflicts sustain the momentum for change by stimulating new learning. Acknowledging paradox introduces difference into the limit cycle. A mix of several contrary pairs will act like strange attractors. But where is the order in this disorderly mixture?

2.3   Avoiding errors of the third kind—the paradoxes of 'Chaos management'

Good solutions to the wrong problems are particularly prevalent in messy problem settings. The planner faced with an ill structured environment must be concerned with the validity of the planning process as well as its consistency.

Mitroff and Featheringham, 1974[35]

Hindsight is a wonderful thing. Looking back on past mistakes frequently shows that failure was caused by implementing the right solution to the wrong problem. Errors of the third kind, like this, are commonplace, but hard to avoid. We struggle to get to grips with the full dimensions of a problem, because of the sheer volume of dilemmas that abound in any value system. Indeed, the number of dilemmas is only limited by the number of distinctions one chooses to make.[36] Attempting to resolve them all would quickly produce total disorder; tackling a few at random is ineffectual. Errors of the third kind are what you get for trying to unravel the paradoxical strands of the spaghetti when they are covered in sauce. The knack is to know which group of dilemmas are having the most influence on the system—go for the hottest, tastiest ones first! Following the lessons of Chaos theory, there is a simple way to identify which forces bring order to apparent disorder. Look for the commonality on different scales. Fractals are the product of a few iterative rules governing the interaction of the forces in the system. By extension then a set of strategic paradoxes that can be shown to apply consistently to various levels of society and business should provide a strong control framework, while still permitting the latitude necessary for infinite variety. Variety comes from the interpretation of core paradoxes at each level, because outcomes differ based on subtle differences in the ambient conditions. Yet evaluating decisions against a common set of unvarying criteria brings an overall order to what otherwise could be an arbitrary process. Decisions guided by iterations of these principles will scatter the seeds of a new order in fertile soil. Paradoxical management, in this form, can provide a new mechanism for Chaos control in business.

The rest of this chapter is a search for the pervasive paradoxes affecting the circulation of global energy across the scales of society, business and daily life. There are five major paradoxes. Resolving them produces five primary objectives for transformation. The following sections of this chapter explore each of the conflicts in turn, explain how they are derived from the fundamental points of strategic control seen in Fig. 1.1, and then consider how the tension can be turned into a positive directive for transformation planning. A variety of analogies from both business and daily life, show how these dilemmas are relevant across the scales. In the last section, the tensions are assembled into a productive cycle of evolutionary revolution that converts conflict into continuous learning. This process of Chaos management becomes an unending cycle of accelerated learning.

2.4   Sharing strategic responsibility

> No man is an island, entire of itself; every man is a peace of the Continent, a part of the maine . . . Any man's deathe diminishes me, because I am involved in Mankinde; and therefore, never send to know for whom the bell tolls; it tolls for thee.
>
> *Devotions*, John Donne

Whatever your status in life, there is always some higher power to be answered to. There are dominant economies and struggling third world countries; there are governments and people, societies and industries; there are bosses and employees, parents and teenagers, teachers and pupils and even children and their younger siblings. The responsibilities of each differ across the scales, but, in the end, each pair has a common interest in cohabiting to their mutual benefit. In every case, the success of their strategy for survival and growth is intimately associated with that of their correspondent in the pairing. This being the case, responsibility for the direction and outcome of any action ought to be shared. Objectively, the nature of each party's contribution to the relationship is irrelevant. In other words, so long as each contributes their best, there is no difference in the quality and value of their participation. Yet, in our society, thinking and leading accrue a disproportionate amount of power, compared to their complementary activities. In practice, this is a dangerously subjective course of action. Certainly, the world could not advance without its leaders and thinkers, but equally it could not survive without the followers and doers.

In business, the balance of power in this paradox is often out of alignment. The extent and direction of the misalignment varies according to the specifics of the relationship. However, any sub-standard power immediately puts a relationship at a disadvantage in conditions of complexity and uncertainty. Whether it is shareholders and the Board, directors and departmental manager, or project leaders and their teams, it is equally important to make sure that both top and bottom share responsibility for strategic direction and are allowed to contribute their utmost to the relationship. Leaders have the task of providing direction and guidance to coordinate effectively the efforts of those in the ranks. However, their commission does not make them infallible, nor does it give them perfect understanding. In situations of open-ended change, it is those closest to the detail who are best positioned to identify the crucial change indicators, and to adjust direction to avoid the pitfalls. Their contribution is invaluable to the health of both parties. If the leader is too rigidly authoritarian, then the offerings of his staff are likely to be undervalued or ignored. Authoritarian leaders do not empower their work groups (see points 1 and 6 in Fig. 1.1). This is dangerous in the Chaos of business. Anyone who directs from the top without listening to the troops is more likely to lead them into danger than to safety, because his vision is out of kilter with changing reality. A top-level perspective frequently overlooks critical details which quickly hamper the progress of those on the ground. It is imperative that an organization make provision for accurate and unimpeded information supply lines and heeds the messages that they convey, otherwise the transformation process will surely flounder.

Nor should distance from the source of information become a means of avoiding the difficult responsibility of leadership. The view from higher ground extends further and covers the angles that are invisible when one is bogged down in the detail. Those at the sharp end will not work effectively as a team without some unifying objective, guidance and discipline from above. It is essential that the focus moves backwards and forwards between the scales. In this respect, the dilemma is also applicable to each individual. In other words it can be internalized. Full understanding of any situation requires a good overview, involvement in the detail, and then a reconciliation of the two and a revision of the outlook. Even the process of personal learning has to cycle continuously between the scales.

Managing people can be compared to raising children. The parallels provide some salutary lessons. In each case the objective is the same—to develop talented individuals who are capable of independent thinking in increasingly more demanding situations. The management parameters are the same too. Control and authority teach obedience; permissiveness and freedom allow independence and creativity. The trick is to find the right balance that *safely* exposes the growing person to increasing risk. In other words to create an environment for controlled innovation. This is the primary business objective for transformation too. What happens if either side has too much power. The exercise of too much parental authority produces two types of offspring, neither of which are desirable. Either the children grow into adults who cannot think independently— yes men and women—or they rebel as soon as they get into a position where they have some power of their own—strikers, saboteurs and troublemakers. Too little parental control produces equally obnoxious progeny—freewheelers who will never take any responsibility, or arrogant domineering adults who think the world owes them a living. Clearly, the illustrations are extreme, but they make a point. Businesses would be reluctant to employ anyone exhibiting these traits, but, in many organizations, managerial practices are committed to fostering them!

The time has come for everyone to stand up and bear their rightful share of strategic responsibility. Developing a true partnership between top and bottom is the first objective of every transformation programme and the first step on the road to changing behaviour. Far better than downsizing too (Re-engineering Myth 1), because it concentrates on the positive. Enabling every part of the organization to work to its full potential is far healthier in the long term than amputation. To make this happen, organizations will have to put in place new procedures and structural mechanisms, that both encourage shared responsibility as well as measure progress along the way.

2.5   Planning for the unknown

The best laid schemes o' mice an' men, gang aft a-gley.

To a Mouse, Robert Burns

Whatever your position, it makes sense to plan ahead in order to make the most of the limited resources at your disposal. Competition from any source compromises survival; strategy is an attempt to outmanoeuvre those threatening forces. Even paleolithic man must have made some primitive plans to make sure he had enough food for the winter, or enough protection from the wild animals who might also fancy his food. Of course, environmental conditions are always changing. When we can predict those changes, we can formalize the plans and pool our resources with others to gain more power over circumstances. When something totally unforeseen happens, real survivors have to be nimble enough to modify the original plan and look for ways to make the most of changed circumstances. If man had not had enough ingenuity to reassess his food plan when the Ice Age came, we might not be here today to wrestle with the knotty problems of business. Of course, it is not as simple as that. It is easy to make gradual adaptive changes over long periods of time. The difficulty today is that timescales have been compressed, so few people have the luxury of long periods of reflection to work out how to respond. Consequently, formal structured planning exercises are fraught with difficulty. Strategy has to be in a constant state of flux as it adapts to the constantly changing conditions. This is the paradox. How can we plan for the unknown? Somehow, managers have to reconcile the need to organize resources through formal competitive planning for the known, with the need for a nimble response to uncontrollable changes that pop up at random in the business environment (see points 2 and 7 in Fig. 1.1). Complete competitive manoeuvrability is vital. Otherwise the organization will become a dinosaur, destined for extinction.

This planned versus random response is also part of the learning process. There are two ways to learn: to hypothesize, test logically, and then evaluate the results, or to have sudden insights that spark new understandings. The planned programme works from predetermined assumptions, the unplanned breaks out of those constraints and finds a higher-level reality. However, that higher-level reality has to become the next proposition to be tested, to ensure that the new insights are not so esoteric as to be out of touch with reality.

The resolution of this paradox is not only relevant to business learning. This second paradox also holds true across all the scales. Individuals plan their career path, but frequently have to revise their plans to build in factors such as redundancy, takeover and sickness. Whole government departments are involved in analysing the future of world trade and finance in order to plan an effective national economic strategy that fulfils their social responsibility. Those plans need constant retuning and the policies need constant retesting to keep them in line with the demands of sudden unpredictable fluctuations in exchange rates and share prices brought about by the corporate hunt for profit.

The challenge facing society, organizations and individuals is how to plan for enhanced manoeuvrability in the face of turbulent environmental conditions. Analogy often proves illuminating, when the way forward is unclear. Think of the organization as an aircraft, that has to conform to certain aerodynamic principles in order to get off the ground. Once in the air, the objective is to pilot it as smoothly and economically as possible. It is constantly being buffeted by the whole gamut of weather conditions. How can the pilot adapt the flight plan and the resources built into the aircraft (flaps, engine, rudder, etc.) to fly most efficiently? In flight, the options are limited by the design of the aircraft, which is built to accommodate macro conditions. The broad tolerances necessary to make a plane safe for commercial flight make it cumbersome; human limitations slow the response time. Watching a jumbo jet take off, one wonders how such a lumbering piece of machinery can ever get airborne. Yet, when engineers got the chance to redesign an aircraft using the latest in technology, they produced an inherently unstable frame that mimics the infinite flexibility of a bird in flight. Ironically, the instability produces greater efficiency, but makes the pilot dependent on the rapid feedback provided by the on-board computers. With the assistance of computer technology, the aircraft can make rapid responses to events that would otherwise throw it off course.

Businesses currently have a similar golden opportunity to improve competitive manoeuvrability, by incorporating into their organizational planning and control system the sort of technology that will help them make a real time response to changes in market conditions. Here is the second objective for transformation—fly more competitively by installing technology that will feed back the essential control parameters for manoeuvrability. Later chapters of this book will take a brief look at some examples of available technologies that can be integrated into the planning and control system. Consultants have much to contribute to the selection and understanding process. However, upgrading strategic manoeuvrability is such a crucial refit that companies cannot afford to leave the design to outsiders, who only have a general background in aerodynamics principles and partial understanding of the properties of the structural components (Re-engineering Myth 2). This is not to say that consultants cannot be useful. They are ideally placed to introduce some instability into the system, by coming in as secondary resources to question the designer's assumptions and act as a convenient devil's advocate.

2.6 Putting ideals into practice

Companies that do come up with an innovative approach find them watered down by political infighting during the implementation's stage.

Hall, Rosenthal and Wade, 1993[37]

A political community will resist a prospective violation of its integrity whatever the rationality of the approach.

Burton Swanson, 1983[38]

Societies are groups of people with common interest banded together for the greater benefit of everyone involved. The same can be said of corporations, functional specialisms, churches, tribes, and even packs of animals. Each grouping develops its own identity, described by a set of ideals, a territory and their combined resources. Each community will try to arrange their resources to produce the greatest added value to their members (see point 3 in Fig. 1.1). Small wonder that they will defend their rationale for existence when these things are so intimately tied to their identity and their future. Conflicts of interest between the various communities are inevitable, considering the complexity of interactions between different segments of society and industry. In primitive societies, the first line of defence would be physical force. Money, to buy your way out of trouble, is perhaps a slightly more sophisticated response, but frequently the balance of power is such that this is not an option. Negotiation then becomes the only practical alternative. Politics are the mechanism of a civilized society for reconciling the differing interests of conflicting groups and sub-groups (see point 8 in Fig. 1.1). Depending on how they are used, politics can be a positive or a negative force for change.

In their most negative sense, politics are irrational, self-interested and protective. Negative politics are usually covert underground activities. This sort of usage has given politics a bad name; to describe a manager as a political animal is often seen as an affront. Yet, politics was once a noble art. It did not start out as stabbing your colleague in the back, or subversive intrigue, rather it meant service to the people. That is hardly an insult. In fact, used constructively in the interests of others, politics is a positive force. Negotiation and debate are an effective means of getting a feel for the major trends in attitudes and activities that will ultimately affect the body of the community. Putting the principle into a specific context should make this clearer.

There was a period in the history of the Ford Motor Company, when the paradox between ideals and practicalities was seriously out of balance. The effect was highly detrimental to the fortunes of the company. In the 1970s the management team was dominated by a financial élite which ruled through strictly rational criteria of added-value measurement. The strategic objectives were profit optimization, based on logical analysis and minimal risk. The rigour with which these policies were pursued overrode all practical necessities, and seriously clouded corporate judgement. The rest of the organization abandoned productive effort and resorted to political backstabbing in an attempt to gain 'points' in the eyes of the ruling junta. Protectionism and turf wars effectively quashed all cooperation between the various functions and what started as sound business practice degraded into out and out political warfare as a result of excessive profit rationalization. Decisions based purely on political expediency do not contribute to higher standards or greater added value. They are dangerous compromises that, in the end, block the path to creativity and the benefits of new alternatives.

It took the fresh outlook of a new CEO at Ford to ease the constraint upon effective strategy imposed by idealized financial status. By giving more recognition to the contribution of other departments and removing profit as the *only* criteria for decision, specialists were empowered to negotiate productively and fulfil the most important demands upon their skills. This, in turn, allowed them to help the organization react to the forces in the system that were shaping the corporate future. Ironically, underplaying the emphasis on financial criteria actually produced results that more fully satisfied the original desire of the finance function—optimal allocation of scarce resources. In fact, collaboration should have been the unifying ideal for every department.

There is a subtle political lesson to be learned here. Less direct pressure often produces more effect. Political activity is most effective when it is not driven by one ideal. Achievement of the shared goal that benefits everyone happens spontaneously when political activity is used productively to order the impact of subsidiary interests in the community. It is the Butterfly Effect in action.

The operational viability of strategy at any level is dependent on a balance between theory and practice, ideals and realities. It must be a reconciliation between the interests of the whole body and those of the individual constituencies.

When politics outweighs global rationality, things can go equally wrong. The healthcare debate in the USA is but one example of how too much political power can hinder change for the common good. The various insurance, legal, and medical lobbies are at loggerheads, protecting their own interests, while the people without access to primary care continue to suffer.

Businesses encounter this challenge at various levels in the organization. The process of new product development is but one example. Goods designed in isolation from manufacturing realities usually encounter major problems in production. Design engineers have a different perspective on a product than manufacturing engineers. Research chemists have different criteria to the operations manager when it comes to assessing the viability of their invention. When the balance of power is inequitable these differences either result in products too costly to make, or research results that do not scale up to a marketable output. Organizations often employ someone who can act as a 'boundary spanner'. This individual rationalizes the incompatible goals of each group by introducing some unifying focus, outside of the individual interests. As an objective intermediary who understands both the engineering or scientific theory and the practicalities of manufacturing, the responsibility of the boundary spanner is to find some workable compromise that satisfies a higher ideal.

This same argument echoes around the hallowed halls of all institutions of higher learning. Too much idealism may produce highly innovative research, but if the results cannot be applied then what is the real contribution to society as a whole? Can highly abstract theory really contribute to the institution's complementary role of teaching? In some ways it compromises freedom of thought if results must always be pragmatic. Yet, when the two arguments are viewed as complementary elements in a learning cycle it is possible to see how blue sky theory and down to earth research can work together to their mutual benefit. It is a symbiotic relationship.

Thus we come to the third objective of transformation. To ensure that the programme for change synthesizes the vision of an ideal future for the whole community, with the current political realities in the various constituencies. This is precisely the reason why IT-enabled transformation cannot be delegated solely to the IT function (Re-engineering Myth 3). Too much emphasis on one lower level ideal neglects the important contributions of other parts of the business.

2.7   Looking out for internal structure

> The learning organization possesses an openness to the outside world . . . The need for openness to outside ideas has a great impact on how the firm is structured.
>
> Quinn Mills and Friesen, 1992[39]

All organisms are engaged in a two-way exchange between their internal and external environment. The human body is constantly adapting to hot and cold, danger and security, pollution, food shortage, stress and many other variables. Some of those adaptations are temporary, others become more permanent as the basic structure of life, cellular DNA, changes. When environmental changes are within known limits, most bodies are fit enough to cope with changing conditions, because they were designed specifically to do so. However, if the outside changes go beyond predicted tolerances the internal structure has to change. Either new life forms evolve or mutations occur. Of course, Man stands alone in the animal kingdom as being able to manipulate the outside world for his own benefit. This is what has given him his competitive edge in the process of evolution. Intelligence is what gives mankind the power to manage the environment. Passive adaptation is not the only option. With foresight, it is possible to look outwards and forwards to envision a range of futures and then make the necessary interventions to bring about more favourable conditions. Housing, heating and air filtering systems, entertainment for relaxation are all inventions designed to insulate man from severe environmental changes.

Businesses are in a similar situation. They have a fairly stable internal structure that fits them to cope with the demands of their chosen industry. They have regulating mechanisms that help them adapt to hot or cold market conditions, perceive threats and assess security levels (see point 4 in Fig. 1.1). However, global conditions throughout the business world can suddenly impinge on the quality of their environment—outside predators take a liking to the spoils of the industry, technological change alters the balance of power in the market, natural resources are exhausted or customers change their habitat (see point 9 in Fig. 1.1). Then the organization has to consider evolving a new internal structure to compensate for these crises.

It is an unfortunate fact, that most organizations only consider one side of this equation. They have become expert at designing the most efficient resource structures for prevailing conditions. But all too frequently they neglect the fact that with a little intelligence they could manipulate that environment for their own benefit.

For example, United Parcel Service (UPS) had always defined itself as the most efficient road courier. The company developed the best network of lorries and a highly efficient support structure. Rigorous physical training made it the fittest carrier on the road. But it was still overtaken. Affordable air transport gave Federal Express an opportunity to overcome environmental limitations. By introducing new developments from outside the parcel carrying industry, Federal Express was able to shape the competitive environment to suit its own agenda. UPS had to scramble to catch up, or die.

Most organizations eventually react to new conditions. It would be hard for any business to survive if it had not taken a few steps along the information super highway. E mail, voice mail, digital answering systems all provided competitive advantage for some, for a short time; yet, once they became an integral part of most operations, the advantage was gone. In the end, adapting to outside stimuli is never more than a catching up exercise. However, when revolutionaries dare to stand back and look at the forces in operation beyond the borders of their industry and then imagine how they can use these apparently unrelated elements to their best advantage, they can create the conditions for true transformation. Manipulating outside forces is the way to get ahead.

Of course, it is useless to manipulate the environment and not assimilate the effects. Even those at the forefront of change are not protected from adapting. The entrepreneurial spirit of Steve Jobs turned Apple into a serious player in the home computer market and shook the safe environment that IBM had created for itself, but as the momentum grew, Apple tripped up continuously until it put in place a structure that allowed it to cope with its own success.

The paradox is this. Any structural configuration that an organization adopts is intimately linked to its strategic performance, but that internal framework immediately limits future strategic direction, by precluding certain incompatible options. To cope with this paradox, the organization has two alternatives. Either undergo major restructuring at regular intervals with all the associated upheaval, or it uses its intelligence to enact 'active, intrusive strategy'.[40] Perhaps it is the uncertainty surrounding most of the environmental variables that makes this option unattractive to many managers. Historically, strategy is the result of analysing the outside conditions and adapting the organization to fit, but complexity makes the environment inherently unanalysable, or so the argument goes. However, Chaos theory has something to offer in this situation too. We do not need to understand the whole system. All we need to do is mimic that butterfly in Brazil. Flexing the corporate muscles just enough to take flight will have a cascade effect throughout the business system. Active, intrusive strategy does not have to be on a grand scale, but it must be a continuous process: flex the muscles, adapt to the change, flex the muscles again, and see how the changes accumulate to create a storm that will catch the competition unawares.

This suggests a fourth objective for transformation. Redesign the organization so that it becomes a 'dissipative structure', that is one that can transfer energy back into the environment while retaining its internal integrity. The energy in question is information and knowledge. So, in the context of learning, new internal processes must be designed to create what has been termed an information 'gradient exchange' with the environment. Bring it in, process it and then use it to change the outside world. This is why business Re-engineering is not only about redesigning internal processes (Re-engineering Myth 4). It is about looking *out* for internal structure.

2.8 Building unity from diversity

If a house be divided against itself, that house cannot stand.

St Mark's Gospel 3: 25

Communities need stability; businesses must create diversity in order to keep improving results. The two objectives are in conflict (see points 5 and 10 in Fig. 1.1). When the influence of one exceeds the power of the other, bad things happen. For example, Americans can shop for seven days a week for at least 11 hours a day. Grocery stores open 24 hours a day, 364 days a year. Retailers are giving individuals every possible opportunity to consume in their drive for more sales. But, what does this push for more service offerings do for society? Indirectly it causes instability. More shopping requires more money. More money means more work. More work and more shopping means less time for the family. Family time is squeezed and a major stabilizing influence in society is undermined.

Certainly, the growing influx of new products produce new and more comfortable ways of living, but new lifestyles require more money to support them. The diversity of possible outlets for the average family income has proliferated; most couples need two incomes to sustain the sort of living standards that are displayed through the various media channels. Few people can afford all that they see on offer. This provides a new profitable business opportunity—to expand credit, with the result that personal debt escalates. Arguments over money are one of the major sources of marital disputes and breakdown. Society suffers. In the end, the cost of *uncontrolled* diversity and *unlimited* credit is out of proportion to the satisfaction derived from the original expansion. In other words, the negative effects have been amplified by the system. Everyone ends up paying to police the increasing delinquency of their dissatisfied citizens. Unstable family backgrounds, the status attributed to material possessions and the sheer impossibility of keeping up with the range of available options divide people from one another. Then one communal stabilizing influence is lost.

This is not to say that business is the only one at fault. The Church is often accused of remaining so stable that it is out of touch with the issues of the day. Congregations have dwindled, and as a result the influence of the Church has declined. Strong spiritual values could have provided the necessary counterbalance to the excesses of materialism.

Just like nations and societies, organizations develop their own cultures and social norms. These are a vital unifying force, but that culture must not be a constraint on necessary change. Groups can, however, become so united that they are a danger to themselves and others. Overly strong cultures place the life of the group above all other considerations. This produces delusions of invulnerability, and infallibility. When Kennedy and his advisers blundered into the Bay of Pigs invasion they showed all the signs of what Janis[41] termed 'group think'. A group of extremely clever men managed to conveniently filter out all the danger signs, override any internal disagreements and come to a unanimous decision that was totally wrong. In an organization, group think obstructs change.

Hewlett Packard (HP) was an organization with an exceptionally strong culture. The 'HP Way' was humanitarian and nurturing. People came first in the belief that secure, motivated staff will be committed employees, who can think and act independently. However, when unpleasant change became an economic necessity for HP, the culture became an overweighty burden that dragged the organization down. HP's way was a success from 1957 until the early 1980s. But, when the diversity of their computer business needed consolidating and refining, policies such as no redundancy, complete divisional and management autonomy, and exceptionally civilized behaviour prevented them from taking the necessary action to remove superfluous fat. HP had to introduce some harder business counterbalances to offset its soft humanitarianism in order to maintain status and reputation as a solidly successful company.

Too much unity and normalcy stops change at any level. If the harmony of its existence is so strong, a culture instinctively protects itself against outside violation. So, even though a corporate owner insists that a recently purchased subsidiary adopt different procedures and implement new corporate policies, once the immediate pressure for change is reduced, subsidiary members will slip back into the old way of doing things, just like a piece of elastic that has been temporarily stretched out of shape. One way to halt the slide back towards cultural comfort zones is to introduce conflict in the form of paradox. This maintains tension and encourages controlled stretch.

Of course, too much change, even in the name of progress, can tear previously stable institutions apart. The fall of the Berlin wall was the first step towards a unified Germany in a united European federation. Reunification placed enormous strains on German society and intolerable stress on the most stable currency in the European monetary system. One change might have been manageable, but other global events, such as the demise of the USSR, the Danish vote against the Maastricht Treaty, and a stagnant Japanese economy, all combined to put an intolerable burden of change on the band widths of the snake.* In October 1992, the dollar/sterling exchange rate fell from $1.9 to $1.7 in the space of a few hours, and Britain withdrew from the Exchange Rate Mechanism (ERM). By August 1993, the entire European monetary union was in a state of collapse.

Individuals can also show signs of mental collapse when change overwhelms them. Phobias, obsessive behaviour, depression and apathy are all psychological by-products of too much dislocation and change. However, not everyone reacts in the same way in the face of far-reaching change. Survivors of tornadoes in Florida, earthquakes in California and floods in the lowlands of northern Europe all suffered the loss of homes and possessions. Some collapsed under the strain of the trauma, others saw it as a challenge and picked themselves up ready to start all over again. The original group challenged their original fixed view of the world and learned anew. Clearly, some people are more resilient to change than others, and more open to new learning.

This brings us to the fifth objective for transformation: to develop a community of individuals who are resilient enough to cope with substantial change and then take control over it and use it to promote further change. If Re-engineering is a process of completely obliterating the frame of reference by which people have lived for years, it is destined for failure because the change is too radical (Re-engineering Myth 5). People will either be too traumatized to be productive or in time they will slip back into their old ways. However, if it is designated as a programme of steadily developing the capacity to change, of creating a culture that is predisposed to change, then it can succeed.

2.9   Evolutionary revolution—cycles of strategic learning

> One sensible operating rule is that whenever organizations adopt one prescription, they should adopt a second prescription that contradicts the first. Contradictory prescriptions remind an organization that each prescription is a misleading oversimplification that ought not to be carried to excess.
>
> Greve, Starbuck and Hedberg, 1978[42]

This examination of international, business and personal problems has produced five recurrent dilemmas that are consistently influencing outcomes within the whole human system (see Fig. 2.5). The question is why

---

*A system of interconnected exchange rates for the European Union countries.

		Modus omnibus rebus optimus est habitu		
		Moderation in all things	Plautus c200 BC	
Top down direction	1	**Elements of strategic responsibility**	Bottom up initiatives	6
Structured competitive planning	2	**Components of competitive manoeuvrability**	Random opportunism	7
Global resource rationality	3	**Issues of operational viability**	Political bargaining	8
Internal framework	4	**Facets of physical fitness for the environment**	External orientation	9
Social norms & standards	5	**Constituents of elastic strength**	Organizational change	10

Fig. 2.5   Complementary opposites in the transformation process

five? Why not six, seven or ten dilemmas? Referring back to Fig. 1.1, we find 10 individual functional disciplines that are reflections of 10 strategic themes, consistently identified by various authors, in virtually that order, over the past 30 years. A closer examination of these points of control has shown that they are paired aspects of the five dilemmas that have ordered societal and personal interactions over the millennia. Here is the order amidst disorder.

These five paradoxes have produced five important strategic objectives for transformation. Build an organization that:

- Shares strategic responsibility across all levels of the organization.
- Has the information circuits to be competitively manoeuvrable.
- Reconciles the goals of the community with those of the various constituencies in order to produce viable plans that benefit everyone.
- Absorbs information from the environment and uses it constructively to manipulate conditions and ensure that the organization achieves peak physical fitness.
- Is a community of diverse but resilient individuals dedicated to employing their combined skills in the service of continuous change.

The variety produced by the constant fulfilment of these objectives *in combination* across the levels of the organization should be the equivalent of an organizational strange attractor. A mixed-up ball of spaghetti (Fig. 2.6) that eventually transforms the behaviour of every individual in the system.

The circle is reputed to be the most efficient shape in the universe. It has been said that 'most managers get into trouble because they forget to think in circles'[43] so a management process that is deliberately organized in a circle should be ideal for ensuring that a revolution does not get into trouble. However, in order for the circle to remain true, the values at each of its spokes must be equally weighted. In other words, only a perfect tension between complementary opposites will permit easy revolution. Any imbalance will distort the circumference of the wheel and hinder its learning cycles. This is where the central ideas of paradox and learning come in.

How is it possible to make sure that the wheel stays in balance? In the end it comes down to resolving the paradoxes (see point 11 in Fig. 2.6).

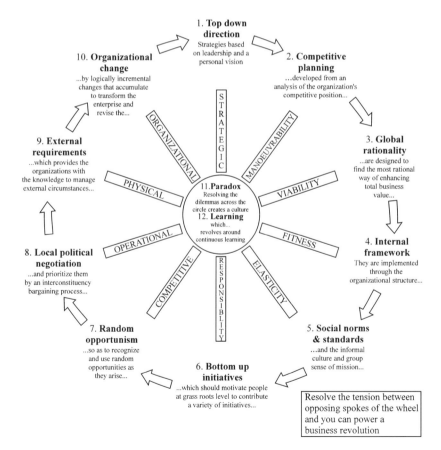

1. Top down direction
Strategies based on leadership and a personal vision

10. Organizational change
...by logically incremental changes that accumulate to transform the enterprise and revise the...

2. Competitive planning
...developed from an analysis of the organization's competitive position...

9. External requirements
...which provides the organizations with the knowledge to manage external circumstances...

3. Global rationality
...are designed to find the most rational way of enhancing total business value...

ORGANIZATIONAL

MANOEUVRABILITY

STRATEGIC

PHYSICAL

VIABILITY

11. Paradox
Resolving the dilemmas across the circle creates a culture

12. Learning
which... revolves around continuous learning

8. Local political negotiation
...and prioritize them by an interconstituency bargaining process...

OPERATIONAL

FITNESS

4. Internal framework
They are implemented through the organizational structure...

COMPETITIVE

RESPONSIBILITY

ELASTICITY

7. Random opportunism
...so as to recognize and use random opportunities as they arise...

6. Bottom up initiatives
...which should motivate people at grass roots level to contribute a variety of initiatives...

5. Social norms & standards
...and the informal culture and group sense of mission...

Resolve the tension between opposing spokes of the wheel and you can power a business revolution

Fig. 2.6 A paradigm for 'evolutionary revolution'

The first step towards that goal is to expose the exact mixture of imbalances currently inhibiting the organization. Because the paradoxical forces can be quantified by use of Hampden Turner's dilemma template, it is possible to turn the core dilemmas into a simple questionnaire (Appendix A) that can be used to explore the dimensions of the corporate personality at every level in the organization. Every business will have a different personality, caused by its own individual idiosyncrasies. The unique profile that emerges will show where there is uniformity and where there are dislocations between the levels and the organization. Chapter 7 will look in detail at how this tool can be used to understand the psychology of the organization, and to pinpoint the type of action needed to rectify the imbalances so that the organization can function as a completely balanced but unique entity in a rapidly changing world.

As we saw earlier in this chapter reconciling dilemmas has long been acknowledged as a worthwhile route to learning. When an organization focuses all its energy on managing all the strategic points of control as paradoxes, it automatically generates new perspectives and creates learning (see point 12 in Fig. 2.6). Such learning becomes the power which drives the revolutions of the wheel. So, revolution evolves from repetitive cycles of paradoxical management. Effectively, the two central points are the hub of this new process. Later on, the reader will see that the circle changes to a star. This acts as a reminder that the result of managing by this process will be sudden explosive transformation derived from conflict management and learning.

Having no end is an important attribute of a circular framework. Transformation is not a one-off activity produced by a single revolution. It is a continuous process of evolution, of making small but *significant* modifications across the scales, and reconciling all of them into purposeful action that carries the organization forward. The nature of paradox will amplify the learning generated in each revolution of strategy to produce spontaneous change throughout the system.

The message of this chapter is simple. Always keep both sides of every argument in mind. The mental tension thus generated will save you from the dangers of extremism, as well as helping you to think in constructive circles.

The next chapter will look at the paradoxes in action by considering a widely acknowledged case of successful transformation. However, because the framework was not explicit, and management was not thinking in circles, the transformation was underpowered and slow. The case of the American Hospital Supply Corporation may be old hat, but it does contain several useful lessons that can be used to improve the speed and efficiency of future revolutions.

How the revolution evolved at the American Hospital Supply Corporation (AHSC)*

A distinctive characteristic of this case is AHSC–Baxter's ability to proactively make the literally hundreds of small incremental redesigns of internal work processes and information technology necessary to improve its overall service level and business relationship with customers. A second distinctive characteristic was Baxter's ability to reconceptualize its primary business relationship with hospitals.

Short and Venkatraman, 1992[44]

At this point, it is worthwhile testing the wheel against a real case to see what it tells us about paradox in operation. Perhaps the most publicized case of transformation on record is that of the American Hospital Supply Corporation (AHSC), now Baxter Healthcare. Over a 30-year period, continuous cycles of change took a middle-of-the-road local distributor of hospital supplies and turned it into the market leader in the healthcare industry. Although progress was not as quick as most organizations today would expect, that does not mean that there aren't useful lessons to be learned. As an example of an organization that successfully revolutionized its business with the help of IT, it should, in theory, display all of the components of the five paradoxes. How the dilemmas were resolved provides a clue for would-be revolutionaries about how to speed up the transformation process. First, however, it is important to understand how the tale evolved.

3.1 A brief history of AHSC/Baxter

This is the story of a far-sighted organization which removed its blinkers to look beyond simple process improvements to become one of the first companies to reconfigure both its business network and the competitive conditions in its market. Years before the idea of business Re-engineering had ever been heard of, AHSC transformed its own personality and in the process transformed an entire industry.

*The evidence for this chapter comes predominantly from an article in the *Sloan Management Review*.[44]

Surprisingly, the first step came neither from the top nor from some far-reaching competitive ideals. The seeds of change were sown by a local manager trying to satisfy a customer. In 1957, AHSC had been focusing on ways to reduce the cost of order entry at the distribution centres, and had found the answer in IBM tab card machines. The objective was simply to improve internal efficiency by automating certain activities. In 1963, AHSC started experiencing problems servicing Stanford Medical Centre because the centre had moved to a unique inventory numbering system that was incompatible with that of their supplier. A local AHSC manager saw the synergy between circumstances in AHSC and the customer needs and devised a simple but effective solution. He supplied the Stanford purchasing department with IBM cards that had the AHSC product number pre-punched on them and the corresponding Stanford number written in the corner. This small action set the wheels of change in motion. Buying from AHSC was made easier than from any other supplier. Not only did the process improve order efficiency, it also locked in the customer. AHSC quickly recognized the importance of this innovation to future business strategy. Endorsement came when the idea was incorporated into a more formal strategy and investment resources were allocated to the project. The now famous Analytic Systems Automated Purchasing (ASAP) process was really the product of an experimental response to a customer problem.

For this low-level innovation to bring corporate advantage, however, changes in the political power base were necessary. Although the Chairman of AHSC, Karl Bays, had long had a vision of what IT could do for the future of the business, others would need to change their perception of the role and contribution of IT. The symbolic action of taking IT out from under the wing of the accounting function and reallocating the resources to marketing and distribution was enough to refocus attention. IT began to be viewed as a strategic business resource rather than an administrative support system. People began to see how information systems could add value to corporate activities.

Even though AHSC's corporate IT department was given the job of turning what had been known as the 'Tel American' system into a corporate asset, Bays did not ease off the pressure. He demonstrated his commitment to the system and to IT as a strategic resource by his dedicated participation in monthly review meetings. In time, his effort paid off and one man's initiative evolved into an organization-wide order entry system, based on touch-tone phone technology. However, although the system revolutionized the process of placing and receiving an order, it did not provide the necessary linkage between the sales representatives, the hospital customers and AHSC administration. Furthermore, there were no hard copies for order verification. This was a serious limitation from the customer's perspective, so the next step was for AHSC to enhance the system further to meet outside requirements.

Version two of the ASAP system contained the seeds of partnership between customer and supplier, between inside configuration and outside needs. ASAP2 produced a printed copy of the order via teletype machines installed in the customer sites. Customers paid for the machines and AHSC paid the call charges.

ASAP3 took this cooperation with the customer a stage further. In the early 1970s, automated materials and supply management was uncommon, and most hospitals were struggling with the cost and complexity of managing their materials purchasing. The third-generation system provided a customizable ordering programme that allowed buyers to use their own purchasing formats, create standing order files and incorporate economic order quantities back into their own system.

This was an entirely new service in the industry; it saved the customer money and provided the sort of bespoke system that hospitals could not afford to develop for themselves. Obviously, it became very popular. By the mid 1970s AHSC was producing 'customer purchase analyses' for key accounts, and providing larger hospitals with a small team of sales marketing, distribution and IT personnel to analyse their paper flow and find process improvements. The knowledge gained during these activities was fed back into new service offerings for other customers. Eventually, the service level provided by AHSC became an industry standard that changed the rules of competition.

The growing competitive advantage of the ASAP system was helped by two fortuitous developments.

In the late 1960s and early 1970s government spending was growing at a phenomenal rate, as a result of the Medicare/Medicaid legislation in the US. Purchasing budgets for medical supplies and equipment were increasing by 10 per cent per annum, and sales to hospitals grew from $2.14 billion in 1970 to $22.5 billion in 1986. This frightening growth focused hospitals more on cost and less on quality. The ASAP strategy supported their pressing need for cost control; the success of the system brought positive feedback into the organization to bolster the perception of IT as a strategic resource.

During the late 1970s and early 1980s, hospitals became more computerized. Gradually developments in technology made it possible to eliminate manual intervention in the order process. The ASAP4 enhancements took advantage of better communication technology to create a direct electronic link between the AHSC computers and the hospitals' internal systems.

As a materials distributor, AHSC recognized that improving their customers' purchasing function would contribute to their own success. Over time this became another unifying objective. Everyone believed and worked towards becoming the 'prime vendor of choice' with all the major hospitals. Prime vendor status meant that hospitals agreed to purchase specific volumes, mainly at a fixed price, which saved them time and effort in the long run. The benefit to AHSC was to shift the emphasis away from price towards service, which was their strength. The concept of prime vendor was to become an integral part of the corporate culture, and a powerful driver for change.

Obviously, competitors were not standing still all this time. They, too, were scrabbling for a piece of this growing market. Several companies developed localized systems, but none of them found it easy to overcome AHSC's early penetration advantage. Nonetheless, AHSC managers were under no illusions as how quickly their advantage could be eroded. Competitive analysis showed that AHSC's unique advantage was their broad product line, not the ASAP platform. A combination of the two factors would offer the customer a very attractive 'one stop shopping approach'. The ASAP infrastructure and the vast product range of AHSC, was a formidable barrier to entry. In fact, AHSC's competitors were doubly disadvantaged. Regional fragmentation prevented them from fielding the same level of resources as AHSC and the inertia brought on by their own historical characteristics and structural idiosyncrasies seriously hindered their progress. Some tried litigation, accusing AHSC of unfair trade restrictions, but the courts eventually exonerated the corporation in December 1983.

Gradually the ASAP platform became an integral part of a much wider strategic focus, and management was constantly redesigning other structures and processes to make the integration seamless.

Baxter, Travenol Laboratories recognized the benefits of the AHSC set up. They acquired AHSC, in 1985, in a strategic bid to control the most powerful route into hospital purchasing departments—the ASAP distribution network. This action changed the competitive dynamics of the industry totally. Johnson & Johnson, Abbot and several other, smaller companies who had previously sold products through AHSC, suddenly found that their erstwhile distributor was no longer a complementary organization in the industry value chain, but part of a major competitor. As a result, several major suppliers removed their products from the ASAP system and started developing their own seriously competitive versions.

Baxter's range of products and the 80 per cent hardware penetration made it difficult for even the largest competitor to promote a proprietary system, so new entrants had to be *multi-vendor systems*. Their scramble to catch up reinstated them as important players in the market, but they spurred Baxter to make further system enhancements, adding features such as electronic funds transfer and off-line order creation. Unfortunately, by 1988, there were more than 50 order entry/materials management systems competing for hospital interest. The more incompatible systems there were, the more hospitals feared that their purchasing efficiency would be eroded, so there was a growing cry for a common order entry platform.

To deal with this new problem Baxter first developed ASAP Express, a multi-vendor system designed to link to other network providers. They continued to move away from dedicated systems with proprietary architecture until, in 1990, ASAP Express Powerbase 1990 was launched. This was an all-vendor electronic purchasing system that would run on any 386 computer with a modem. It included gateways to other network providers and added-value network products. By this time the strategic emphasis was being reshaped again. The prime vendor concept was giving way to the idea of an added-value information-based relationship between the company and the hospitals. Once again, a change in strategic direction wrongfooted the competition.

In 1990 Baxter deployed Valuelink. This was a fully integrated logistics system that ensured customized packaging and Just In Time (JIT) supply to the point of use, every day of the week. The concept was a whole new approach to managing the purchasing, inventory control, invoicing and payment cycle that makes up customer–supplier relationships. What had started as an order entry system had become a value-added materials management service. The rationale behind such a move was that distributors are the best people to manage the purchase/inventory part of the cycle, but they can only do that if the customer will commit to product and service purchasing quotas. This is a true strategic partnership, a win/win situation in which both sides accrue benefits and minimize their disadvantages. This willingness to merge Baxter's strategic objectives with those of customer organizations rather than seeing them as exclusive alternatives, represents one example of synergy.

The lesson here is that transforming corporate direction and changing the dynamics of the marketplace was an accumulation of change actions, which evolved flexibility and the capacity to continuously re-evaluate the *status quo* translated a simple distributor into an extension of the hospitals' inventory management programme. When enough evolutionary changes filter through into strategy, structure, culture, politics and individual actions, the revolution occurs spontaneously.

3.2   Lessons from the field

From Fig. 3.1 we can see how AHSC activities satisfy all the criteria in the paradoxical framework. AHSC shared strategic responsibility by incorporating low-level initiatives into future strategic direction (1/6 paradox). Competitive analysis combined the value of IT with the value of product range to produce a manoeuvrable strategy that made the most of environmental opportunities (2/7 paradox). The attitude to the AHSC–hospital relationship brought added-value to both participants, once the pressure to use IT was intensified by a realignment of political power

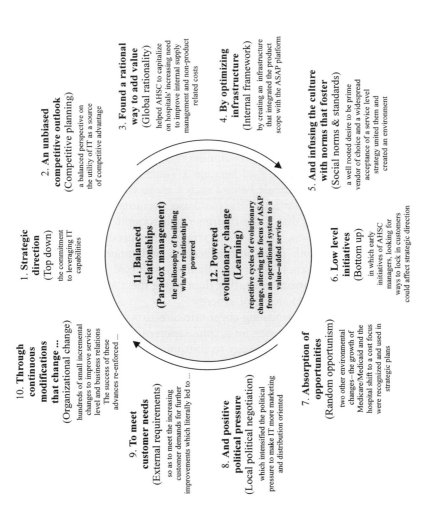

Fig. 3.1 The complete AHSC cycle. By reading clockwise around the circle, we get a complete picture of the AHSC transformation process.

(3/7 paradox). A flexible internal infrastructure and an open technology platform enabled AHSC to accommodate the customer as well as change external conditions for their competitiors (4/9 paradox). Cultural beliefs about the nature of the business relationship drove hundreds of incremental changes that eventually transformed not only the organization but also fed back into a reconceptualization of the cultural credos (5/10 paradox).

Looking back over this case, what is immediately striking is the nature of the triggers for change. Although the Chairman and his strategy team saw the potential of IT, those at the top of the organization were not the primary innovators. The technological changes were triggered by humble sales managers, random circumstances, or customer requirements. Later, the triggers were incorporated into the formal strategy as management recognized how important the innovations were to the production and maintenance of competitive advantage for the benefit of the whole organization. This is the first important lesson for anyone using the wheel of paradox. Energy to start the wheel in motion does not have to come from the top alone. Even though the spokes of the wheel have been numbered sequentially from one to ten in this book, this is purely a convention. It is not necessary to start from the top and work around. Any one of the 10 aspects around the wheel can act as the initial trigger for a change in strategic direction, so long as managers have an eye open for the opportunities.

This conclusion must be taken one stage further. Aspects are not used in isolation either. Often a combination of several is required. In everyday life aspects overlap and recommendations fit more than one problem. Fig. 3.1 isolated the activity at AHSC Baxter into discrete examples of each strategic aspect. However, this is a convenient theoretical refinement in the interests of clarity. In practice, the aspects were operating in dynamic equilibrium all the time. Pressure from the Chairman (1), a grassroots initiative (6), and political restructuring (8) allowed the organization to obtain strategic value from IT (3) by capitalizing on unforeseen opportunities at large (7) and feeding them back into formal strategy (2); cooperation with the customer (9) drove internal change (4) in logically incremental steps (10) which could be absorbed by the community into a cultural belief (5) that would transform the entire strategic direction (1) of the corporation.

As change activity continues, the focus of attention does not move sequentially from the trigger point, around the elements. Energy can cycle back and forth across a few spokes for a time, before it affects aspects further around the circumference of the wheel. It all depends on the strength of the various forces and the unique set of circumstances prevailing at the time. AHSC's development showed a lot of activity along the internal/external dimension, as they read their environment, altered the internal structure of the system to fit with the changes and then used the changes to further alter market conditions. A major factor in Baxter's success is that management did not let organizational boundaries restrict its perspective. Focus on business processes was not excessively introverted because it was driven by an external customer orientation. Concentrating on the connection with the customer was a stimulus to question the implicit industry assumptions. The external outlook provided the necessary counterbalance to the dangers of introversion that are associated with internal process change. Other organizations may already have such counterbalances but might have shown more activity in, say, the cultural or political areas, where a redistribution of energy was necessary.

The point is that there is a third dimension to the framework, which is not immediately obvious. It is not simply a revolving wheel held in tension by its spokes, but a dynamic molecular structure with energy flowing backwards and forwards across the bands as well as around the circumference. Practicalities make it difficult to depict the full complexity of the wheel in operation in all the diagrams in the book. Fig. 3.2 is an idealized version of the process in action.

This case also confirms other important points made earlier. Transformation is a continuous process. It must be viewed as a means not an end in itself. The competitive advantage brought by the first cycle of change would not have been sustainable without ongoing revolutions of the wheel. Revolution is an interesting word. It can mean radical change and upheaval, but it also means a turn of the wheel and an action that brings us full circle. The goal of organizational revolution will come

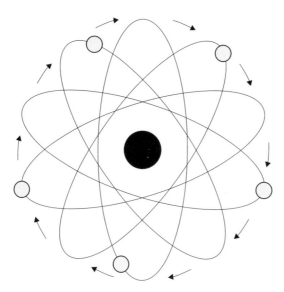

Fig. 3.2 Dynamic energy flows as values interact

from cycles of strategic activity that organize the components of business interaction into conflicting patterns and then resolve the tensions in such a way as to propel the company further along the road to transformation. The propulsion comes from learning and the Baxter case exhibits all the aspects that, in the end, combine to produce an organizational learning culture.

What made the process so slow

Organizations embarking on the transformation process today have several advantages over AHSC Baxter, not least of which is foreknowledge of strategic intent.[45] AHSC did not set out deliberately to transform anything. The ideas of business Re-engineering had yet to be defined. Nonetheless, AHSC Baxter still managed to completely reconceptualize the role of the organization in the whole business system several times. It redefined its role from that of efficient distributor to prime vendor, to electronic supply networker and finally to value-added partner for the hospitals it served. In parallel, AHSC Baxter had to redefine the strategic contribution of IT. What started out as a 'business led IT response', became a customized systems strategy dedicated to customer service and, finally, an open systems architecture that added value by carrying organizational expertise beyond the boundaries of the organization. However, if management had originally been motivated by a far-reaching intent to transform activities their actions would have been designed to 'stretch' the company's strategic ability more and get more 'leverage'[46] from its resources. This would have helped to compress the timeframe from initiative to transformation.

Certainly the corporate transformation was the product of various process redesigns, but the trigger for each step-change was the reconceptualization—that sudden 'Eureka', that alters the perspective so that a mass of detail becomes an illuminating three-dimensional image. It is rather like the 'Magic Eye' pictures that are so popular today. At first glance they are multi-coloured patterns on a flat page, but if you look beyond the detail there is a solid figure hidden in the disorderly mass. Admittedly, focusing on the detail of internal process brought early competitive advantage, however, to sustain its advantage AHSC had to look beyond the obvious and visualize new forms of business relationships and a new scope for its operations. In other words, AHSC tackled the process back to front, climbing the ladder sequentially because no-one knew any better. If it had tackled the relationship and process changes synchronously coming from the deeper perspective of reconceptualized scope, the journey could have been shorter.

Of course, conditions in the 1990s are more favourable for transformation because the ambient rate of change is greater. Many of the farthest stretches of imagination will probably be realized in 10–15 years from now. Greater energy in the environment can be channelled back into the organization.

A further factor that slowed the rate of change at AHSC was the way the organization chose to manage the implicit paradoxes that make up the strategic wheel. There are four basic ways to handle a dilemma: accept the contradiction and learn to live with it (this often means conflict goes underground); keep the conflicting elements in separate physical or social compartments (i.e. functional disciplines, or isolating the supplier from the buyer by organizational boundaries); separate the differences in time (i.e. put one value in the background until later and concentrate on the other for now; cycle back and forth between the two over time); or synthesize the requirements of each party to produce an entirely new dimension that incorporates both perspectives. For the first 25 years at least, AHSC Baxter managed the paradoxes by separating the conflicts either in space or time. This works, but it is a slower way to finding the common denominators that form the basis of a transformed picture. Effectively, the organization works its way gradually up and around the spiral shown in Fig. 3.3, rather taking the direct route to point 10/10.

However, the root of the success of AHSC Baxter lies in its ability to reconcile all its experiences into a pattern that produces continuous *learning*. At each stage, it has examined the forces constraining the situation, honestly faced its own limitations and set about fixing them in an innovative way that kept the organization one step ahead of the competition. What is the secret? Two things: openness to continuous criticism and upheaval, and never assuming the journey is over, never saying 'we are there, so let's rest'. The journey continues to this day. Recent history suggests, however, that paradoxical forces may have got too far separated in time and space, leading the Baxter organization astray into errors of extremism. Only time will tell whether it can redress the balance.

The next chapter will look at five important principles designed to induce the irritations and openness so essential to learning.

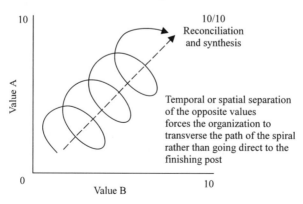

Fig. 3.3 Managing paradox

Five principles of evolutionary revolution

4.1   Introduction

There are several very important preconditions necessary to create a favourable setting for corporate transformation. Each principle on its own expands the potential for organizational learning and enhances the corporate capacity to reconcile an associated strategic paradox. Together the five principles work to re-energize the whole body of the corporation. The problem is that most of the time they fly in the face of conventional business practice, and change the task of management entirely. This chapter considers the principles of *evolutionary revolution* in the same order as the paradoxes in Chapter 2.

4.2   Federating knowledge *(top down/bottom up)*

> In an economy where the only certainty is uncertainty, the one sure source of lasting competitive advantage is knowledge. When markets shift, technologies proliferate, competitors multiply and products become obsolete overnight, successful companies are those that consistently create knowledge and disseminate it widely throughout the organization.
>
> Nonaka, 1991[47]

How can an organization encourage people to take an equal share of the responsibility for strategic direction? The answer is deceptively simple: by giving them the power to do so. Of the three basic sources of power, knowledge is the only logical choice for the circumstances. However, the practice of federating knowledge is not easy. In order to maintain perfect tension between the top and bottom, between vision and action, there must be open access to information as the raw material of knowledge. No secrets, no playing things close to your chest as a lever against others! Further, once the information is in circulation, everyone must feel equally empowered to 'tell it as it is', in response. This is the only way to sustain a balanced energy exchange between the levels. How rarely that happens in practice!

There are two requirements here. The first is an organizational issue, the second is a more personal one. Organizationally, businesses need a formula for coordination that still leaves room for independence—a way of uniting that does not deprive individuals or subgroups of their power. At the personal level, individuals have to feel psychologically comfortable enough really to 'tell it as it is'.

Nations use federalism as a mechanism for banding together without losing their individual identity or local power. Canada, Europe, USA, and the United Nations all work along federal lines. Some businesses are following the trend.[48] Organizations such as Ciba, Coca-Cola, General Electric, IBM, Johnson & Johnson, Royal Dutch Shell, and Unilever, have all moved to federal structures to help them manage the complexity of their operations. Taking the idea one stage further, it is possible to view every organization as a federal union, in that it is made up of bands of experts. Expert groups need to maintain their identity and power, otherwise their expertise can be devalued. For a federation to remain a meaningful institution for its participants, however, power has to remain at the lowest level. The principle being that the most effective decisions are made by those closest to the detail. This maxim is fundamental to shared strategic responsibility. Those at the top are not in the best position to make informed decisions, because of their distance from the detail, so they have to accede to those who are better qualified.

However, no members can be allowed a disproportionate share of power or they will start to usurp the role of the central body. Pluralism and *inter*dependence spread the power load effectively in a federation. By extension, these are necessary attributes of an organization.

Somehow, the federation has to coordinate the consequent mass of disparate decisions into a coherent direction for the syndicate. If top management is to fulfil that role it too must have access to open channels that transfer new knowledge and learning from the source to the coordination point and back again; information must also flow freely between members, and the channels must be 'clean'. There are three qualities essential to keeping these circuits open and unpolluted: honesty, trust and communication, or more specifically, common communication standards.

When it comes down to the line, real honesty can stir up some very disagreeable situations—that most people would prefer to avoid. It is never pleasant to have to deal with criticism, or to face unpalatable truths. However, in terms of results, it is actually quicker and less destructive to meet the truth head on rather than beat about the bush implementing the right solution to the wrong problem. The right solution to the real problem has been stated as everyone in the organization changing their behaviour. In many cases, the most fruitful place to start is with the counterproductive behaviour that makes people shy away from unpleasant facts. That is not easy when no-one wants to tell the bosses they are wrong.

Unfortunately, it is often the high powered, well educated executives at the head of the organization who most need to reflect on their behaviour. As Argyris has pointed out,[49] these are the people who are often the least skilled at double loop learning. In other words they rarely challenge their own behaviour let alone change it and then crystallize the results into a new management style. The track record of success that got them into their position usually means that they are relative strangers to failure. Many executives have never been taught how to learn from mistakes. Consequently, when the first cycle of strategy goes wrong they become defensive, justifying their actions or looking for a scapegoat. Such defensive activity consumes so much energy that it diverts them away from a critical examination of their own contribution to the problem. Hence they never start off around the second learning loop. How often have you watched your organization commit to a strategy and then change it as soon as it runs into problems? Over a period of five to ten years, some organizations blithely adopt six or more new strategies without ever questioning why the earlier ones failed, or understanding what the new strategy does to correct those failings.[50] What sort of message does that communicate back to the grassroots? Hardly a clear coherent direction, more like confused uncertainty. This inability to learn increases the ambiguity and unpredictability already present in the chaotic business system, but the energy input is negative and destructive.

Argyris spent 15 years studying consultants, whom he considered to be 'the epitome of highly educated professionals'.[50] What he found was surprising. Although, they were enthusiastic about learning in a generic sense, and spent their lives transferring knowledge to others, they were usually the biggest obstacle to change in their own organizations, because they were unwilling to question their own behaviour. As soon as the spotlight turned on them, the consultants felt threatened. Guilty and embarrassed when they were found to be less than perfect, they shied away from criticism, and erected a protective wall that prevented honest self-assessment.

Honesty does not have to be brutal. It can be gentle, yet incisive. There are ways to present a truth without destroying the dignity of the listener, however painful the facts are. Integrity and respect for the individual is tied up in this whole thing. Counsellors and therapists are expert at encouraging people to be honest with themselves in a non-threatening way. The hard truth is that if management wants to successfully transform an organization, it is going to have to start incorporating some of these softer techniques into its own portfolio. Peter Senge[51] suggests that organizational learning requires a *shared* vision. Visions that come down from above do not have the commitment of those below, so they fail; the idea of visions arising from below is equally impractical. To develop a joint vision, the leaders will have to adopt a new role as facilitator, arbitrator and (Socratic) teacher; the bulk of the contributions will have to come from local knowledge and decisions. Valuable local contributions are only produced when individuals are given the freedom and power to act independently. This requires trust. Although it often doesn't feel like it, trust is a two way thing. The manager whose head is on the block, has to trust that his staff will not mess up. The staff have to trust not only that the manager really will allow them the freedom to decide for themselves, but also that he has enough experience to put safe limits on that freedom. Further, the credibility of management efforts to fulfil its new role will depend on whether managers start to make themselves vulnerable by opening up their performance to the scrutiny of those whom they are leading. The smartest people in the organization have to be open to criticism in order to learn the basic mechanics of the second learning loop. The benefit is that leadership vulnerability sows the first seeds of trust that enable others to improve their learning capacity.

Trust is essential to the working of an information economy and the economics of information are critical to the fortunes of every subgroup within the federation, as well as to the wealth of the syndicate as a whole. It has already been said that knowledge grows when it is shared. Without trust people are unwilling to share the information resource. Unfortunately, when information is secreted away and jealously guarded, like cash stuffed in a mattress, it cannot appreciate, and eventually is devalued. When a group is excluded from the knowledge loop, it is unable to make a worthwhile contribution to the community affairs. Consequently, it will be isolated from future participation and what little currency reserves it did have will be even further devalued. This is the start of a vicious circle.

It is an unfortunate fact of life that people tend to hoard information like they hoard money because it gives them status and power. Giving away information is like giving up one's financial security; it makes people feel vulnerable. So people become defensive and protective and only share part of their intellectual property.[49] Unfortunately, the bit that is kept private is usually the most valuable nugget of information, the one that touches them personally, or the one that will stir up conflict. The end result is that everyone is going around either making decisions based on superficial understandings and incomplete information, or making no decision at all. Is it any wonder that Chaos is so difficult to manage?

Strategic value is locked up in these disparate pockets of knowledge. Even if each person is only withholding one tiny but significant fact the total loss to the organization is enormous. In fact, if individuals could only overcome their fear, they would find that in the end, pooling their resources makes everyone stronger. Under what conditions do people feel strong enough to make themselves vulnerable? Usually, it is as simple as feeling secure in their surroundings. What does management do to make employees feel secure? Keep their own intentions hidden under the guise of a confidentiality, send out ambiguous messages like, '*Yes you have my authority to go ahead, but remember it is your responsibility!'* agree to something and then have a change of mind two weeks later, or make changes that affect subordinates but protect themselves from the pain— pay rises for the boss, pay cuts for the workers. How secure would anyone feel under those conditions?

Even worse, the whole fiasco is generally brushed under the carpet. Everyone pretends that it is normal to live in a world of veiled threats, half truths and false harmony. No-one admits that there is a crisis of trust, and so no-one challenges it. When a company appoints a divisional president, it is buying experience and knowledge. Ostensibly, the organization puts its trust in that foundation, and give the president authority to run his operation. Yet, often, as soon as an important issue comes up, HQ pulls rank and interferes. After the event, HQ still expects the divisional president to act independently, and insists that he is running his own show. The interference is motivated by insecurity. Out of fear (going under the misnomer of respect) the president does not *openly* question the dual standard. Of course, that sort of blighted exchange is not solely confined to business—it happens in social clubs, marriages, parent–child relationships and any other communal institutions where power is distributed. People go out of their way to insulate themselves from the pain of learning. The tendency is to hold steadfastly to the comfortable and familiar and desperately look for a way to avoid admitting imperfection, thereby limiting their ability to question the implicit assumptions that colour their picture of reality. Prejudice, intransigence, illusion and extremism will persist, unless organizations create a safe learning environment.

How can management weed out these destructive forces? The process starts with one word—honesty. The answer is simple, the practice is much more difficult. However, paradox can be a powerful assistant.

There is also an important and complementary value that supports the move to more ethical behaviour, namely commitment. Ethical behaviour is only credible when it is consistent. Trust takes a long time to gain, but only a second to lose. In the real world, there are many temptations to allow standards to lapse. It is easy to justify minor dishonesty or keep information to yourself, '*I didn't want to hurt his feelings*', '*the staff wouldn't understand, it's too complicated to explain*'—'*I have more experience in this, so I'm in a better position to make a decision anyway*' — but it is a dangerous pretence. Staff sense the inconsistent message and dismiss the sincerity of the original intentions. In fact, when people are treated fairly, they usually rise to the occasion and prove more adept than expected.

However, if the leaders are not truly committed to following through with what is effectively a power sharing exercise, particularly when the going gets tough, as it undoubtedly will, then there is no point in starting out on the journey. In fact, a half-hearted attempt at honesty and fairness will do more harm than good because it will harden attitudes for the future.

This discussion can be framed as a general principle for transformation. Knowledge power must be disseminated through unobstructed information channels. A management commitment to basic ethical principles, such as honesty, integrity and consistency, will clear the worst blockages and increase the information flow along the channels. To convince others that intentions are genuine, the first step is for management to make itself vulnerable to criticism from below.

4.3   Relinquishing direct control *(competitive planning/random opportunism)*

> Control is an amplifying activity that spreads new perspectives through an organization . . . those at the top of the organization can create the necessary conditions for bounded instability, but they cannot control outcomes.
>
> Stacey, 1992[52]

How does anyone plan for the unknown? It sounds incongruous to be devising a strategy that will cope with the unforeseen, however, it is not without precedent. Adventurers and explorers throughout history did it and thought nothing of it. Christopher Columbus and his crew set sail to find a westerly route to the Indies, without knowing what lay in store. Some people thought they would fall off the edge of the earth, but they didn't; instead they found America. Nothing daunted, others set sail to in pursuit of Columbus's dream. In 1521, Magellan finally chanced on the route around America into the Pacific, and so became the first to sail around the world. Sailors are particularly adept at resolving the paradox between planning and opportunism because they are familiar with managing Nature's Chaos. Columbus and Magellan knew the general direction in which they were heading, but they had to sail with the wind, an element largely outside of their direct control. There are lessons here for modern captains of industry. One of the first requirements is somehow to revive the corporate spirit of adventure.

In many respects the world has become an open book since the days of Columbus and Magellan. There are few uncharted areas to explore, few unclimbed mountains, and few challenges that have not already been conquered by someone. The amount of knowledge accrued since the 1500s is phenomenal. Scientists have already mapped large areas of the human genome. People and machinery have been launched into outer space, bringing back vast amounts of information about matters beyond our world. We know how to obliterate our existing world several times over. We also have all manner of financial instruments and techniques at our disposal for controlling business. With all this available knowledge, surely it is not unreasonable to expect people to have the power to control their tiny section of the world? Management has reams of business information at its disposal and years of accumulated business knowledge, surely it should have control of the situation? Sadly, such arrogance will be our downfall in the end, both in society and in business. No-one can ever have perfect knowledge. The human brain struggles to handle more than seven different concepts at one time. How can anyone possibly expect to attain perfect understanding under such narrow constraints?

In fact, this is one of the fundamental perversities of life, the more knowledge there is, the less in control we really are. Why? Because as knowledge increases, so does ambiguity. Life is a paradox. There are two sides to every argument. Consequently, as facts multiply, the sharp contrast between black and white starts to blur into an indecipherable shade of grey that fogs the vision and makes it more difficult to be decisive.

In defence, organizations have become so buttoned down, so focused on a singular objective that the spirit of adventure has been lost. The objective is profit, why waste time diverting off down unexplored avenues when we 'know' this is the road? We have been down it before and it led us to the money. Many companies of the 1990s are still pursuing strategies of the 1980s, dressed up in the guise of transformation or Re-engineering. No-one would argue that cutting costs, downsizing, and rationalization were appropriate when organizations were fat and flabby, but once they are lean and mean, further strictures start to cut muscle. If management does not exercise caution and question the continuing validity of a strict regime then strategies become narrow, inflexible and extremely dangerous. They also pass over the tastiest morsels—the adventures and diversions that often produce something new and extremely valuable.

So, how does an organization recapture the spirit of adventure—that entrepreneurial flair exhibited by young innovative companies, such as Virgin and Apple? Once again, the explorers of old have a tale or two to tell.

Setting off into the unknown requires two things: courage and careful planning. Part of the courage comes from the explorer's own conviction, the 'because it was there' attitude. Often, that conviction will be at odds with the majority world view, but adventurers are unconventional thinkers, larger than life people who will not be confined by the mundane, so it doesn't matter. However, they must be able to convince crew members that the risk in joining them does not outweigh the benefits, if only to get the crew on board. Of course, it is possible to 'shanghai' them, but there is always the danger of mutiny lurking beneath that strategy. Careful provisioning is a more convincing strategy. That should not be translated to mean trimming resources to the bare minimum, so that the crew are constantly scraping the bottom of the barrel. A starved crew will be too weak to sail the ship home. Careful provisioning means having enough for most eventualities—spare capacity, enough contingency supplies to cover emergencies or diversions. Spare capacity? Contingency funds? Is that not the fat that most organizations are so busily cutting in the name of transformation?

Nor is it any use having a crew that is frightened to take risks. As soon as any danger threatens it will quickly want to turn for home. It is the captain's responsibility to build a brave and confident crew, which is capable of independent risk assessment and concerted action as a team. It is in his own interests too. When the elements threaten, the captain's own life is in the hands of his crew.

Grand strategies and holding rigidly to a predetermined course do not help control a ship that is being blown around in a gale. In stormy conditions, the only control left to the captain is to rely on the fact that he has trained his crew well. Careful provisioning also means that he will have prepared his human resources to make the best of the circumstances and manoeuvre the ship to safe harbour. Then he can replot his course towards the original objective.

Some organizations/departments/teams have good captains, who inspire their group with far-reaching competitive strategies, train them rigorously in the skills needed to pilot the ship and then delegate effectively once underway. Some staff are naturally more risk-averse than others, but most, if placed in a position to use their skills, will do so to the best of their ability, and often come up with some surprising solutions that no-one had thought of previously. The exercise of putting their abilities to the test actually refines those skills further. The task of transformation managers is to give people that opportunity.

Thus, we have a generic principle relevant to planning for the unknown. However much knowledge power you have, direct control is impossible. Control in uncertainty comes not from following ambitious predetermined strategies, but from careful resource preparation. Unconventional thinking and a spirit of adventure are the stimuli that inspire people to greater feats of learning. These forms of indirect control are all that can be hoped for in the middle of Chaos.

4.4   Rationalizing the democracy (global rationality/local political bargaining)

> You can never have a revolution in order to establish a democracy. You must have democracy in order to have a revolution.
>
> Gilbert Chesterton, *Tremendous Trifles*

Putting ideals into practice is also going to need some painful reflection on the role of management. The task is to reconcile the goals of the organization with those of its various constituencies so as to produce a viable plan that benefits everyone. A tough call!

Honesty, commitment, integrity and trust, resource preparation and delegation of control—in other words the principles developed by reconciling the first two paradoxes—undoubtedly lay the right foundation for a democratic organization in which political activity determines the path to most corporate added value; but there is more to it than that.

What is added value? What returns bring benefit for the community as a whole? It depends on the context. For a lonely old person it is the companionship that they get from a paid home help, for the home help it could be the unsolicited wisdom of an older generation. For company shareholders, it is profit returned as dividends or increased share value exceeding market averages, for staff it can be the satisfaction they get above and beyond the money they earn. Each has got something from the other that was more than their due. People will remain in an arrangement that satisfies their needs. They will enthusiastically nurture one that mutually gives them more than that. On the largest scale, the most added value for the society as a whole comes when all the interrelationships are organized so as to exceed mere satisfaction. Satisfying this principle across the scales brings order to the disorder of society.

Perversely, rationalizing the democratic output actually means enlarging the democracy itself. It is all a question of connections. The more connections, the greater the likelihood of making the intervention that transforms the organization: new ideas come from word associations— mental connections between different subjects; new relationships come from networking, mixing and making connection with a whole range of people; new capabilities come from combining skills and expertise. Of course, not every connection is valuable. Some mental associations are blind alleys, some relationships are dead ends. However, the more you experiment the more chance there is of finding the worthwhile connection. Certainly there is an element of luck involved, but to some degree you can make your own luck. Looking for connections amongst local people, or only within your field of mental expertise will throw up possibilities, but they are contained. The farther you range outside the walls of your own limitations, the greater the chance of finding the strange attractor that will transform the operation of the system.

Clearly, the only possible way to coordinate such interrelationships is to allow the various parties to negotiate between themselves. Stacey[10] argues that political negotiation is the best and only way to find the most rational outcome amidst Chaos. Through negotiation, groups find their common interests, if they are actively looking for the synergy between their values, so as to reach some mutual agreement. When all the various constituencies are effectively jostling for position the majority forces will emerge, making it easier to detect the combinations of energy that are most likely to benefit the corporate climate. Politics can be refined into an effective forecasting tool. Close examination of the combined interactions will give the strategist a clearer picture of the Butterfly forces in action. Later in this book, the reader will find some powerful tools to assist in this difficult process (see Chapter 8 in particular).

Conflict is inevitable once you break out of the narrow confines of existing relationships. New ideas and new people are unlikely to fit conveniently into the old patterns. Some re-arrangement will be necessary. As long as the conflict is handled constructively, it can be productive. The first principle of productive conflict is 'no blame'. Blame produces an emotional and defensive response that instantly diverts participants into patterns of destructive behaviour. No blame may sound soft, but it is harder than you think. No blame does not mean benevolent acceptance of failure, it means dispassionate analysis of the underlying causes. No blame does not mean accepting superficial answers to avoid an argument, it means carrying on the discussion until everyone accepts. In the Chaos of an organization, the underlying causes and the reconciliatory conclusion emerge from a combination of actions. The solution cannot be the responsibility of one person alone. The answer may take a long time to unravel, but time spent now is time saved later, when unresolved problems and wrong solutions cause unnecessary turbulence in the system.

The general principle for putting ideals into practice can be summarized in this way. Break out of cosy compartments and argue productively if you want to uncover the rationale that satisfies the most people.

4.5   Managing environmental limitations
   (internal/external)

Tomorrow's Hall of Fame companies are working on new organisational forms today.

Miles and Snow, 1984[53]

How do we bring the organization to the peak of physical fitness? Corporate fitness depends on a healthy internal structure that is well adapted to outside conditions. Unfortunately, the people who create the outside conditions, customers, shareholders, governments and regulatory agencies, have a nasty habit of constantly moving the goal posts. It would be a waste of energy to keep re-organizing to accommodate every stimulus. Getting one step ahead, by identifying the environmental limitations in advance is one way to reduce the constant stresses upon structural integrity. The previous principle for putting ideals into practice required more involvement from more people; this inevitably puts more strain on information systems. What sort of structure will allow the organization to use the huge volume of information it absorbs to best manage the world outside?

Fractals are structures naturally adapted to the task. Lungs and trees are designed to capture the most input and produce the most output with a minimum amount of coordination. Applying the principle to organizations requires a little ingenuity, but the result will be a flexible structure that permits almost infinite operational variety, within a finite organizational form, thus managing both the internal and external conditions to best effect.

Figure 4.1 shows a simple fractal shape. The recipe is simple. Take an equilateral triangle. On each side place another equilateral triangle one-third the size of the original. Repeat *ad infinitum*. The result is a shape with an infinitely long boundary that can still be contained within the finite area of a circle surrounding the original triangle.

A moment's reflection and it is possible to see how the principle can work for organizational structures. Outsourcing, partnering, strategic alliances, internal associations and project teams are all ways to connect skills around the core competencies necessary to support basic existence. This statement is applicable across the levels of organization. The surface area of the many nodes will capture the maximum amount of information from the environment. The heart of the organization can process and distribute the information to the various branches. The complex mesh of information clues that result enables the organization to interpret and manage the environment more effectively. Companies such as Apple, Corning, DEC and Johnson & Johnson are already doing this; extending their structure beyond the confines of normal organizational boundaries and experimenting with ways to couple and uncouple companies into and out of their structure.[54] In this way, they can form flexible and infinitely

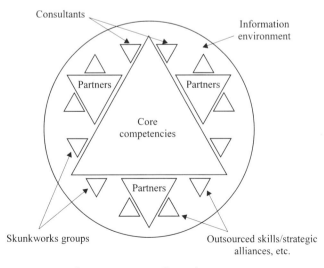

Fig. 4.1   Infinite variety in finite form

varied 'best of everything' businesses, without the burden of a bureaucratic structure. The result has been dubbed the 'Virtual Corporation'.

What is obviously essential is an efficient distribution system. An open information systems architecture with common communication standards is a fundamental necessity. These standards must capture the key interacting variables that affect the energy flows in the environment. Rather like Saltzman's three equations for convection describe the Butterfly Effect for weather, the organization needs to identify a few simple but non-linear parameters affecting outside conditions. Then it can track the climatic changes. The objective is to use information to minimize the restrictions on future options. With knowledge of the limits in organizational competency and the environmental constraints, it becomes possible to align with outsiders to overcome the restrictions and reduce the risk associated with unforeseen change.

Obviously, there has to be some restraint upon the value of diversity. Lungs have to fit into the chest cavity. Trees can only support the weight of so many leaves or they fall. There is no easy way to set a size or complexity rule for every organization. Each one will be different, just as every tree is different. However, the quality that ensures that differentiation does not become burdensome is *discrimination*. With all the information flowing and the interactions sparking new ideas, the management team needs to develop the facility of discriminating between opportunities. Otherwise resources will be spread too thinly. The yardstick has to be how much a change will improve service to the ultimate customer, and whether internal resources are the appropriate conduit. The concept of benchmarking against 'best of breed' outside the industry can provide a meaningful comparative measure for this assessment. It is a simple question. If someone outside can do it better, then use them. If they cannot, do it yourself.

Once again, we need to formulate this into a governing principle relevant at any scale. Maximize the organization's exposure to the environment by adopting nature's flexible structures. The form of that structure will be decided by resource limitations inside and outside the organization.

4.6   Removing the barriers inhibiting change
(social norms and standards/organizational change)

Don't push growth; remove the factors limiting growth.

Senge, 1990[51]

The advice of Senge in the quote above applies equally to the process of change. For every action there is an equal and opposite reaction. The more you push change through direct intervention, the more resistance you will generate. In the end, it is possible to create the very anomaly you are trying to remove. Too much change and people run backwards towards the known.

The only way to build unity from diversity and resolve the paradox between stabilizing and destabilizing forces is to act passively. This sounds ridiculous, but it is possible. Transformation will occur spontaneously when eyes are opened and barriers removed. It is much the same as Socrates' teaching philosophy. Highlight the inconsistencies then learning will occur naturally.

One of the biggest inhibitors to change is past experience. Our history conditions our view of the world. The accumulated experiences of an organization conditions its response to change. The old war stories, the myths and legends of corporate life have a strong influence on spontaneous reactions to any proposal. For example, Xerox firmly believed that, whatever happened, a photocopier must *never* harm an original document. The myth was probably the result of some earlier disastrous experience, but this one minor event was allowed to colour the whole outlook on design. Staff vehemently rejected any idea of mechanical document handling. In the end, this perspective blinded Xerox to change. By the mid 1970s customers had got used to concept of copying, but were getting tired of the time it took. In their minds, the need to speed up the copying process far outweighed the risk of damage to the odd piece of paper. Competitors, uninhibited by past history, responded to this need for change. Kodak added a recirculating document handler to their copiers, which greatly increased throughput rate. Xerox subsequently lost a lot of major customers to Kodak.

The experience of introducing IT into business activities has been a painful one. A difference in personalities between IT personnel and other parts of the business has produced a cultural chasm that separates IT specialists from their compatriots in other areas.[55] Obviously this is a severe barrier to effective change. Yet IT is expected to be one of the primary enablers of transformation. Consequently, the author has spent the past three years talking to managers from a wide range of organizations about the issues that cause friction between the two camps. From these discussions and from the literature on the subject, it was possible to identify 10 particularly prevalent issues on which the groups were divided. Based on the earlier application of Chaos theory, it was assumed that resolving the most frequently occurring tensions would contribute most to restoring order to the current disorder. This is the subject of the next chapter. Chapter 5 examines the 10 most frequently occurring paradoxes hindering the integration of IT into business activities and relates them to the main paradoxes of a transformation strategy, outlined in Chapter 2, and their associated principles, derived from this chapter.

To remove the barriers inhibiting change, corporations need to develop two further qualities: communication and a progressive outlook. A progressive character has two meanings. Firstly, it means 'in stages'. In other words, achieving transformation requires many evolutionary cycles that accumulate incremental changes into a pattern for revolution. Secondly, it has connotations of being forward-looking and open to novelty. Both of these attributes depend on intensive communication. Intensifying communication brings out the conflicting ideas needed to produce novelty, as well as creating the propulsion to drive successive cycles of change. It also provides an outlet for the tension generated. There are many ways that an organization can encourage communication, but the maxim is undoubtedly 'the more the merrier'. Corporations such as NEC, Phillips, Procter and Gamble, and Unilever successfully combine the two characteristics. They concentrate on developing progressive communication strategies that reconfigure knowledge and idea flows rather than redesigning process flows for parts or components. Communication takes the form of regular job rotations, inter-unit forums, pooled resources and changing meeting locations so as to alter the mix of participants.

The Japanese place an equal emphasis on informal communication.[34] In large Japanese corporations all recruits joining the firm in the same year maintain contact with one another throughout their employment, regardless of their ultimate status in the company. They socialize together outside working hours; lubricated by sake and beer they exchange information outside the restrictions of formal channels. Members can talk to one another with 'honto' (unreserved openness) and express their true feelings without fear of retribution. This brings us full circle back to the issue that expands vision and enables grassroots initiatives—federating knowledge.

The final principle of *evolutionary revolution* can be stated as follows: remove the frictions that slow progressive cycles of change by extensive communication.

This chapter has developed five management principles designed to help an organization resolve the five transformation paradoxes developed in Chapter 2. For convenience, these have been summarized in Fig. 4.2.

Any organization interested in starting out on the road to transformation, must start out with a good supply of these qualities. The diagnostic questionnaire in Appendix A contains a section that will help pinpoint where deficiencies currently exist. With that knowledge the organization is poised to take the necessary remedial action to improve its chances of success.

When present, the qualities work in harmony to create the self-sustaining conditions in which transformation can occur spontaneously.

The next chapter will look in more depth at a set of underlying cultural divisions that can act as a brake upon the cycles of change.

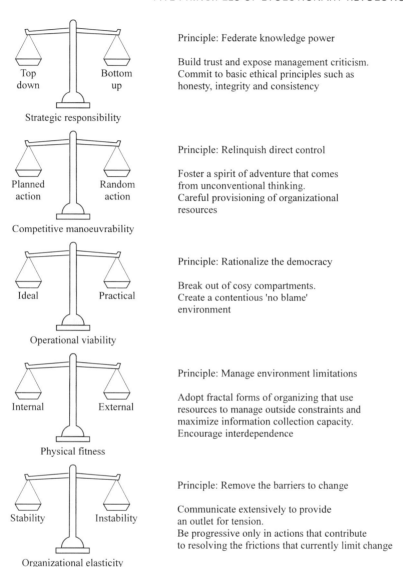

Principle: Federate knowledge power

Build trust and expose management criticism.
Commit to basic ethical principles such as
honesty, integrity and consistency

Principle: Relinquish direct control

Foster a spirit of adventure that comes
from unconventional thinking.
Careful provisioning of organizational
resources

Principle: Rationalize the democracy

Break out of cosy compartments.
Create a contentious 'no blame'
environment

Principle: Manage environment limitations

Adopt fractal forms of organizing that use
resources to manage outside constraints and
maximize information collection capacity.
Encourage interdependence

Principle: Remove the barriers to change

Communicate extensively to provide
an outlet for tension.
Be progressive only in actions that contribute
to resolving the frictions that currently limit change

Fig. 4.2   Creating balanced conditions for change

Underlying frictions that slow the cycles of change

5

5.1   Introduction

Friction is a nuisance. Bowling would certainly be an easier game without it; business management would be a lot simpler too. Friction introduces an unfortunate complication into what otherwise could be a nice neat world. By interfering in the cause and effect relationship, it makes outcomes very difficult to predict. For example, if it were not for friction, a simple linear equation could tell you exactly how much energy to use to get a bowling ball down an alley and knock all the pins down. In practice, it is impossible to calculate exactly how hard to throw because the speed of the ball is limited by friction, but the friction itself fluctuates with speed of the ball. In other words, 'the act of playing the games changes the rules'.[4] In business, friction in relationships has the same effect. As managers soothe a conflict in one area they alter the dynamics of others. This is non-linearity; this is where Chaos begins. Yet, if good bowlers can surmount this problem and regularly achieve perfect games, businesses can too. Of course, bowling alleys oil the lanes to help the ball slide along the first half of its journey. This increases the speed of the ball, so that when it hits the unoiled part it has more momentum. The question is, how can business people oil the wheels of change to smooth the road to transformation? The first step is to resolve the interpersonal frictions that act as a brake upon revolution.

This chapter will take a look at 10 particularly troublesome frictions (Fig. 5.1) that have dogged the smooth integration of human and technological systems for many years. Unresolved they create substantial resistance to any proposed change, and reduce the momentum for learning. Any organization that can successfully remove these obstacles will be doing much to smooth the road to faster and better transformation. The act of resolving these paradoxes can contribute much towards the development of the revolutionary characteristics outlined in Chapter 4.

There is one tension for every aspect of the main paradox wheel. Depth of vision affects strategic direction; biased judgements on investment resources dull the edge of competitive planning; rationality is unbalanced without both analysis and intuition; structural flexibility needs both

Short term view	**Depth of vision**	Long term view
Product/service value	**Competitive acuity**	IT value
Analysis	**Complete rationality**	Intuition
Central integration	**Structural flexibility**	Decentral diversification
Elaborating	**Communication quality**	Abbreviating
Deciding	**Participative scope**	Discussing
Organizational benefits	**Goal sharing**	Personal aspirations
Resisting	**Arbitration skills**	Surrendering
Precision	**Service quality**	Speed
Safe support	**Technological utility**	Risky transformation

Fig. 5.1 Frictions creating resistance in the system

centralized and decentralized resources and so on around the wheel (Fig. 5.2).

Do not be deceived by the apparent simplicity of the associations. In practice, the forces are dynamically interdependent. This means that they operate in a complex three-dimensional pattern that is too elaborate to represent in a flat half-page picture. Some idea of how the forces interact will emerge from this chapter. However, an organization can see the patterns in action by use of the diagnostic questionnaire in Appendix A to profile its organizational character. Over time, monitoring the fluctuations will provide a clear picture of what imbalances are inhibiting real behavioural change.

Starting from the top of the wheel in Fig. 5.2 and working clockwise, this chapter will look at each underlying paradox in turn, to find how its resolution contributes to more efficient transformation.

5.2   Conflicting priorities limiting depth of vision

short term   TOP DOWN DIRECTION   long term

Short termism governs our share prices. It governs our decisions and our investment policies. The trick in IT is to build the long term survival structure using profitable short term bricks. This way you do not need to bridge the culture gap, because you've got instant agreement.

Grindley, 1991[55]

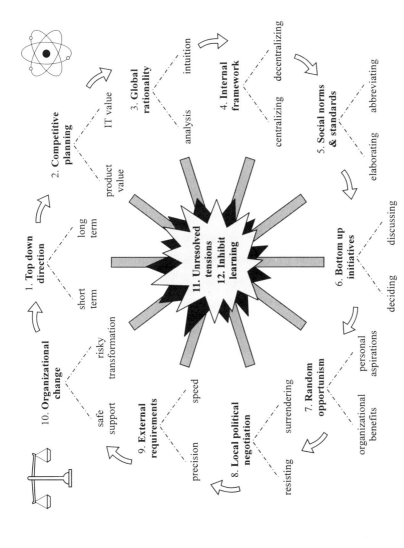

Fig. 5.2 Underlying frictions slowing the cycle of change

The quality of leadership depends very much on how well a group director manages to reconcile the conflicting pulls of short and long term goals. To acquire full depth of vision, a leader needs the skill to keep both the short term foreground and the long term background in focus simultaneously.

Short termism dominates Western business. At the extreme, long term commitments to quality, customer service and learning are frequently sacrificed on the altar of quarterly profit figures and stock market reporting requirements. American and British investors look for quick investment returns. Japanese and German investors look further out, so companies can afford to take a longer term perspective on their strategies for growth. American corporations such as General Electric, United Technologies and Westinghouse shortsightedly abandoned their forays into robotics because return on investment would be too slow for market tolerance. Foreign competitors took up the challenge. Steadier market expectations gave them the space to extend their time horizons. Eventually they will win the technology race, just as the tortoise beat the hare in Aesop's fable. Allocating part of an investment portfolio to technologies of the future dilutes share performance in the short term, but in the end better, long term results will compensate.

This focus on the short term is exacerbated by the way many Western organizations judge performance. Most senior managers are under more pressure to produce profits than to develop the skills of their staff or increase learning. If profit is the principal measure of job performance then personal survival quickly becomes tied up with short term objectives. Under such conditions, any leader's commitment to long term goals is bound to be strained. When the two objectives conflict, the leader is going to plump for the safe short term option, particularly when quantifying the long term is such a subjective process.

It may also be tempting to view transformation programmes as a short term fix. In fact, they are a long term commitment to IT-enabled, behavioural change that may actually have a detrimental effect on performance in the short term. If managers hare off in a race for transformation, without acknowledging this paradox, they will undoubtedly have another abandoned strategy to add to their collection!

This dilemma of timescales has long bedeviled the business–IT relationship too. Business managers want immediate results, but, although IT is a primary agent in the transformation process, often the benefits take a while to materialize. In some cases, the dearth of measurable short term returns from IT investments has induced a fundamental mistrust of performance. Further, many managers have had their fingers burned by IT projects that have mushroomed from sensible investments into monolithic, intergalactic designs that tried to be all things to all people. Systems specifications include so many 'just in case' requirements that the end product becomes cumbersome and unprofitable. Thorough analysis for large information systems takes a long time, but circumstances are changing even as the design is developing. The natural inclination is to handle this by covering *every* foreseeable contingency; unfortunately it also produces systems too complex to program or test comprehensively. Cost and time overruns are a common complaint. In fact, consultants will tell you that anything over a $20 million budget is almost doomed to failure. Projects like that make managers nervous and then they over-compensate by cutting other projects. IT directors frequently complain that strategic projects get axed because short-sighted managers are too quickly swayed by operational frustrations during planning or testing.

Of course, the dilemma relates to more than just IT. Transformation requires behavioural change too. In Chapter 4 commitment to power sharing was identified as an essential leadership quality for reconciling the paradox of shared strategic responsibility. Unfortunately, the risk associated with power sharing is very likely to prejudice leaders towards short term activities until they gain the confidence to trust their own future to grassroots activists. Severe uncertainty quickly discourages commitment and fosters insecurity. Insecurity focuses attention on the short term, where people believe that they have some semblance of control. Soon, managers retreat to the safety of closed and contained changes and ordinary management techniques, jettisoning all notions of extraordinary management methods, such as paradox and open-ended change, all of which is entirely contrary to the requirements for transformation.

Sadly, leaders who fix their eyes solely on distant horizons and shut out the foreground issues are equally troublesome. Steve Jobs was a visionary, with his sights set on the future, but he was often blind to short term practicalities. Apple sensibly introduced a counterbalance—a business manager who would deal with the day-to-day details that keep things on track.

Alleviating the friction caused by this paradox means aligning long term and short term objectives, so that activities satisfy the requirements of both. The simple solution is to break the whole down into manageable and profitable subsections that can deliver short term satisfaction in pursuit of long term goals. A leader's strategic intent should be supported by short term achievements. A steady accumulation of satisfactory contributions builds commitment to long term objectives but still leaves room for modifications as circumstances change. Perversely, it now becomes very important to monitor results, but assessments must be viewed as milestones on the road to the ultimate goal, not the be-all and end-all of the project.

5.3 Dissonance that takes the edge off competitive acuity

product value   COMPETITIVE PLANNING   IT value

◄───►

> Most companies . . . do not give those providing analytical input enough power to actually apply sufficient influence. It is no use having a group of information gatherers run by a manager who is disregarded.
>
> Stacey, 1990[56]

An incisive strategy cuts to the heart of the competitive situation. By analysing strengths, weaknesses, opportunities and threats, an organization can plan how to maximize, minimize, use and defuse the four variables, respectively. However, breaking with convention, challenging the assumptions that currently shape the world is a necessary precondition for novel strategies. Chapter 4 made it clear that an unconventional perspective and a spirit of adventure were important attributes in the early stages of this voyage of transformation. The status of IT in the resource hierarchy is one of the first conventions that needs to be smashed if IT-enabled transformation is to occur spontaneously.

Traditionally, information services have held a relatively menial status in competitive terms. Products and services are direct revenue generators, so related assets sit proudly on the balance sheet as evidence of the organization's investment in the future. Information, on the other hand, is an intangible asset, with unquantifiable value, and technology is merely an administrative support system that carries the information. Since attributing measurable worth to information's contribution is highly subjective, the asset remains hidden, while those who manage information are often deprived of the appropriate amount of power. For as long as there have been IT directors, they have been fighting a rearguard action to defend their position and justify their worth. This is an almost impossible task because information value only materializes when it is used by others, and so the act of using it often changes the rules of the game. In other words its effect is non-linear and inherently unpredictable.

Many IT directors that the author spoke to were wrestling with the problem of how to build trust in IT as a catalyst for profitability. Why do IT projects frequently require 40 pages of justification as opposed to four for the average product-related investment? Why do IT projects get cut prematurely, while R&D projects lumber on for years? It seems that managerial instinct channels thinking down narrow well worn tracks. Managers are well versed in appraising projects which involve new factories, takeovers or new product lines, so they have the confidence to assess the risks underlying the figures. Of course, their good judgement is only an illusion. Rapid change consistently devalues the predictive capacity of experience. Environmental Chaos makes all estimates of bottom line returns equally as tentative as those for IT-based change.

IT experts are also fighting for their own survival, which exacerbates the conflict. Some consultancies and industry writers are predicting that the position of Chief Information Officer (CIO) will eventually disappear as other business directors assume increasing responsibility for IT. One journalist quipped that 'CIO is starting to stand for Career Is Over!'[57] Why is the IT expert being singled out? Does anyone ever question the need for a marketing director or a manufacturing director? Without someone in the role, how will the organization keep track of the dizzying pace of technological change and who would have the knowledge or authority to follow information flows across organization frontiers?

Unfortunately, this prejudice against information distributors will adversely affect competitive manoeuvrability in a knowledge society if it is not resolved. The Luddites of the nineteenth century destroyed the looms and spinning jennies, because they feared the consequences of a mechanized future. If twentieth-century Luddites discriminate against computer technology then the competitive position of an organization in the information economy will be seriously damaged. This is not to suggest that the organization get carried away with unbridled enthusiasm for investing in IT. Nothing could be more dangerous. A violent swing to the opposite extreme is likely to reinforce the destructive IT–business divide by making IT arch rivals of other business disciplines. Just as too much emphasis on financial control pushed Ford executives into destructive political one-upmanship, too much emphasis on IT is likely to have a negative impact on strategic manoeuvrability.

The tension between IT and other revenue-generating functions distorts competitive judgement. Until managers redress this prejudice, they are discriminating against a key resource that could influence competitive manoeuvrability. To fulfil its strategic role in the transformation process, IT must be given equal access to investment funds and equal negotiating power.

5.4 Subconscious restrictions to the quality of complete rationality

analysis   GLOBAL RATIONALITY   intuition

<--->

Logic and order are not vehicles for yielding a new product—they can never produce anything but what is already implicit in the premises. Rather they are the tools of testing and are useless unless you have fecundity to impose on them.

Elbow, 1986[58]

Rationality is often viewed as synonymous with logic. But this is only half the picture. To expect that ideals for improving added value will come from logical analysis alone is narrow-minded. Logic is rooted in old assumptions; it holds thinking into cosy mental compartments, but, as Chapter 4 concluded, breaking out of compartments is a prerequisite for solving the ideals versus practice dilemma. This is where intuition is so essential. There are many studies that show how important intuition is in the creative process. Logic is a testing tool that is destructive and limiting without a rich source of intuitive hunches to which it may be applied.

Unfortunately, managers somehow mistrust decisions based on intuition. They speak of intuition disparagingly. Mere mention of the word usually brings forth terms of derision such as 'seat of the pants management' or 'gut feel' and pompous statements such as 'we don't rely on hunches around here'. It is unscientific and irrational.

In fact, intuition is not the irrational force that everyone believes. It is simply the result of grouping information into patterns by a process of association. Chunking together information speeds up and short-circuits the logical process of 'if x then y' type reasoning, by compressing the data. In addition, associations between blocks of information often spark new and unusual ideas that provide a higher level of understanding. A creative person uses intuition to break out of the confines of deductive reasoning and find the order on a different scale. Take the example of chess Grand Masters. One would instinctively class them as highly analytical and logical thinkers; all their actions are circumscribed by a fixed set of rules. Yet some of their skill can only be explained by intuition. Studies show[59] that a chess Grand Master can handle 50 games simultaneously without affecting the quality or the speed of play. This would be impossible if they relied solely on step-by-step analysis of alternative moves.

The speed of electronic logic allows expert systems to compete favourably against the basic deductive reasoning skills of a chess player. However, computers can still be beaten by an intuitive master. It is not the speed but the quality of response that is so important. Computers are rigidly limited by the rules. They cannot challenge the assumptions programmed into them, so they cannot be unpredictable. The chess Grand Master can reason beyond the restrictions of probabilities and logic, and take the mental leap to produce innovative strategies that improve the chances of success. Intuition is a powerful tool that can also help businesses to develop creative strategies for the future, if it is not continually undervalued.

In conditions of Chaos, intuition also gives humans the edge over computers too. Stacey[11] sees intuition as an essential attribute for the management of open-ended change, where incomplete information and discontinuity make it impossible to follow patterns of logical reasoning. In closed and contained change, knowledge of the facts permits rational assessment. In open-ended change, the environment is no longer an open book, rather it resembles 'an entire library of encyclopedias under perpetual revision'.[60] So information is always incomplete. Some data fields will be empty. A computer cannot function under such conditions. In fact, computers alone cannot manage Chaos. Set to the task of solving the equations describing the Butterfly Effect, computers search for an answer for ever, even though non-linear feedback makes one answer a logical impossibility. A computer follows the logic unendingly, creating more and more intricate patterns, whereas the human brain will look for a reasonable pattern that provides a clue to an acceptable solution.

In chaotic conditions intuitive jumps of reasoning will contribute as much to added value as logic, because they break out of cosy compartments.

5.5   Warring factions inhibiting structural flexibility

centralized   INTERNAL FRAMEWORK   decentralized

◄──►

> In a monarchy power is centralized and departments have less autonomy over information policies . . . Information anarchy emerges when the centralized approaches to information break down . . . In a feudal model, individual executives and their departments generally control information acquisition, storage distribution and analysis . . . Feudal actions diminish central authority's power to make informed decisions for the Common Good.
>
> Davenport, Eccles and Prusak, 1992[61]

Structural flexibility is an essential component of organizational fitness. A healthy response to environmental limitations will combine the benefits of integration (e.g. economies of scale) with those of diversification. If the dilemma between centralized and decentralized power is not reconciled then the disaster is inevitable—a 'big brother' bureaucracy or information anarchy. Chapter 4 suggested that organizations develop a fractal quality based on a complex web of *inter*dependent relationships. The more relationship-orientated people become, the easier it is to create *unique* competitive advantage. However, management will have to alter the power structure in order to make this happen. The pendulum swings of re-organization that waste so much time and money without generating any added value must stop.

How does this affect the way IT is integrated into the business. Clearly a 'centrally/decentralized' approach[30] needs a compatible information structure. Some kind of central function is needed to maintain a broad overview of business activities; this would be responsible for defining common information collection standards. However, there must be restrictions on the central body to prevent it growing into an entrenched bureaucracy that is inherently unresponsive. A complementary decentralized service organization can provide the necessary counterbalance. Of course, it would be equally bad if decentralized services dominated the picture. Overdiversification leaves information scattered all across the organization with no hope of coordinating it. It is possible to create a more nimble structure by an appropriate division of responsibility. Central staff should control infrastructure, both technical and human, because these facilities are needed by everyone. Staff in the field should be developing applications in accordance with local user requirements and budgetary restrictions. The responsibility is appropriately split between resource mechanisms that provide a common service and response mechanisms customized for differences in ambient conditions.

The dilemma applies at all levels of operation, but will be resolved in different ways:

- Someone needs to keep a central service honest. One company resolved the dilemma for IT services by temporarily assigning accountancy trainees to the information systems department. Their task was to develop and review budgets and charge-back formulae. When they returned to their division they could personally vouch for the fairness of IS cost allocation across the divisions.
- Someone needs to keep decentralized staff on their toes. Highly diversified companies sometimes set up a central customer service unit that crosses divisional lines of authority and acts as a single point of contact with the outside customers. Service representatives deal with technical, operational and administrative queries for their customer base. Specialist departments are still responsible for putting the problem right, and have to answer for their own performance. Centralizing the decentralized responsibilities in this way presents a united front to the external customer, but also acts as an internal conscience to improve decentralized performance.

The way to create structural flexibility is to encourage cross border relationships that exert bidirectional influence. Then the organization can respond effectively to outside influences.

5.6   Interference in the quality of communication

elaborating   SOCIAL NORMS and STANDARDS   abbreviating
◄──►

A little inaccuracy sometimes saves tons of explanation.
Saki, *The Comments of Maung Ka*

Chapter 4 argued that strong communication was a necessary stabilizing influence during organizational change. Clearly, better information dissemination will support the learning process, but the way it is achieved influences and is influenced by cultural conditions. Greater dialogue must be meaningful in order to be productive. Simply multiplying communication without improving the quality of the transmission leads to even greater confusion. 'Send reinforcements we are going to advance' will quickly become garbled and sound like 'Send three and four pence we are going to a dance!'.

Communication quality is dependent upon the sender balancing succinctness against the need for enough detail to convey the right message. Too much detail becomes information overload and the listener switches off, too little and the listener receives incomprehensibly cryptic code. In essence, communication is a simple encoding and decoding process; inaccurate encoding and decoding produces misunderstanding. For example, if the boss says '*When are you going to get that report done?*', an employee may interpret the message as '*He's dissatisfied with my performance*'. If he says '*I need that report in the next 24 hours to meet my deadline*' then the subordinate understands that the boss needs his support. In fact, that was probably the intention of the first message, however it was so abrupt that it got misinterpreted. Imagine the repercussions down the line from this one simple misunderstanding. A good employee may look for another job, waste time dredging up support elsewhere or be so distracted that he commits a serious mistake. Ineffective communication aggravates Chaos; it sets in motion vicious circles of mistrust and confusion. However, when the boss makes the effort to elaborate a little, the message gets through accurately.

This does not mean go overboard with unnecessary detail. It simply means 'spell out precisely what you mean'. Most organizations have their own cultural language to help them do this. This includes jargon, acronyms and abbreviations that have meaning to the organizational members. This is invaluable for making communication succinct, so long as the recipient knows the terms. However, for those outside the brotherhood it can be rather like listening to a foreign language. Too much abbreviation confuses rather than enlightens.

The issue of terminology may seem a trivial point, but if readers reflect on the multiplicity of abbreviations surrounding IT, they will no doubt remember many occasions where they have resulted in people talking at cross purposes. It is hard to find two people with a consistent definition of Open Systems Interconnection (OSI), or even two who agree on what the term Information Systems (IS) covers. One person's understanding of Business Process Re-engineering is unlikely to be the same as anothers. The problem has to have reached serious proportions for Keen to devote a whole book to defining the terminology.[62] Indeed, the difficulties surrounding this communication dilemma prompted the John Lewis Partnership to establish a policy on technical abbreviations. Fully elaborated terms were mandated until a new concept was completely absorbed into the culture, then abbreviations became acceptable. Staff were encouraged to pick up on premature use of jargon and publicly to question the perpetrators, whatever their status.

The paradox can manifest itself in subtle forms, as when staff try to communicate their dislike of a policy or a manager by silence (an extreme form of abbreviation). The recipient senses that there is dissension, but does not understand the reason. Consequently, they feel compelled to provide over elaborate justifications of their actions, in an attempt to communicate more accurately. This becomes a vicious circle of incomprehension, as the original dissenters switch off, and no message gets through.

Managers should be on the look out for the symptoms of communication breakdown—over elaboration or excessive abruptness. The symptoms are indicative of people avoiding productive conflict and the pain of learning. This is an unhealthy situation and is clearly detrimental to the process of transformation.

Resolving the paradox is a matter of establishing a common language in a no blame environment, where conflict can be dealt with objectively but compassionately. A communicative culture of this nature is strong enough to withstand frequent change.

5.7   Hidden constraints on participative scope

deciding   BOTTOM UP INITIATIVES   discussing
◄──►

A riot is at bottom the language of the unheard.
Revd Martin Luther King, *Chaos & Community*, 1967

Given that strategic responsibility should be shared and knowledge power widely disseminated, the organization immediately faces the question of when to stop exploring different viewpoints and when to take action. Too much discussion and opportunity will be lost; too little and inappropriate decisions will be made and people will be disenfranchised.

Deciding quickly limits complexity by eliminating options; it also precludes widespread involvement and, in the extreme, represents dictatorship. Discussion, listening to everyone's point of view, without pressuring them to accept yours expands the available options, fosters innovation and commitment, but it is notoriously slow. One only has to look at the way universities and business colleges operate. The discussion between intelligent equals often goes round and round without anyone reaching a conclusion. Traditionally, businesses have left decision power at the top of the pyramid, because it is quicker. The problem is that autocratic decisions do not produce ownership amongst those who have to im-plement the decision. Punishment or reward have to be used to foster compliance, and this lays the foundations for an adversarial control system. In the long run, early simplification leads to later complications. The time spent in the inevitable cycle of hostility and placation is not productive. Trust is lost and the whole process undermines responsibility sharing.

Sadly, individualistic machismo Western managers usually scorn the non-decisive approach, dismissing it as soft and weak. Action is prized more highly. Japanese managers, on the other hand, have no qualms about adopting a more supportive, discursive style, because reflection and harmony are part of their culture. In the end, neither proposition on its own can cope successfully with the today's rapid change. Both are showing signs of failure.

The answer, as always, is to use both simultaneously and consistently; then the paradox can be resolved. Discussion becomes decision, but the decision subsequently becomes a subject of further discussion. This cycle means that the earliest facts are not excluded, but become the back-ground for further discussion. Thus over a period of time, organizations build increasingly complex strategic visions, and emergent initiatives are guided by a rich tapestry of supporting evidence.

5.8   Subliminal resistance obstructing goal sharing

organizational benefits	RANDOM OPPORTUNISM	personal aspirations

◄───►

> Resilience is the ability to absorb high levels of disruptive change, without displaying dysfunctional behaviour. Resilient people are positive, focused, flexible organized and proactive.
>
> Conner, 1992[63]

The captain's job is to instill his crew with confidence in the face of danger. A risk-averse crew will not boldly seek out new opportunities; a resilient crew, on the other hand, will make the most of any circum-stances. What makes a person resilient to change? In some respects it is a matter of perspective. Resilient people see adversity or failure as a chal-lenge, a stimulus to learning or development. Others are crushed by the shame or inequity associated with it. Somehow, organizations have to create an environment which encourages people to overcome the stigma of failure. A no blame environment has already been identified as one precondition, however there are other positive steps that an organization can take to overcome the handicap. Harmonizing organizational benefits with individual aspirations makes an important contribution towards building resilience. When both desires are satisfied, it sets in motion a virtuous circle of trust and support.

People are always concerned with the fairness of any relationship. They want an equitable return on their personal investment—be that time, effort, knowledge or practical skill. A business relationship has to satisfy the needs of the individual as well as the organization if it is to function effectively. The trade does not have to be monetarily equal, only just and fair in the eyes of both participants. For some successful businesses this principle is so important that the entire work ethos is organized around it. Chapparal Steel is one such organization, and its performance is testimony to the success of the approach.[64] The Vice President of Administration, Dennis Beach, admitted that the whole organization is designed around Maslow's hierarchy of needs, in other words, it accepts that once people have satisfied basic needs for food, safety and community, they are motivated by a search for self-esteem and eventually self-actualization. The Chapparal Steel management policy is dedicated to satisfying those needs for growth in its employees.

The company holds many records in the US steel industry, despite only being the tenth largest producer. In 1982 Chapparal Steel set a world record for production tonnage; in 1984 it was cited as one of the 10 best managed factories in the US (*Fortune*, May 28th); in 1989 it produced more tons of steel per worker than any other Japanese or American competitor. Chapparal Steel was the first US company to be awarded the Japanese Industrial Standard Certification, and over a period of 20 years it has consistently outperformed the industry in terms of new innovations. One of the main premises on which the company is built is that people should be encouraged to see risk as positive. When they employ people they look for people with an innate willingness to challenge their own and others' thinking. But having employed an individual, Chapparal Steel makes sure that it invests in him by continuously looking for ways to help the employee become 'self-actualized'. Foremen rotate into teaching roles; security guards are trained paramedics and do data entry on night shift. Line managers can authorize large sums of money to try out new ideas, rewards are geared to skill improvements as well as performance. An egalitarian attitude to all employees is the hallmark of the company. Of course, success is rooted in trust. Trust that the employees will not abuse the power that they so obviously have, and trust that the management will look after a loyal staff. Clearly, this relationship is so important that anyone who is not trustworthy must immediately be removed, so as not to rock the boat. A hard line to follow, but one that the company adheres to.

The case study of New United Motor Manufacturing Inc (NUMMI), in Chapter 9, also contains similar pertinent lessons. Although it resolved this dilemma of goal alignment in a different way, by allowing work groups to specify the standards that they would work to and so regain control of their own destiny, NUMMI still satisfied both organizational and individual needs. People who feel in charge of their own destiny are more confident and resilient towards change.

Of course, the two sides of the conflict can co-exist in one person. Loyal committed employees are often obliged to put the organization before their own personal needs. The result is severe stress and dysfunctional behaviour. Executives of the 1990s are always battling to reconcile heavy work commitments with family responsibilities. Mostly work has to come first. In the end, broken homes and the strained emotional relationships inflicted by this conflict of allegiance are more expensive than most corporations realize. They undermine concentration, cause resentment, illness, inefficiency, and poor decisions. If there is not a give and take attitude, constant pressure demoralizes and depresses.

The time has come for a dose of realism. Realism means not only stretching people, but making sure that they feel comfortable being stretched. Feeling comfortable will allow their spirit of adventure to blossom naturally.

5.9   Underground currents affecting arbitration

resisting   LOCAL POLITICAL NEGOTIATION   surrendering

> Politics should be realistic; politics should be idealistic: two principles which are true when they complement one another and wrong when they are kept apart.
>
> Johann Kaspar Bluntschli, *Politiks als Wissenchaft*

Chapter 4 urged managers to create a contentious no blame environment in order to resolve the tension between ideals and practice. Arbitration skills become more and more essential under the circumstances. This next dilemma is the very essence of political decision making, and exists in even the most egalitarian circumstances. When to resist and when to capitulate. Departmental, organizational and even mental protective boundaries are under attack. Everyone has to decide when to defend the value of their experience and specialist knowledge in resistance to change, and when surrender is in the general interest. Expertise is devalued if principles and standards are not upheld. Specialists have a duty to defend their knowledge. However, standards become outmoded and principles get out of date. Then compromise is necessary.

This issue causes friction between IT and other business professionals where technology investment is concerned. IT experts fight for the benefits of improved hardware; business people are often more interested in applications, so long as existing technology is reliable and simple. The conflict can spread further. Take the example of a business redesigning the electronic interface for customer order processing. Key account sales people will defend the hardware choice that links easily to their major customers' computers, even if it is outdated or awkward for everyone else. General sales people are likely to want an interface that is adaptable and state of the art, because it must make a wider range of connections. If key account specialists dominate, they lock in a few customers, but at the expense of lost opportunity among the general customer base. If specialists are ignored, their expert understanding of the customer is wasted and major customers may go elsewhere if their interests are not served.

The organization has to find a solution that recognizes the arguments of key customers but does not stifle broad spectrum opportunity. Often the way to reconcile this difficulty is to bring in an outsider to arbitrate. Involving the external obstacles to change in the debate can also help. By including major customer representatives in the technology debate, the organization weakens the emotional strangle hold by demonstrating its commitment to major customers, but improves its own chances of negotiating a more flexible alternative.

This same paradox is at the heart of the healthcare debate in the USA. Doctors favour the current system because they are defending one of the highest standards of care in the world. Others want to see affordable care for a wider section of the community. The outside pressure inhibiting any compromise is the legal lobby, which exerts pressure on doctors to over-prescribe, through fear of expensive negligence suits. This unnecessarily inflates the cost of all healthcare. When lawyers generally base their fee on a percentage of the settlement, it is in their interests to fight for exorbitant damages. A compromise is unlikely to be found until new legislation limits malpractice suits, in other words when an extraneous control is introduced into the conflict.

When political negotiation hits a stalemate, the general answer is either to bring in an impartial outsider or look for the source of the conflict outside the immediate combatants, and defuse their power. Manipulating the balance of power by altering some external influence ensures that contention is used productively to put ideals into practice.

5.10   Opposing demands in service quality

precision   EXTERNAL REQUIREMENTS   speed
◀───▶

Chapter 4 argued that discrimination has an important role to play in the resolution of the internal–external tension; responding to all the changes in outside forces would run managers ragged. Satisfying external requirements is a quality issue which has two opposing parameters: precision and timeliness. Precision can be anything from coding accuracy when the IT department serves another department, to delivering the exact product the customer requested. Remember, for an internal service function, other parts of the business are the same as an outside customer. Customers always want exactly what they asked for, but they also want it promptly. If precision means it takes months to fulfil exact requirements then customers will get fed up and go elsewhere. Rushing the job and giving them half of what they need, or a substandard product, means that the customer feels cheated and will go elsewhere next time. Either way a customer is lost.

It is the job of management to insist that both parameters are upheld. Consequently, performance measurements must emphasize both speed and accuracy. If manufacturing is judged only on output then the quality of the end product suffers. If quality standards are unrealistic, either sales will suffer because there will not be enough material to sell, or people will just ignore the standards. The same paradox applies to information handling too. Looking for dead certainty will suppress prompt action; a quick and dirty decision is just that—uniformed and imprecise.

Managers need to assess constantly which way the organization is leaning with respect to this friction. Solutions may vary. For manufacturing it may be a question of finding where most faults occur, in other words where the risk is highest. The answer could be to move quality assurance so that checks are done right after that point. This way inherently faulty products are not processed further, so time is not wasted finishing and then reworking the finished product. For decision making, it is a question of minimizing the danger by getting more information on the variables that carry most risk, and accepting the others at face value.

In the end, it all comes down to risk management. This is the key to a discriminating personality, and the best way to ensure that a business remains fit for outside conditions.

5.11   Cultural blinkers to technological utility

risky

safe support   ORGANIZATIONAL CHANGE   transformation

◄───►

Information and technology, of themselves are neither tactical nor strategic. They are merely operational in both contexts.

McKenzie, 1991[65]

Many managers have a blinkered outlook on technological utility. They want to categorize it as either a support function or as something that can differentiate the organization from its competitors. One represents safety, the other risk. This prejudice often blinds them to what is really happening. Most technological advances differentiate the organization that invented them for a while, but then the idea becomes an accepted support system that is a standard across the industry. Differentiation is not a permanent attribute; it eventually degrades into a cost of entry into the industry. This statement does not relate only to IT or organizations, it applies equally well to the latest in any form of technology and on any scale; robotics, guided missiles, nuclear fission, even the jet engine all brought competitive advantage to the first users. These were the people who were prepared to take an initial risk. Others prefer the safety of following, but this puts them in a position of constantly having to catch up in order to remain a player.

Chapter 4 identified a progressive outlook as the final attribute for transformation. It contributes to the elasticity that comes from resolving the stability–change paradox. How progressive an organization is able to be, will depend to a large extent on how well it reconciles this underlying dilemma. Do managers have a balanced attitude towards technological advancement? Are they eager to explore the potential of new developments, or have they closed minds? Sometimes, success can be as bad as failure. Often, the most successful companies have been at the forefront of technology for a while; they feel comfortable that they have differentiated themselves well enough, but they forget that technology does not stand still. If managers rest smugly on their laurels they will quickly find themselves sliding down the wrong side of the wheel of fortune, champagne glass in hand! (Fig. 1.2c).

A progressive organization is one that is constantly on the look out for improvement, continually challenging its own success, and demanding even more of its employees. New inventions, new knowledge and new behaviour are all essential to the process of transformation.

5.12   Conclusion

There are certainly a lot of factors to be managed. We now have 15 key paradoxes to attend to. Five of them are strategic imperatives and the other 10 are frictions holding back revolution. Unfortunately, reality is generally more complex than we want to conceive. Simple actions containing prejudice might seem easier, but they generate eddies to which others will react negatively. The accumulation of negative energy expended resisting managerial bias can offset any positive efforts to effect transformation. That is counterproductive. In the end, the root cause of the difficulties remains, and the consequence of destructive activity will have been magnified by the chaotic system, making real transformation even more difficult. However, if we tackle the most serious frictions early on by integrating the forces into constructive feedback loops, all the energy is channelled into positive action that will be amplified in the system to generate spontaneous transformation.

Fig. 5.3 overleaf on page 102 indicates that the forces are interactive. However the text only describes the dynamics across the primary connections. In fact, the reality is that all 15 paradoxes are one of a piece. We cannot get away from the fact that, whatever we do, it is all unity, part of an infinitely complex and larger whole than we can ever imagine.

The paradox wheel at the start of this chapter (Fig. 5.2) cannot provide the answers. They must come from individual managers as they face the dilemmas and find their own unique solutions. What the wheel does offer is a flexible framework that organizes the most important forces operating in business into a consistent pattern. If the organization resolves the 15 paradoxes in this framework, it will have developed a sufficiently balanced corporate personality to cope with the vicissitudes of business life in the twenty-first century.

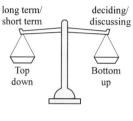

Is strategic responsibility shared?

Equitably shared strategic responsibility depends on how well TOP management balance LONG TERM and SHORT TERM demands through a cyclical process of DISCUSSION and DECISION between themselves and those at the BOTTOM

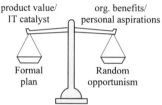

How competitively manoeuvrable is the organization?

Competitive manoeuvrability relies on comparisons between PRODUCTS & SERVICES and IT-based profit CATALYSTS being unbiased and objective so that everyone is motivated to maximize ORGANIZATIONAL BENEFITS by feeding back OPPORTUNITIES into the FORMAL PLAN without compromising their PERSONAL ASPIRATIONS

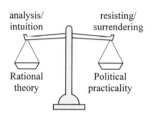

How operationally viable is the plan?

Reconciling what is THEORETICALLY BEST for the organization as a whole with PRACTICAL options that satisfy disparate POLITICAL agendas requires a balanced mix of ANALYSIS and INTUITION to break down RESISTANCE and integrate the different perspectives into an ACCEPTABLE COMPROMISE

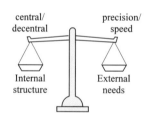

How fit is the organization?

A CENTRALLY DECENTRALIZED organization can react with both PRECISION and SPEED to changing EXTERNAL CONDITIONS by manipulating its INTERNAL STRUCTURE to create new EXTERNAL environments

How elastic is the organization?

Effective communication standards that find the right balance between ELABORATE DETAIL and ABBREVIATION are a CULTURAL necessity to support accurate transfer of information concerning ORGANIZATIONAL CHANGE. The quality of this information transfer influences the organization's ability to balance SECURITY against the TECHNOLOGICAL RISK associated with IT-enabled BUSINESS CHANGE

Fig. 5.3   An interactive policy

A model of a balanced corporate personality—the Xerox transformation*

*It is in the failure to achieve integration . . . that
personalities often make shipwreck, wither, breaking
down (physically or mentally) under the strain of conflict
or abandoning any real desire for an effective synthesis.*
Charles E Raven, *The Creator Spirit*

6.1   Introduction

Balanced personalities do not come ready formed. Integrating what are often divergent traits takes a lot of hard work and soul searching for any person. It is no good pretending that it will be easier for businesses. Corporate transformation represents a substantial change in business behaviour. The nature of the change will differ from corporation to corporation, although every organization will need a good supply of the characteristics identified in Chapters 4 and 5 and summarized in Fig. 6.1. Don't forget, however, that these are the attributes of a revolutionary; radicals are usually disastrous when it comes to managing day to day circumstances. Unfortunately, this is where we return to 'the land of paradox' again. With one exception (ethical behaviour) an excess of any of these attributes would be equally as disastrous as an absence of them. Take the following caricature of an unrestrained revolutionary—committed to the cause beyond the bounds of realism, unorthodox to the point of rebellion, demolishes conventions without a thought for the consequence, uses relationships for his own ends, is a great orator who never listens, over confident, thick skinned, loud and argumentative, tries to do too much at once, and rides roughshod over anyone that gets in his way as he single mindedly drives the revolution forward. Not a pretty picture, but in truth not an unrealistic portrait of an evangelical transformation manager!

Management by paradox is the only way to develop a balanced business character capable of coping with revolutionary change as well as day to day activities. However, the conflict and upheaval needed to integrate diverse personality traits is likely to prove unmanageable, if trust and candour are not an unshakable management ethic. Trusting relationships

*The evidence for this chapter is taken from the book *Prophets in the Dark*[66] which describes the detailed history of the Xerox transformation.

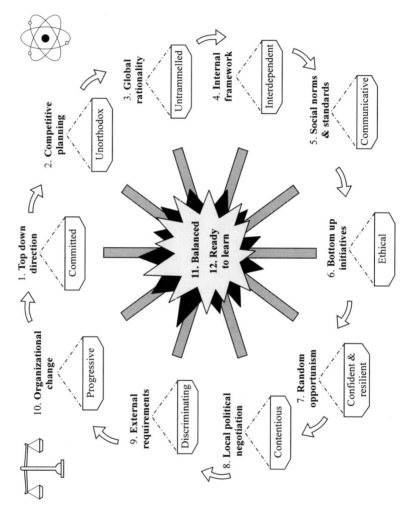

Fig. 6.1 Characteristics of an effective revolutionary

are necessary to the health of every sector of society; organizations are not immune, as they break new ground in their search to manage Chaos.

Ethical qualities are perhaps the one redeeming feature in the mysterious land of paradox. Navigating through this shadowy realm often feels similar to driving through thick fog. It is extremely disorientating, familiar objects are hard to pick out or appear blurred at the edges, and discerning the right path through the swirling mist is not easy. However, truth and integrity provide a quick and reliable navigation aid because they can be used as a yardstick against which to assess each move. Truth and integrity are incontrovertible qualities that provide a moral foundation for most societies; measuring decisions and solutions against something solid is reassuring, and a practical way for managers to judge whether they are going in the right direction. Truth and integrity are also preconditions for trust. It is interesting to look back over Chapter 5 and see how often mistrust lies at the heart of friction. Remove mistrust and each conflict becomes productive—a route to creativity. In fact, the primary task of all managers is not to organize or to make decisions, it is to build trust. None of the other revolutionary qualities can have the desired effect if trust is absent.

Trust may sound a soft and wishy-washy objective for senior executives to pursue, but when Re-engineering is about building productive relationships, it becomes an obvious necessity. In fact, trust does have undeniable benefits. Trust engenders loyalty and loyalty is a profitable commodity.[67] Loyal employees stay with a company, which saves wasting money repeatedly hiring replacements and moving them up the learning curve; loyal employees learn and share their learning, which keeps the business changing with the times; customers also like loyal employees, because their contact with the supplier is through a knowledgeable ally, rather than a succession of different representatives who have to be continuously brought up to date with the details of the relationship. Customer retention is higher when contact is consistently with the same person, repeat business is greater and less costly to obtain. Ironically, the service industries, such as accountancy and consultancy, which ought to be good at relationship-building, are particularly guilty of low customer retention rates. Auditors change from year to year, so the poor finance manager or financial director finds himself going over the same old details again and again. Consultancy partnerships frequently use different staff for consecutive client projects; even worse, when different consultants turn up they have not even seen a client history file because it is jealously guarded in someone else's domain. In both cases, the client is rightly frustrated, but worse he has no incentive to use the same service provider next time. Then the relationship becomes a simple matter of economics, and a source of advantage gets wasted.

Corporate behaviour is the product of corporate personality. Many organizations behave badly because they have developed some unfortunate prejudices. Others simply break down under the strain of a severely disturbed mentality. Perhaps it is now a good time to look at the nature of the therapy that transformed one company into a more complete and balanced corporation. The ordeal will be different for everyone, but there are some invaluable lessons to be learned from an experienced traveller on the road to transformation.

6.2 The Xerox history

The Rank Xerox story is the tale of a company that totally rejuvenated itself on a global scale in the space of seven years. An astounding feat when one considers the size of the organization and realize that, in 1982, Xerox was in such a poor condition that its new CEO, David Kearns, believed that Xerox was on its way out of business. There is no doubt that the revolution was painful and difficult, but perseverance and a commitment to quality made the pain productive, because by 1989 Xerox was back in shape and ready to face the challenges of the 1990s.

The evidence shows that the history of the corporation before 1982 created a totally unbalanced environment. Xerox's subsequent problems arose because some corporate traits were so overpowering as to be disabling. Other important attributes were completely absent. This accumulation of disabilities was the cause of a vicious circle of decline that lead Kearns to fear for the future of the company.

The first and perhaps the biggest mistake the corporation made was to permit assumptions developed in the 1960s to colour its outlook permanently. Environments are not stable and what appeared to work once can easily become a noose around the neck in the future. Xerox was a 'prisoner of its past' and a successful past at that. The birth of the 914 copier made the corporation one of the biggest success stories of the early 1960s. Sales growth reached astounding proportions—rising from $32 million in 1959 to $1.125 billion in 1968—and profits poured in at an awesome rate. Operating in an expanding market with virtually no competition, the corporation learned that selling copiers was easy and that they were doing the customer a big favour by 'democratizing information'. People in the organization were so accustomed to rapid growth and easy profits that they came to believe in their own infallibility. Xerox became over confident, but in the end its confidence blinded the organization to opportunity rather than encouraging a spirit of adventure. David Kearns compares the corporation to a flock of pigeons trained to repeat the same old routine, without ever understanding why.

The culture of arrogance that ensued shut out various important aspects of changing reality. Customer requirements and attitudes were not taken into consideration, in the belief that Xerox knew best. For example, Xerox had never once asked their customers whether the machine damaging their original document was really their worst nightmare. Yet, this was the unquestioning assumption on which they based the design of new photocopiers. In this, the company was also blind to technological advances. The value of an original to a typist, with no means of recreating it, is high, however, the advent of golf ball typewriters in the late 1970s and early 1980s meant a page could be stored in memory and reproduced without retyping; now a lost original was not the catastophe it once had been. Inevitably these unfounded beliefs and blinkered attitudes held Xerox back while competitors developed compact, user-friendly machines with document handlers.

In fact, Xerox never paid much attention to anything the competition was doing. The next jolt to its complacency came when IBM unveiled a new sales policy, called Top Stop pricing, for its improved Copier II. Pricing policies at Xerox had originally been designed to allow the customer to pay according to usage, but because this kept profits rolling in, the company had got caught up in its own cleverness. Scale rates per copy became so complex and detailed that they alienated rather than pleased the customer. Under Top Stop pricing, IBM customers paid a known price for a fixed number of copies and then charges stopped.

Xerox studiously ignored issues of customer satisfaction too. If it had been more open-minded, customer complaints should have been a stimulus to solve real design faults. As it was, service maintenance became more and more a retrofit exercise, despite the inconvenience to the customer of having a machine out of action. Sadly, at Xerox, little money was set aside for developing improvements in what was assumed to be a mature market; customer dissatisfaction with problems of reliability, low user-friendliness, 'dirt levels' (the amount of loose toner in the machine and around the print room) and overall quality were given a relatively low priority. Xerox deluded themselves that customers would stay loyal, however they were treated.

As if this blind arrogance was not enough of a handicap, the death of Joe Wilson, Xerox's visionary leader, brought to power some ambitious financial wizards trained in the stables of the highly successful Ford Motor Company. This may have seemed a timely move in a company whose fortunes had run away with them. However the introduction of extremely rigid controls, authoritarian discipline and a steep hierarchical structure generated trauma so severe as to almost tear the company apart. The nature of the change also compounded the bad habits already bedeviling the organization.

Certainly, the Ford men imposed order upon a company that had little financial discipline, but the swing to structured financial planning was so violent that it often overrode the possibility of reacting to changing market circumstances. Complex computerized financial planning models started to inhibit market decisions. When the marketing department wanted to change prices or introduce new products they had to provide 3500 input assumptions for a model that would predict to three decimal places the impact on profits! Further, the financial experts began to believe that they knew more than the marketeers and would run the model with their own assumptions to compare them with those of marketing. Mistrust fuelled irrational behaviour. The result was a huge overload in internal communication, all of which was counterproductive. The excesses of supposed rationality that the financial people tried to impose resulted in intense political battles between themselves and more market orientated groups. To win the battles, marketing recruited their own finance people, to act as interpreters; all that did was re-enforce the power that was the root of the problem by creating a structure more heavily weighted in favour of finance and less focused on the customer.

The new President, Archie McCardell, aggravated the communication problem by his management style. His introverted nature and dislike of debating things in front of management quickly blocked vital communication channels. Meetings, which should have been a centre for lively debate and challenge were meek inconclusive affairs. McCardell preferred to collect the financial data, hear the arguments from his management and then retreat to his office to analyse it and reach his own conclusions. Although people were uncomfortable with the fact that the McCardell administration spent so much effort measuring things and too little time sharing decision making, meetings remained civil, with little in the way of honest, bidirectional communication. In fact, even information gathered directly from customers was discounted as 'feel' for the marketplace, in the face of the unassailable logic of the financial 'White Papers' as they came to be called. Sales heroes of the 1960s were chastised for 'hunches' and the 'culture became less tolerant of the absurd act'. In fact, the motto of the company became 'if it can't be analysed it isn't true'.

This led to increasing centralization and branch managers lost much of their power. Effectively, the company's ability to react to the symptoms of environmental Chaos was increasingly being whittled away by some overbearing characteristics.

Outside circumstances and the arrogance of the corporation combined to aggravate these bad habits. Xerox had a long-standing philosophy of being an 'enlightened employer and a responsible corporate citizen'. When the Federal Trade Commission accused Xerox of using unfair trading practices to artificially sustain its monopoly of the photocopier market, the company felt obliged to defend its reputation. The resulting legal battles and antitrust suits had two detrimental effects. Firstly, it shook the confidence of many in the organization in the wrong areas, making them more tentative about excursions into the outside world. Secondly, it brought the lawyers to power, and their involvement in almost every aspect of business created a stranglehold on the company's ability to react to the increasing competition from Japan at the low end of the market, and the likes of Kodak and IBM in the upper end.

After the death of Joe Wilson, Peter McColough became Chairman and CEO. Certainly, he was a timely counterbalance to the shortsightedness of current attitudes, but one shift in the forces was not enough. McColough saw his role as less operational and more strategic, so he handed over much of the day-to-day control to McCardell. McColough spent time looking at the future and outlining a long term vision for the organization. He foresaw the need for an 'architecture of information'—a structure and interactive support system that would streamline communications. Clearly, Xerox was positioned to play a central role in satisfying such a need by offering a suite of compatible office products that together would speed up the flow of information. Unfortunately, the vision was totally disconnected from the central beliefs of operational managers, who saw information and document processing as a rather boring but essential support function. Uninspired by McColough's vision, they did not have the commitment to implement it in any form. McColough tried to make his vision a reality by diversifying out of just xerography. In a bid to gain a foothold in the digital technology that would eventually support his vision of an architecture of information, he purchased SDS a small computer company on the west coast of America.

Unfortunately, as is often the case, independent action without the backing of other managers is a mistake. SDS became the Palo Alto Research Centre (PARC). PARC was a constant irritation to the staid and arrogant East Coast Xerox culture. PARC people viewed copier people as stodgy and out of touch. Copier people saw PARC people as expensive ideas men who did not produce anything that was commercially viable. Naturally, there was competition for resources, and whenever this clash of the Titans occurred the result was acrimonious political dogfights that wounded the corporation in many ways.

New technologies were rejected on principle rather than on their merits; groups fought for their honour, rather than for a higher corporate objective; mistrust clouded every judgement. Balancing factional loyalties often led to erroneous decisions. Good people were lost to the corporation because they could not tolerate the politics and, worst of all, because the PARC research was extraneous to the mainline business there was no way of building upon PARC innovations to stimulate progressive improvements in the corporate direction and performance. Work on the west coast never became an integral part of the corporate strategy so there was no way to use the synergy between the contributions of each side. Unresolved, the difference in personalities turned into a bitter and destructive war between the two camps, with no benefit for the whole organization. The effect of this rift was exacerbated by the fact that what talent did exist in mainstream operations was under utilized. Xerox made little use of the clever people that they employed because the company rarely asked for their input, so east coast personnel felt undervalued, disempowered and resentful. McColough had recognized this as a serious limitation back in 1976 when he was studying the Japanese work methods. He tried to rectify the imbalance by introducing employee participation, however, the culture of Xerox was so backward that even the CEO failed to get anything moving on this front for a full three years.

All these faults started to take their toll on the Xerox results. Japanese direct sales at the low end of the market were becoming increasingly painful, as Xerox customers changed to decentralized copying on higher quality small machines. In addition, the appeal of Xerox's traditional leasing arrangements was declining both for the customer and the Xerox salesman; pushing sales was a short term fix for a poor quarter, in direct opposition financial people actively discouraged sales. Leasing meant a continuous predictable flow of profits, sales were tantamount to eating your own seed corn because the customer was no longer obliged to pay by the copy. To sustain growth on a sales base was a geometric progression that required more and more intensive effort, particularly in the area of new product development. Unfortunately, Xerox was not used to creating the necessary innovations in the copier market to support regular new sales, neither was the rigid control culture an ideal environment in which innovation could thrive.

As the company entered the 1980s margins had dropped from 70 per cent to 10 per cent and the Japanese were now increasing the pressure by moving upmarket. Prospects were bleak and the company needed a complete overhaul if it was to survive.

1. Vacillating	Committed	○ Dogmatic
2. Orthodox	○ Unorthodox	Rebellious
3. Narrow minded	○ Untrammelled	Reckless
4. Independent	○ Interdependent/democratic	Manipulative
5. Uncommunicative	○ Communicative	Bombastic/arrogant
6. Devious/underhand	○ Ethical	Over zealous
7. Fearful/shaky	Confident/resilient	○ Thick skinned
8. Avoids an argument	○ Contentious	Aggressively argumentative
9. Distracted	Discriminating	○ Deluded
10. Staid	○ Progressive	A steam roller

Fig. 6.2   A profile of an unbalanced personality

Fig. 6.2 shows how unbalanced the corporation truly was, with respect to the sort of characteristics needed for extraordinary management. The actual positions on the scale are only estimates, based on the textual description of activities. Ideally, one would use the questionnaire in Appendix A to evaluate the corporate character. In fact the actual position is not so important. What is important is the overall tendency to extremes, manifested by the company and its management. The left-hand column represents the opposite qualities of revolutionary. Some of the terms may seem derogatory, but in fact they are an honest description of many traditional management values when taken to the extreme. Vacillating is often described as 'being flexible'; devious and underhand is often considered to be smart and crafty; uncommunicative may be strong and silent, or autocratic. The right-hand column describes the effect of taking revolutionary values too far.

The personality disorder in Xerox meant that its actions put the paradoxes around the learning wheel completely out of balance (Fig. 6.3).

Unfortunately, the unresolved frictions at the lower level (Fig. 6.4) were also severe and the combination of the two completely stopped any chance of the organization learning new behaviour. Of course, not all companies demonstrate imbalances along all of the tensions around both circles. The fact that Xerox exhibited a weakness in all of the principle strategic dilemmas shown in Fig. 6.3 and most of the underlying inhibitors to revolution (Fig. 6.4) is testimony to the severity of its problems.

Modus omnibus rebus optimus est habitu Moderation in all things Plautus c200 BC		
Vision at top disconnected from operational focus	**1 Sharing strategic responsibility 6**	Suppressed grassroots initiatives
Little fear of competition and rigid financial justifications	**2 Competitive manoeuvrability 7**	Restricted ability to take advantage of circumstances
Constrained thinking and perpetuated wrong assumptions	**3 Operational viability 8**	Created bitter political battles
A very steep hierarchical structure	**4 Physical fitness for the environment 9**	Focused interest away from customer requirements
A culture of arrogance and ineffective communication	**5 Elastic strength 10**	Left no incentive or stimulus for continuous improvement

Fig. 6.3   The warring factors at Xerox

Items in CAPITALS represent excesses		Items in text represent omissions
FOCUS ON ANNUAL FINANCIALS	**Depth of vision**	The obverse of quality
INFORMATION IS BORING	**Competitive acuity**	No one listens to common sense
ALL DECISIONS NEED LOTS OF ANALYSIS	**Holistic rationality**	"We don't act on hunches"
HIGHLY CENTRALIZED	**Structural flexibility**	Little local power
HUGE MEETINGS FOSTERED ORATORY	**Communication quality**	No limit to rambling and irrelevant "war stories"
DECISIONS TAKEN ALONE	**Participative scope**	Little discussion
No clearly accepted goals no quality benefits	**Goal congruence**	No incentives and no personal reward
HIGH RESISTANCE TO "PARC" IDEAS	**Arbitration skills**	East/West divide could find no compromise
Not even a consideration	**Customer service quality**	Not even a consideration
INFORMATION ONLY A SUPPORT FUNCTION	**Technological utility**	No interest in differentiation

Fig. 6.4 Severe imbalances are a powerful inhibitor to change

Not all the inhibiting paradoxes highlighted in Fig. 6.4 have been detailed in the foregoing précis of Xerox's history. However, the quotes and descriptions supporting the paradoxes come directly from Kearns' own account of the problem. He clearly identifies the over emphases (shown in capitals) and the weaknesses (shown in lower case) as factors that directly contributed to the crisis facing Xerox. He and David Nadler, head of Delta Consulting Group took on the mantle of business revolutionaries and successfully turned the company around. It will become clear that their remedial actions introduced most of the previously identified management qualities (Fig. 6.1) and addressed the unreconciled dilemmas that were holding the company back. The end result was behavioural transformation.

Correcting the deficiencies

The first stirring of change began right at the bottom of the organization, where little had moved for years. In 1979, three years after McColough's insight, a man called Harold Tragash was given the task of improving employee involvement.

Tragash was a man of academic orientation who had kept a relatively low profile in the organization until then. His knowledge of the corporation was extensive but underneath his pedantic style lay 'a quiet revolutionary'. To start with all he could do was to plant some seeds and cultivate the small shoots that grew, but this was the right approach;

radical intervention would have stirred up an equal and opposite resistance, and never have achieved the desired effect.

Tragash recruited David Nadler as an advisor early in the employee involvement exercise, because Nadler had been working on employee participation at Columbia's Graduate School of Business. Nadler's introduction to the company was less than overwhelmingly enthusiastic. Only 17 people turned up to the first meeting on employee participation. He quickly concluded that a massive corporate initiative would immediately die a death from apathy. Besides, he knew that:

> organizations long used to doing things one way, did not readily accept a new direction.

Consequently, he recommended to Kearns, now president of Xerox, that a low level effort would be more effective. Tragash and Nadler therefore started the process of steadily building the pressure that would eventually explode employee's entrenched attitudes. They used educational seminars, they created the position of quality facilitator, and they dragged managers off to see examples of enlightened organizations where self-management was the norm. Unfortunately, their work was hampered by the fact that the employee involvement issue was not given a particularly high priority by top management. Kearns himself admits that although he was in favour of the concept, at the time he did not see it as the way to turn the company around; his sights remained firmly fixed on costs and the Japanese.

However, two things changed his perspective. The first was the findings of the team sent to investigate why Japan could undercut price and still achieve 7–8 per cent gains, when most American companies only made 2–3 per cent per annum. The results were so shocking that they stopped Xerox management in its tracks. Japanese competitors carried six to eight times less inventory. The quality of purchased parts was 99.5 per cent compared with 95 per cent at Xerox. Xerox carried 1.3 overhead workers per direct worker, the Japanese needed only 0.6. In general, for every factor they compared the Japanese were usually at least 100 per cent better.

The second insight that altered Kearns' perspective was a chance reading of an article while he was *en route* to Japan for one of his regular educational visits. The Western press was pouring scorn on General Motor's strategy for change. It was incredulous that GM would invest $3 billion on quality and expect real returns. Yet, when Kearns arrived in Japan, he found that the competition had copies of the article pasted on the walls of their plants. *They* were convinced that the GM programme would be successful, so they were taking appropriate action. All GM's own countrymen could do was to pour scorn on the idea. Kearns realized that this difference in expectations was key to the whole issue. The

Japanese expected progressive improvement, whereas Western organizations were sceptical that even a massive investment in quality   could change a company's fortunes.

> As I chewed this over in my mind, I realized that we were fine tuning a bad product—the bad product being our management system—and by doing nothing more than fine tuning it, we were not going to change anything at all.

Linking these insights into Japanese attitudes with the idea of employee involvement, Kearns set out to define a meaningful vision for Xerox. The mission he outlined was appropriately general. It was to improve business effectiveness by increasing expectation levels. Unlike McColough's vision of an 'architecture of information' Kearns' concept of business effectiveness was not so far removed from practicalities that it could not inspire commitment. It was also good counterbalance to offset the many of the excesses that had been strangling the company.

The change in direction was no radical swing away from structured controls back to woolly opportunism; that would have been dangerous. Instead, it was a programme of firm goals and strict targets, that were forward and outward looking. Control parameters would no longer be internally generated financial ones. Instead they would reflect outside determinants of the corporate future. Kearns immediately initiated a process of benchmarking against best of breed organization. Quality had previously been measured against the specifications of earlier Xerox products, now it would be measured against the best competitors products. Every facet of the organization was encouraged to measure itself against the best performer in their industry. So, for example, in distribution, Xerox took LL Bean, the clothing distributors as the model, and in data processing John Deere, the earthmoving company, was the benchmark.

The philosophy of business effectiveness was underpinned by the notion of employee involvement, so that, finally, those at the sharp end of the business would have a say in defining what changes were needed. In 1980, Kearns provided a clear demonstration of his conviction for the idea of cooperation with the employees by agreeing to a union request to guarantee specific people's jobs, during the change process. The benefit he gained from this simple action of satisfying the employees' natural desire for security was to give the quality programme a vital lift that drove the concept deeper into the organizational consciousness. Kearns was starting to build trust.

This proved useful when the time came to cut manufacturing costs. The threat of closure at the Webster, New York, facility combined with Kearns' previous actions gave New York plant workers the confidence to use the idea of employee involvement in a bid to save their jobs. They asked for a chance to develop their own plan to save the

$3 million in operating costs that closure would achieve. Although they could only find $2.3 million at the first pass, Kearns agreed to spare the plant. In the end his faith was justified because the $2.3 million was later improved to savings of $2.9 million. The boost to the employee participation programme from this effort was a crucial step in the turn-around strategy, and worth far more than the missed $100,000. The fact that Kearns was consistent demonstrated the integrity of his intentions. Often a symbolic act of commitment is more effective than mere words.

A McKinsey study in 1981, also helped to rebalance the power distribution further. The company was re-organized into a series of decentralized business units. Redistributing power weakened the central bureaucracy that had been strangling the organization. However, central influence was not completely negated; Kearns recognized that central support for the quality initiative needed a boost if things were going to happen at an acceptable rate. Changing the culture solely from the bottom up was going to be too slow a process.

To this end, Kearns installed a master of business politics, Norm Rickards, as head of his business effectiveness office. Tragash and Rickards spent two months designing a programme called Commitment to Excellence, which they felt had to become the driving philosophy of the company. It was a vision without specifics, but Kearns approved it.

By now, McColough had retired, and Kearns was Chairman and CEO, Even the power of his combined office meant nothing without a constituency of support amongst the right people. So Rickards began testing the waters. Firstly, he targeted the most senior managers. He spent time explaining the concept of Commitment to Excellence and trying to get their support for this long term change. Unfortunately, few of them believed that quality ideals were the way to improve the financial problems that Xerox was facing. Fortunately, at the next level down, Rickards found the supporters he needed, and between them they recruited a 'Gang of Eleven' who began plotting the revolution. Subsequently, this was reduced to a 'Gang of Seven', when it was found that 11 people together was too many to be productive.

The underground effort still did not produce results quickly enough. Unfortunately, guerrilla warfare rarely does. So despite an implicit long term commitment to quality Kearns got nervous and took short term measures to prop up corporate performance, until the quality initiative produced results. Kearns decided to diversify and, in September 1982, Xerox bought an insurance company called Crum & Forster for a massive $1.6 billion in cash and stock. Unfortunately, the rationale behind such a move was misinterpreted. Employees saw it as a sign that the copier market was no longer core business, and the reaction on Wall Street was no less catastrophic. Most investors and analysts failed to understand the sense of slashing costs, laying people off, and trimming benefits in the core business and then spending $1.6 million in non-related investment. Institutional investors reacted by dumping stock and the share price was falling dangerously.

The mistake that Kearns made was to send an inconsistent message about his commitment to Xerox as a quality copier company. Unfortunately, such a slip in consistency is easy to make for one visionary working alone. Even so, the setback to the process of revolutionizing Xerox was quite severe. Had Kearns had the benefit of an objective outsider working with him and playing Devil's advocate, he might not have made such an unfortunate error of judgement. A person with no political agenda and no career investment in the company would have had a clearer view of what was required, and be better positioned to tell the CEO when he is wrong, without any fear for his job. The importance of an outsider in the quality process was the lesson that Tony Kobayashi of Fuji Xerox later explained to Tragash and Rickards. This was the cue for David Nadler to enter centre stage.

Nadler met with Kearns and a partnership was born that was to last for seven years and change the whole culture at Xerox. The first phase of their work was to design a structure to handle the process. Like all future steps in the evolution of the Xerox revolution, this phase reflected all the necessary aspects of strategy (Fig. 6.5).

Kearns demonstrated his commitment by heading up the quality team. Together they planned the nature of Xerox's future competitive stance and set it out in what came to be known as 'The Blue Book'. Next they needed a sensible mechanism to spread their ideals company wide. At a big meeting, in their training centre at Leesburg, the whole management roughed out the shape of a new internal framework and defined the sort of informal behaviour needed to support the change. The output was the result of participatory sessions that focused on 34 questions devised by Kearns and Nadler. Much to everyone's surprise it actually produced 34 answers. This was unusual for meetings at Xerox, particularly when, as Nadler observed, the people did not cooperate very well together. This time, however, they managed to use their knowledge of the environment to come up with a sensible package of ideas.

The Leesburg meeting substantially improved Kearns' constituency of support for his new objective. He sensibly used the momentum generated to start the ball rolling on the next phase of the process, by asking managers to volunteer staff for membership in a transition team that would manage the change.

After the completion of this first phase of revolution Xerox went through many more cycles. The second cycle followed a similar pattern (Fig. 6.6).

The transition team obtained a leader who should have been an inspiration in the process of translating 'The Blue Book' into an

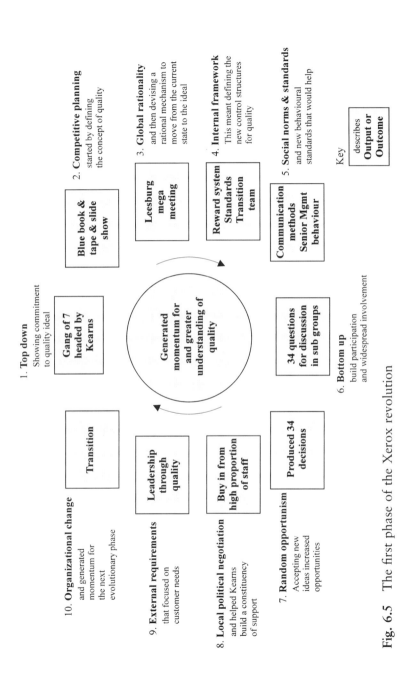

Fig. 6.5 The first phase of the Xerox revolution

1. Top down
Showing commitment
to quality ideal

2. Competitive planning
started by defining
the concept of quality

3. Global rationality
and then devising a
rational mechanism to
move from the current
state to the ideal

4. Internal framework
This meant defining the
new control structures
for quality

5. Social norms & standards
and new behavioural
standards that would help

6. Bottom up
build participation
and widespread involvement

7. Random opportunism
Accepting new
ideas increased
opportunities

8. Local political negotiation
and helped Kearns
build a constituency
of support

9. External requirements
that focused on
customer needs

10. Organizational change
and generated
momentum for
the next
evolutionary phase

Key

describes
**Output or
Outcome**

Gang of 7
headed by
Kearns

Blue book &
tape & slide
show

Leesburg
mega
meeting

Reward system
Standards
Transition
team

Communication
methods
Senior Mgmt
behaviour

Generated
momentum for
and greater
understanding of
quality

Transition

Leadership
through
quality

Buy in from
high proportion
of staff

Produced 34
decisions

34 questions
for discussion
in sub groups

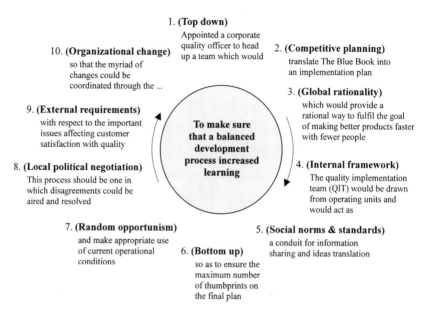

Fig. 6.6   A later evolutionary phase in the Xerox revolution

implementation plan that would deliver added value from quality. Unfortunately, the nature of the quality implementation team (QIT) actually hindered the operation of all subsequent aspects in this phase.

In fact, the same circular pattern emerged as a negative mirror image (Fig. 6.7) of the paradox wheel. The choice of Fred Henderson as the corporate quality officer started a vicious circle that counteracted some of the advances that had already been made. Henderson was too much from the old school, and his method of operation detracted from the value that he brought to the team effort. This was aggravated by the fact that the QIT team members were not the best choices; they were either too young to have the credibility to be change agents, or senior burnouts who were shunted into the team, because no-one knew what else to do with them. Kearns estimated that roughly half of the team were wrong choices. Nadler was adamant that Henderson would not do the job well. However, in the urgency of the moment Kearns accepted his limitations. It was a costly mistake which Kearns admits wasted months of vital time. Because the team did not work well together the members were not prepared to stick their neck out and Henderson's attitude to disagreement and conflict was so contrary to what was needed that the team could not make the significant new advances.

It is worth pointing out at this stage that repetitions of the strategic cycles exhibit a true fractal quality. Chapter 1 noted that fractals are

Fig. 6.7   A vicious circle caused by a counter revolutionary

Nature's way of bringing order to disorder, although still allowing infinite variety in finite form. Since the rules of the circle hold true across the scales, the 'self-similarity' will allow businesses to bring order to the complex process of decision making, without restricting the range of variety. Underneath each aspect on the circle, a similar cycle is being enacted (such as the one in Fig. 6.8).

This is a positive pattern underlying the process of developing 'The Blue Book' shown in aspect 2 of Fig. 6.5. The team went through the same cycle of dilemmas to produce an answer to this one aspect. Unfortunately, sometimes the cycle goes backwards in a mirror image of the process. This creates a vicious circle like the one involving Henderson. Ultimately, the whole complex mass of interacting dilemmas look something like the fractal in Fig. 6.9.

The overall remedy for all the problems that Xerox faced was an infinite variety of small changes that tackled particular personality weaknesses. Fig. 6.10 outlines a selection of the remedies that Xerox employed. It was the interaction of all of them which created an environment in which learning gradually took root.

Fig. 6.11 indicates how the various management qualities manifested themselves. All of the qualities were present to some degree, some of them are not easily supportable by one quote, but are suggested by combinations of actions and overall attitudes (e.g. trust, integrity and respect).

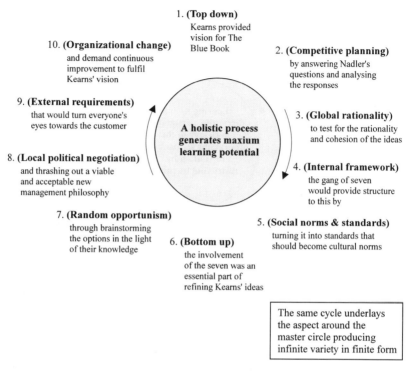

1. (Top down)
Kearns provided vision for The Blue Book

2. (Competitive planning)
by answering Nadler's questions and analysing the responses

10. (Organizational change)
and demand continuous improvement to fulfil Kearns' vision

9. (External requirements)
that would turn everyone's eyes towards the customer

A holistic process generates maximum learning potential

3. (Global rationality)
to test for the rationality and cohesion of the ideas

8. (Local political negotiation)
and thrashing out a viable and acceptable new management philosophy

4. (Internal framework)
the gang of seven would provide structure to this by

7. (Random opportunism)
through brainstorming the options in the light of their knowledge

6. (Bottom up)
the involvement of the seven was an essential part of refining Kearns' ideas

5. (Social norms & standards)
turning it into standards that should become cultural norms

The same cycle underlays the aspect around the master circle producing infinite variety in finite form

Fig. 6.8 A fractal process underlying the quality planning stage

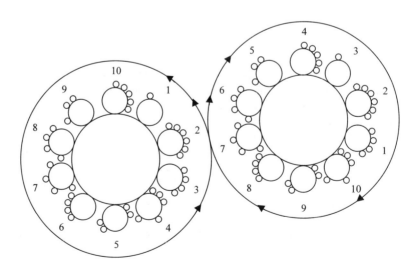

Fig. 6.9 Interacting cycles in the strategy process mimic the patterns of fractals

Top down direction

- Training started at top
- Customer satisfaction given higher priority than ROA or more market share
- Preached consistent message
- Always had quality policy card in his pocket

Competitive planning

- Statistical methods control
- Surveys to see if quality tools used
- Subordinate/Boss evaluation
- In depth studies of project progress
- Systematic people/job plans

Global rationality

- Kearns combined analysis with intuition
- Looked for root causes not symptoms
- Baldrige quality effort
- 15% ROA and market share goods

Internal framework

Social norms & standards

- Product delivery teams
- Use of outside consultant
- Presidential review boards
- Divestment of non core business
- Restructure management team
- Cascade training

- Define 11 interactive skills
- Everyone given small card with quality policy on
- Intensive training—Learn, Use, Teach, Inspect (LUTI)
- Symbols & language to define points of stability
- The Blue Book defined norms

Closed feedback loops
Used Holistic process and balanced the forces
Focused on steady learning

Organizational change

- Defined nine steps to quality improvement
- Recognize it is "race with no finish line"
- Quality in the managerial process breeds quality in operation

External requirements

- Customers can be internal as well as external
- Benchmarking to create dissatisfaction with status quo
- Senior execs take customer complaint calls
- Scheduled meetings must have identifiable customer

Political negotiation

- Nadler plays devil's advocate to Kearns
- Encourage "physical contact sport"
- Tragash/Nadler focus on key power groups

Random opportunism

- Trial and error testing
- Individual job guarantees to give personal security
- Active encouragement of reactions based on principles of quality

Bottom up initiatives

- Participation in planning
- Employee involvement in product development
- Employee projects to drive up satisfaction
- Employee effort prevents plant closure

Fig. 6.10   A sample of the remedies used by Xerox to help the revolution

Commitment (Top down)	Kearns' use of quality card
Unorthodox thinking (Competitive planning)	'Information is structural steel–a new way to frame the building' Kearns' enlightenment when he visited Japan
Breaking out of cosy compartments (Global rationality)	Quality: suppression of financial constraints. Kearns' intuition
Interdependence **Democracy** (Internal framework)	Team working--product delivery teams for new 1090 copier–QIT team for implementation. McKinsey decentralization exercise
Sharing information freely (Social norms & standards)	'A core task of organization design is processing information'
Trust/integrity/respect (Bottom up)	Tragash's employee participation initiative Saving the Webster plant even through the employees did not quite meet $3 million savings targeted
Creating supportive environment for risk taking (Random opportunism)	Individuals guaranteed their jobs as a result of Kearns and unions
Challenging prejudice/ creating contention (Local political negotiation)	'The idea of quality was to provide an open environment in which disagreements could be aired'
Discrimination (External requirements)	'We introduced them to the Japanese notion that there are both external and internal customers'
Progressive **organizational change** (Organizational change)	The accumulation of all the initiatives in Fig. 6.10

Fig. 6.11   Examples of the presence of desirable management qualities

However, what held the whole thing together was the persistence and trust generated by Kearns and Nadler. Kearns often resorted to small symbolic acts to build this trust. For example, he always carried the small card issued to employees that contained the corporate quality statement; he often referred to it in public, which helped convince others that his intentions were genuine. One of Kearns' distinct advantages over McCardell was the fact that he had a more intuitive edge to his personality. He did not mind making decisions, and, as he admits, he was not obsessed with getting 'one more fact' unlike the analysts who had dominated the company before. Kearns and Nadler, with Tragash and Rickards, devoted themselves to a progressive search for new ways to change the culture which had paralysed Xerox in the 1970s.

Despite many doubts and fears as to whether they were on the right track, Kearns and Nadler achieved the turnaround they set out to. In

1990, David Kearns resigned. He handed over the reins to Paul Allaire, a strong supporter of the quality revolution and a forceful participant while he was head of Rank Xerox in Europe.

Allaire then faced an entirely different set of problems and had to consider how to launch his own revolution:

> He wants to rip up the old hierarchical charts, get rid of the restrictive ways in which workers are managed and start afresh. No doubt the circle will turn many more times for Xerox, in the course of the next few years.

Clearly, Xerox knew that the wheel *must* continue to turn. The organization could not stand still and rest smugly on its laurels. Double loop learning lives! The speed of change would vary depending on how effectively Allaire managed to control the frictions that interfered with free revolution, but the transformation must roll on through continuous cycles of challenge, change, crystallize, then challenge the result, change it and recrystallize the effects.

6.3   Lessons of the Xerox story

Do not be tempted to dismiss this case because Xerox encountered its imbalances in the 1970s and resolved them in the 1980s. Paradox is perpetual and endemic, and the cycle remains relevant over time. Indeed, the dilemmas in the model came from discussions with practising managers in the 1990s. The paradoxes chosen were the ones that they considered the most troublesome today. The value of the Xerox case lies in the fact that it exhibits all the paradoxes, repetitively. Had Xerox been working explicitly with a paradoxical model, the change may have occurred in less than seven years.

So, what are the therapeutic lessons to be learned from this study of a personality under change?

- The role of a transformational manager is to introduce changes that strengthen weak areas in the corporate personality, so that these opposite qualities can keep the dominant ones from excess. Remember, love stops power becoming brutality, and strength keeps feeling from becoming sentimentality.
- The introduction of complementary opposites must not be sudden or extensive; gradual progressive stages allow people to come to terms with the new and absorb it rather than reject it. Many remedies are needed to achieve the desired results.
- The process of transformation is continuous and always ongoing. It is a means and never an end.

- The process has a fractal quality. An accumulation of virtuous circles generates behavioural transformation. Vicious circles reverse the momentum.
- The continuity and dynamism of a fractal process means that the leader needs to monitor and rebalance the distribution of power across the paradoxes continuously. The forces are never static because each action indirectly alters the dynamics in apparently unrelated areas.
- Successful transformational leaders cannot turn a company around on their own. They need advisers who keep testing their judgement against standards that they are sometimes too emotionally involved to keep in mind, and they need the support of all political constituencies.
- Leaders do not have to possess all the revolutionary characteristics themselves. However, they need to compensate for the major corporate failings either through their own actions or by delegating the task to the right person (Tragash and Rickards, not Henderson).
- Never take actions that divert attention away from the transformation objective. It sends conflicting messages.

Part 2
THE PRACTICE OF PARADOXICAL MANAGEMENT

Re-energizing your business—tools and techniques for redefining the corporate character

*[Managers and employees] must learn how the very
way they go about defining and solving problems
can be a source of problems in its own right.*
Argyris, 1991[50]

7.1 Introduction

The first part of this book has explored two sets of dilemmas; five strategic control paradoxes that cover the 10 most essential qualities for doing business, and 10 pairs of underlying values. Any unresolved tension at the lower level affects the organization's ability to integrate the top level strategic characteristics into a harmonious whole. Resolving the underlying frictions will help to stimulate the specific revolutionary characteristics identified in Chapter 4.

So, now we have a framework that looks like Fig. 7.1.

The next step is to use the framework to identify the unique pattern of character dislocations that will prevent effective transformation, for each organization.

7.2 Profiling the current imbalances

Profiling the present corporate character is a more valuable starting point for transformation planning than mapping the current information flows. Today's process flows are largely irrelevant to the future; they are simply a manifestation of personality problems that need to be corrected. Treating the disease is more effective than just suppressing the symptoms. Consequently, no organization can make sensible plans for transformation until the most crippling character weaknesses have been identified. Clearly, these are the areas that need attention first.

No two organizations will have the same problems; indeed, the profile of one part of the organization may be completely different from another. This may, in fact, be advantageous if it can be used constructively, so that strengths in one area can be used to offset weaknesses in another.

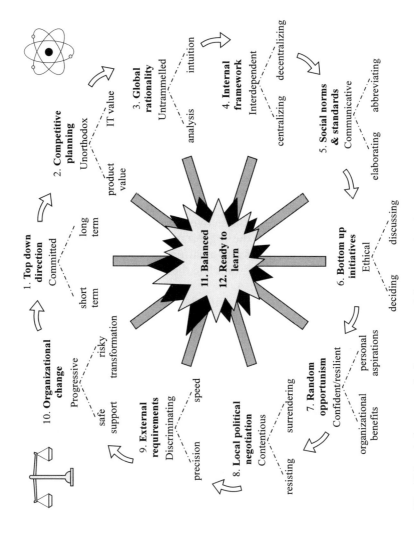

Fig. 7.1 A framework for re-energizing your business

1. **Top down direction**
   Committed
   - short term
   - long term

2. **Competitive planning**
   Unorthodox
   - product value
   - IT value

3. **Global rationality**
   Untrammelled
   - analysis
   - intuition

4. **Internal framework**
   Interdependent
   - centralizing
   - decentralizing

5. **Social norms & standards**
   Communicative
   - elaborating
   - abbreviating

6. **Bottom up initiatives**
   Ethical
   - deciding
   - discussing

7. **Random opportunism**
   Confident/resilient
   - organizational benefits
   - personal aspirations

8. **Local political negotiation**
   Contentious
   - resisting
   - surrendering

9. **External requirements**
   Discriminating
   - precision
   - speed

10. **Organizational change**
    Progressive
    - safe support
    - risky transformation

11. **Balanced**
12. **Ready to learn**

However, if, as in the Xerox case, East Coast and PARC were allowed to remain divided, the organization will suffer. The job of management is to recognize the conflict and then engineer the conditions in which it can be used productively. Dealing with the *mix* of imbalances is important; concentrating on one defect in isolation will not produce the desired results.

How can managers pinpoint the imbalances? Simply by evaluating different parts of the organization using the questionnaire in Appendix A. There are some important provisos attached to its use. Firstly, it must be crystal clear which facet of the business participants are being asked to evaluate. For example, are they being asked to give their opinion on the organization as a whole, the board of directors, the SBU (strategic business unit) in which they work, or their department or project team? This must be spelled out right from the start or the assessments will be misleading. Next, it is important to note that the questions are somewhat different from a normal survey, in that they are bipolar. In other words, the options are not exclusive, and it is perfectly acceptable to rate *both* alternatives simultaneously high or low. The final proviso is perhaps the most awkward. Respondents must be in a position to answer honestly. In other words, peer pressure, fear of reprisals and collusion have to be eliminated. Chapter 9 will consider some IT-based tools that could help introduce the right conditions, however at this stage the first priority is respondent anonymity.

Then there is the question of who ought to answer the questions. Once again this depends on the context in which the questionnaire is being applied. The most important criterion is to get an unprejudiced collection of data, and a cross-section of opinions for comparison. If a company is using this approach to guide organization-wide change then, clearly, input is required from all the management disciplines because they represent all the strategic points of control seen in Fig. 1.1. In the case of departmental or functional change programmes, a representative sample of personnel from all levels should be obtained. Clearly, since there is a fractal dimension to this process it is also possible to collect separate data sets for different functions in the organization and then compare the aggregated results for the corporation as a whole. In fact, it will become clear in the following paragraphs that it is the comparative data that provides some of the most valuable clues to the problems that need resolving. In the end, each organization is likely to use the diagnostic questionnaire in a unique fashion, to explore its profile, and the whole process would be customized to specific objectives.

Clearly, the next question is what to do with the scores once you have them. The first step is to convert them into a dilemmas score. This is a simple calculation that starts by using the answer pairs as coordinates on the graph at the bottom of each page. Let us work through the example of the top down–bottom up tension relevant to sharing strategic responsibility, and assume that the respondents are Board directors (see Fig. 7.2). If the group members feel that the organization as a whole provides good top level direction by visionary guidance then they might answer 8 for part a) of the question. However, if they feel that this vision is largely divorced from grassroots initiatives then part b) may only rate as a 3. The reasons behind this discrepancy can be explored shortly. The score positions the business at point X with respect to sharing strategic responsibility. More autocratic, than participative. The ideal is obviously to maximize the contributions of both the directors and those at the grassroots level. In other words, to reach point 10/10, labelled Z on the graph. To calculate the distance from the ideal we use Pythagoras' theorem (the square of the hypotenuse of a right-angled triangle is equal to the sum of the squares of the two adjacent sides). We can calculate the two adjacent sides by subtracting the score on the appropriate axis from 10, then we simply substitute the figures in the formula and the result is the diagonal line from the actual position to the ideal one (Fig. 7.2). This is the dilemmas score.

Obviously, the higher the resulting number, the worse the situation is. Of course, there could be many reasons for a high score. It could be that there is no mechanism for incorporating grassroots initiatives into corporate direction; perhaps people at the bottom prefer to be led like sheep, and are not very good at producing new ideas, or it could be that the directors don't want to release control. Further enlightenment may be gained by asking the same questions at the grassroots level, and then comparing the results. If lower levels feel that top level guidance is poor, and only give it a 4 then this may be why they do not produce many valuable new ideas. They may be so confused that they don't know how to contribute. Alternatively, lower levels may feel that they really do generate lots of initiatives, but that they are never endorsed by those above. Perhaps directors don't hear about these activities, or perhaps they don't want to hear!

Whatever the answer, the *exact* position on the graph is unimportant. What is important is how far removed from the ideal the organization is, and how the views differ. Comparative intergroup results can produce some stimulating discussion and help uncover the real personality disorders.

Of course, it would be naïve to assume that, just because the organization starts exploring these conflicts, everyone is going to open up and look objectively at the problem. The assessment on the graph may be accurate, but an honest exploration of the underlying reasons may prove difficult. Emotional reactions often cloud the truth. There are several ways to help overcome this problem.

Firstly, an independent arbitrator can be extremely valuable. An outsider, whose job is not at stake, can help everyone, whatever their level, take a more objective look at the real cause of the problem.

1/6 STRATEGIC PLAYERS   *- Sharing strategic responsibility*

Effective strategy requires two types of input

    a) top level direction to provide coherent
       guidance and control

    b) an abundance of grassroot innovations
       in response to chaotic business
       conditions

In the context of strategic responses, please rate your organization,
on BOTH 0 to 10 scales, with respect to how well it

	LOW	HIGH
a) provides top level direction guidance	0 1 2 3 4 5 6 7 ⑧ 9 10	
	and	
b) generates grassroots innovations	0 1 2 ③ 4 5 6 7 8 9 10	

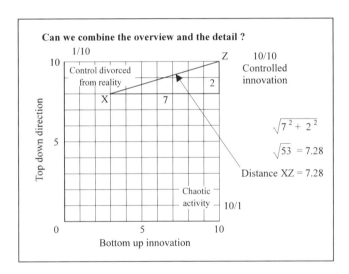

Can we combine the overview and the detail ?

1/10

Control divorced from reality

Z   10/10
Controlled innovation

$\sqrt{7^2 + 2^2}$

$\sqrt{53} = 7.28$

Distance XZ = 7.28

Top down direction

Bottom up innovation

Chaotic activity   10/1

Fig. 7.2   1/6 Strategic players dilemma

Secondly, remember that the dilemmas work dynamically; it is not
enough to look at the results of one dilemma in isolation. Exploring
the interrelationship between them adds depth and understanding. For
example, if strategic responsibility is not shared then one would expect
poor competitive manoeuvrability. However, if the assessment shows
that the organization is good at responding to opportunities, and building
them into a competitive resource plan, the obvious question is why? Is it
because the top managers are extraordinarily good visionaries, or is it
because there is little formal planning, so people just act independently in
their own little domains? The recent failing of the Baring Brothers financial empire would seem to be a timely example of too much independent

action without formal control. Of course, independent action is important, but if it does not feed back into corporate affairs then individual learning never becomes corporate knowledge. That is a waste. Naturally, the viability of the corporate objectives, the fitness of the corporate structure for its environment, and organizational elasticity will all help to refine the objectivity of the interpretation. The revolutionary capacity of the organization depends on all five paradoxes being in dynamic tension.

Thirdly the 10 lower level dilemmas (short term/long term; IT value/ product value/ analysis/intuition, etc.) can provide further enlightenment. An analysis of the five strategic performance indicators provides management with a picture of the major character flaws in the organization, so the areas that need immediate attention can be seen. However, closer examination of the underlying frictions can identify implicit reasons why these flaws are present. So, for example, if corporate vision is weak, and bottom up initiatives are weak, this could be related to the fact that management takes a very short term view of events, but is also indecisive when it comes to action—all discussion and no definite action. If competitive planning is very strong and so is random opportunism, but added value is low, is it because the company is too dependent on logical analysis and extrapolation from the past, with too few creative and intuitive hunches. Really, before making plans, it is important to do a complete character assessment, by looking at the interactions between the various parameters in the 15 paradoxes. Then it becomes possible to make interventions that are the right solution to the real problem. It cannot be emphasized enough that these frictions work interactively not in isolation. One friction has been associated with one top level dilemma in the model (Fig. 7.1), but this is only for the sake of simplicity. In fact, it is the combination of all these unresolved frictions that simultaneously affects each of the individual strategic performance indicators.

The case study presented in Chapter 9, provides a good example of how the dilemmas work together dynamically. Two comparable car manufacturers approached the idea of creating a learning organization from a totally different angle. One combined all 10 aspects of the paradox wheel into a workable method of operation. Consequently, its performance was outstanding in the industry. The other neglected some crucial aspects. The effect of neglecting even one dilemma can subvert the benefits of successfully resolving others. In the end, the unresolved tensions create vicious circles that undermine even the best intentions and, as the case history shows, the effect on performance is damaging.

Some readers may be starting to feel that this is becoming rather complicated. However, it is no more complicated than analysing a set of financial accounts. It's simply a question of familiarity. Just as a good analyst can get a picture of corporate financial health from an annual report, by looking at the combination of events in the profit and loss account, the balance sheet, and the Chairman's report, so a good therapist can get an accurate picture of the organizational character from five strategic performance scores and 10 scores on the performance inhibitors.

After measurement of the 15 paradoxes, the questionnaire contains 10 straightforward questions that ask respondents to assess how strongly the organization exhibits the necessary revolutionary characteristics identified in Chapter 4 on a scale of 0–10. Interpretation of the 10 paradoxical performance inhibitors is enhanced by evidence of the presence or absence of the required revolutionary characteristics. The only potential hiccup in this comparison is the fact that a high score on each revolutionary characteristic indicates the presence of a good quality, whereas a high score on the dilemmas is bad for the organization. Users should keep this polarity in mind. This difference does, in fact, highlight discrepancies. In other words if the calculated depth of vision score is high, indicating that management have not succeeded in reconciling short term and long term objectives, then one would expect commitment scores to be low, because management are vacillating between the two timescales and sending inconsistent messages. If the results are not divergent this indicates that something else is affecting the relationship, and further investigation into the presence or absence of other characteristics may be useful.

The first time the questionnaire is used, the survey will identify the most serious character deficiencies that need to be tackled. This supplies a baseline profile. The questionnaire should be used at regular intervals to monitor progress on the various dilemmas. In addition, it can be used to retune the change programme to reflect the emerging imbalances produced by the first round of transformation activity. In other words, if the second measurement cycle shows progress on all of the five strategic performance indicators, obviously the actions have been successful. However, if there are marked changes in the lower level assessments then maybe some vicious circles are developing and these have not yet shown up as impeded progress. Unaddressed, these negative forces will adversely affect the next phase of transformation. Monitoring the corporate profile in this way provides a consistent but forward looking indicator that helps managers direct the energy in the chaotic system along productive channels. This is infinitely better than relying solely on profit figures which are a historical consolidation of many different variables. Use of the personality profile in conjunction with profit figures gives a more balanced perspective on reality.

7.3   Introducing the appropriate counterbalances

Having identified its character weaknesses, the organization needs to find some way to put them right. Obviously a generic model cannot predict the exact nature of the changes to be made for each organization. However, there are some general rules that can prove helpful.

The way to manage paradox is to be perverse. Don't try to suppress the strongest force, look for the strongest ratings on each of the 15 dilemmas and then deliberately strengthen the weakest value. Let us take the earlier example a step further. In the previous section we envisaged a score of 8 for top down direction and 3 for grassroots action. To resolve the dilemma, the organization needs to initiate a programme that concentrates heavily on encouraging people below the level of directors to take the initiative, and contribute appropriately to strategic direction. In other words, focus on empowerment and endorsement. Without correction, weak, low level input means that strategic direction will become increasingly abstracted from reality, overlooking important details and eventually becoming dangerously divorced from organizational needs. It is a vicious circle which needs to be broken. When few contributions come up from below, those at the top are forced to take uninformed decisions and actions. Those at the grassroots feel uninvolved, so they make even fewer contributions, and so it goes on, getting worse and worse.

Vicious circles are converted into virtuous circles (self-re-enforcing positive feedback cycles) by putting the weakest value first, until such time as such action balances the tension between the two, as the top half of Fig. 7.3 shows. Of course, if the original assessment of the dilemma had shown an over-abundance of lower level activity, and no coordinating objective, it would be most important to strengthen the contribution of the top level management, as the bottom part of Fig. 7.3 shows.

Let us look at another example. What if the company has invested heavily in a sophisticated planning system? Often, this makes it loathe to react unless the proposal has been validated by the planning process. Opportunities are missed, and when that becomes evident, the logical response often seems to be 'beef up the planning efforts, so that we don't miss these opportunities again'. Eventually, this cycle absorbs so much energy that no-one has time to respond to advantageous conditions that pop up unforeseen. If, on the other hand, the company had dared to loosen up the rigid process of strategic predetermination, added a bit of slack to the budget and introduced incentives for spontaneous action, immediately it recognized that opportunities were being missed, the paradox would have reconciled itself. Managers would have been empowered to take advantage of fortuitous events and the planning system would have become flexible enough to cope with the unforeseeable.

Concentrating on the weakest characteristic gives the management an initial idea of where to start making changes. However the exact nature of the therapy will be affected by the weakest factors in the 10 lower level dilemmas. The details of the chosen remedy should correct the most serious imbalances in the underlying frictions. Returning to the earlier

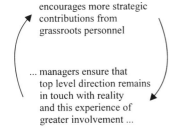

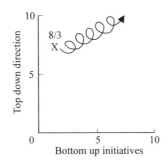

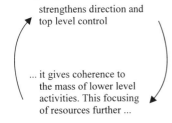

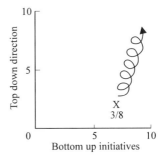

Create virtuous circles by putting the weakest force first and spontaneously drive results towards the synergy of point 10/10.

Fig. 7.3 Reconciling paradox

example, let us assume that, dominated by its directors, the organization is fixated on the short term, values only product investments, uses little intuition, is totally centralized, full of verbiage but takes decisions without consultation. Clearly, it needs a programme to encourage low level activity, but the specifics must concentrate on long term perspectives that introduce information technology, have intuitive credibility, encourage decentralization, concise communication and discussion across the lower levels. In other words, introduce the opposite characteristics at all levels. This is a highly simplistic example, but it conveys the idea that the change programme can be customized to redress the balance at both levels. By concentrating on the development of opposite characteristics rather than encouraging more of the same, behavioural transformation is inevitable. However, the objective is to integrate all the characteristics into a complete and balanced personality, so the task is not finished.

Continual adjustment along all the dimensions is essential if full transformation is to occur. As time goes on, performance on the 15 paradoxes will spiral back and forth, creating an infinitely complex pattern, that requires constant rebalancing to keep progress on the right track. Clearly, managers will not be distributing questionnaires to everyone in the organization on a weekly or monthly basis, but a quarterly review, perhaps alongside the customary quarterly financial reviews would provide valuable information for corrective strategic action. The management then looks forwards as well as backwards to get to the future, which is much more healthy. A quarterly review would only require revisiting the questionnaire with the same representative group of people. One meeting to re-evaluate the results would provide trend data on progress, and pointers on where different action might be required. '*Not another meeting*', is probably the cry! Even this can be made easier. The electronic meeting systems that are discussed in Chapter 9, can actually allow people to join the meeting at different times, and from their own offices, and still discuss the issues in depth. This eliminates diary conflict, captures the data electronically and so provides a ready made organizational memory for future discussions and analysis.

Familiarity with the 15 paradoxes will make their use instinctive. The more managers grow accustomed to thinking paradoxically, the better they will be at assessing accurately whether change activities are creating the necessary balance. They will know whether intuition is still being frowned upon, and whether it is producing more hunches to be tested. They will be aware of whether people are really looking for the synergy between short term and long term objectives. They will have a feel for how effectively others are balancing discussion and decision. Then they will be able to make subtle adjustments as they work, without reference to a formal framework. This will mean that short term control is naturally reconciled with long term activity management. Once paradox permeates through the organization it will become second nature to consider both sides of the coin during meetings, when making decisions, and when dealing with staff. Then, when the various values have become embedded in the corporate culture, the idea of achieving a higher dimension by synthesizing values will become instinctive. At this stage, learning becomes rapid, continuous and highly profitable. Further as soon as managers spot a weakness or an unbalanced paradox, they will be able to turn to the following section of this book, and put into action the appropriate tool to counterbalance the problem.

7.4 Resolving the frictions inhibiting the rate of change

Replicating the exploration outlined so far in this chapter will throw up some imbalances in energy levels around the paradox wheel. These will slow the 'evolution of the revolution'. By use of some of the general outlines for remedial action, identified in Chapters 4, 5 and 6, the company can smooth the progress of transformation. Nonetheless, the wheel can also be used as a tool selector, to point to suitable techniques to remedy a specific weakness. Fig. 7.4 shows some examples of tools and techniques that are helpful for correcting a weakness on the dimension to which the suggestion is attached.

Some of these have already been mentioned—benchmarking helped Xerox look outwards rather than inwards and to do so in a discriminating fashion; fractal geometry has been discussed as a way to build interdependent relationships that give the organization an adaptable structural framework. A brief stroll through the other techniques will show that they have been chosen to help develop the appropriate revolutionary characteristic that can resolve the paradoxes.

Scenarios and games (top down)

Playing games and acting out scenarios is one way to build commitment amidst uncertainty. It works largely on the homily that actions speak louder than words. By running a series of workshops that allow people to explore the implications of a proposed change, before a final decision is made, those involved are able to put the risks into a real context. As an abstract concept, a change often seems more frightening or risky than the reality. Acting out a proposal also reduces the practical risk, because in the process of playing the game, participants grasp details more clearly and then use their knowledge to iron out wrinkles and suggest modifications, before any implementation takes place. The final solution is then better adapted to real world circumstances; those who have to implement it are more committed to the process, because they have seen it in action. Consultants often use this sort of technique, not only to build commitment but also to encourage unorthodox thinking. For example, instead of asking management to suggest improvements to existing processes, consultants will frame the inquiry as a game in which the management are setting up in competition to their own organization, and are trying to design the most effective competitor.

The planning group of Royal Dutch Shell actually computerized such a process.[27] They found that simulating decisions in this way produced many benefits. Participants began to really understand that cause and effect are often separated in time and space, a fact that is not readily acceptable until it has been experienced; hesitance in the face of risk was less because simulated action had no real life implications; this opened the door to more new ideas, so creativity increased. Overall the final solution was more effective.

Running workshops may seem an unnecessary waste of time, but the pay off in the future in terms of strengthened commitment, sounder action and less wasted energy correcting mistakes, will largely compensate for the initial expense.

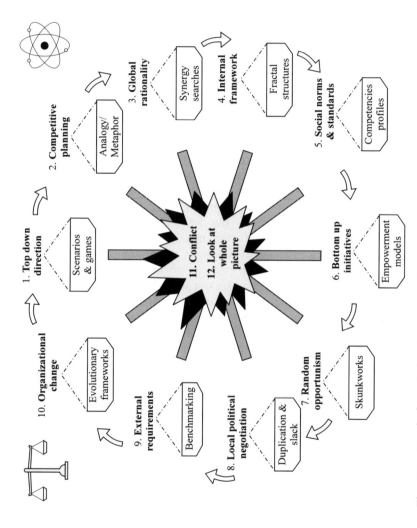

Fig. 7.4 Tools for rebalancing energy flows

Analogy and metaphor (competitive planning)

Analogy and metaphor are tried and tested routes to the sort of unorthodox thinking required in future competitive planning. Analogy moves thought onto a new scale, out of the prosaic and into a new dimension. With a suitable analogy, it is possible to consider a problem without the limitations of existing circumstances impinging on solutions. It is really just a way to look at events from a different angle if there is no 'Devil's advocate' available. Hopefully the reader has already begun to appreciate the value of analogy. This book contains an abundance of them because it is trying to encourage managers to look at business from a different perspective. Western business people often feel uncomfortable with what appear to be flights of fancy, whereas the Japanese are particular good at using analogy and metaphor. Perhaps Westerners prefer a more pragmatic approach, but when innovation and learning are the price of success in today's global markets, it may be time for everyone to open their minds to this oriental strength.

When Canon[47] was designing its desktop photocopier, analogy helped to solve a problem of an over-expensive copier drum. The photosensitive drum inside the copier was the cause of 90 per cent of all maintenance requirements. Obviously, a disposable drum was the most sensible answer, but the design of drum was too expensive to keep throwing it away; customers would balk at regularly replacing what was a high proportion of the total copier costs. What was needed was a cheap, easily manufactured throwaway. A beer can is a disposable aluminium drum. It is cheap and easy to manufacture. By exploring the beer can analogy, Canon designers learned how to solve their disposable drum problem.

Metaphor is a figurative expression that combines two unrelated concepts in one phrase. As such it is similar to analogy, because the attributes of one concept are used to give depth to the understanding of the other. The difference is that by the association of two unrelated concepts metaphor should generate a further unforeseen dimension. Honda,[47] for example, used living organisms as a metaphor for automobile development. Before the Honda City car was designed, engineers started by exploring the unlikely possibility of automobile evolution. By considering how a mechanical object might develop if it was subject to evolutionary forces, they reached the conclusion that a sphere would evolve as the most efficient shape for a car. The subsequent design of the Honda City, first known as 'the Tall Boy' shattered customary assumptions about car design and revolutionized the industry.

Synergy searches (global rationality)

Weak global rationality means that the organization is too compartmentalized, too confined by mental and physical boundaries. Synergy searches are deliberate cross-fertilization mechanisms. All the organization has to do is to give someone the job of looking for the connection between ideas and decisions, across the enterprise—a kind of 'strategic roving reporter', with no operational responsibility other than to look for links. Groups of specialists meet regularly for a variety of reasons—quarterly reviews, sales launches, project appraisals, quality control reviews. Most major meetings are called to initiate changes, deal with a crisis or modify a procedure. All of these factors impinge on strategic transformation. The time to consider the extended consequences of these meetings is when the details are freshest in the minds of those involved, and before any action has been taken. A roving strategic coordinator, could use half an hour at the end of any major meeting to round-up and review the crucial decisions in the context of the transformation agenda. By this one simple action, the organization maximizes the value of meetings, multiplies the opportunities for rationalizing activities, as well as creating a fertile environment for leaps of intuition to occur. The round-up session should be concise and run to a standard format designed only to capture the highlights most relevant to strategic direction; it should not lapse into a rerun of the meeting, or be allowed to reopen closed issues. The process benefits are several; it gives everyone a sense of their involvement in the bigger picture, it opens up the environment to creative thinking and it takes information out of isolated little pockets.

Competencies (social norms and standards)

We have already considered the idea that fractal forms can help expand interdependent relationships (Internal framework, cf. Fig. 4.1), but managers will need new skills to manage connections between equals rather than a boss–subordinate relationship. The idea of core competencies has become popular in recent years, but as organizations move into new markets, and change the scope of their business operations, the core competencies must change. Extending the range of competencies can be an important stabilizing mechanism during the process of change. Working to develop a defined list of desirable competencies gives employees a hook on which to hang their hats, and a common goal to work towards, without introducing social norms that damage elasticity. Formally encouraging the recognition and development of necessary skills is a positive force for change. The process requires the appointment of internal mentors to assist their protégés in getting exposure to new experiences. The mentor–protégé relationship encourages communication between levels and expands the relationships network that holds the company together.

Empowerment (bottom up initiatives)

Empowerment is a relatively recent concept that has obvious relevance to an organization that wants to strengthen contributions from the grassroots level. It is not possible or necessary to go into the whys and wherefores of the idea here when so much has already been written on the subject. The objective is simply to highlight it as a tool for rebalancing an organization that is too top heavy.

Skunkworks (random opportunism)

Skunkworks groups, as the name implies, exist out of the mainstream activity. They are rather non-conformist associations of creative experts who club together outside the confines of the normal bureaucracy. Sort of underground activists. Such groups are known for quick action, unrestricted communication, and experimentation on limited resources— exactly the sort of attributes necessary to respond best to unforeseen opportunities. The enthusiasm of what usually becomes a closeknit group gives it confidence to take risks and try out wild ideas. The existence of various skunkworks groups creates pockets of commitment which act like strange attractors in the organizational weather pattern, to stir up a necessary storm. Their lack of formal budgetary resources ensures that they have to 'make do', which immediately stretches the imagination and encourages creativity. Xerox had a skunkworks group on the East Coast. It was made up of nothing more than nine individualists inhabiting a messy loft in east Rochester. They had no formal place in the hierarchy, no extravagant facilities and little money, but frequently they were the ones who saved the day by sorting out design flaws, solving copying problems and generally producing the rabbit out of the hat. Everyone in the main body of the company was still floundering around looking for the hat!

Duplication and slack (local political negotiation)

Slack or redundancy is a contingency, a buffer against the unforeseen. It is the internal insurance that provides resource cover in an emergency. Most organizations accept the need to buy expensive insurance policies, but they often forget that in many instances they need to self-insure, to set aside some spare capacity, or spare resources to absorb fluctuations in demand. Instead, they rationalize their pared-down resources as cost effective, but then wonder why they hurt when times get tougher. Duplication may sound wasteful but it is a way of turning slack into productive contention. Canon, for example, deliberately introduce duplication into the process of product development. Competing teams work on the same project. Each will find a different solution, and then the teams argue over the pros and cons of each idea, to find a synthesis that draws the best from all of them. The duplication eventually results in greater creativity because each team adopts a different perspective on the problem. The sum of all the perspectives produces a more complex picture, and a more comprehensive representation of the full requirements.

Benchmarking (external requirements)

Benchmarking against best of breed, particularly outside the industry, creates a momentum for improvement that is a more accurate reflection of environmental conditions than internally generated ideals. Paragons of expertise outside the industry are not constrained by assumptions that have ruled procedures in one's own market for decades.

Evolution (organizational change)

The most durable and manageable organizational change will come about when all the previous activities and characteristics are harmonized into an evolutionary process model that is centred on learning. Progressive cycles of double loop learning will result in less wasted effort and, ultimately, more profit because singularly different activities resonate to challenge stultifying assumptions at a rate that people can handle.

These tools and techniques are only one aspect of the model. At a more general level, they can indicate the appropriate focus for analysis and data collection when a business is planning how to strengthen the weak perspective. Fig. 7.5 indicates that top management should be concentrating on pushing out the boundaries of industry models, whereas those at the bottom should be involved in reconfiguring the process flows to adapt to the new industry visions. The industry outlook should, in turn, be influenced by the process flow models. This puts the share of strategic responsibility with those best placed to cope with it, but makes sure that it is interactive.

Planners needed structured models, such as *Portfolios Analysis* (The Boston Consultancy Group's two by two box) or Michael Porter's *Value Chain* and *Five Forces* models, in order to categorize and order the information and assess risk. However, there is still a need for the ad hoc, trial and error data collection. The VIP of worldwide information services for Kentucky Fried Chicken[68] (KFC) vehemently rejects the idea of structured planning and annual strategy documents. He believes in being dynamic, creating an atmosphere of urgency, validating intentions with immediate actions, communicating in 'surround sound', prototyping, and trial and error data planning. It is dangerous to rely *only* on this type of activity because resource coordination is likely to be inefficient, and ultimately throw up shortages. In fact, manoeuvrable planning needs both structured and random planning approaches to complement each other.

International analysis keeps the organization from developing an over-provincial attitude. Economic and national information are essential for keeping the corporation in tune with local interests that will affect its

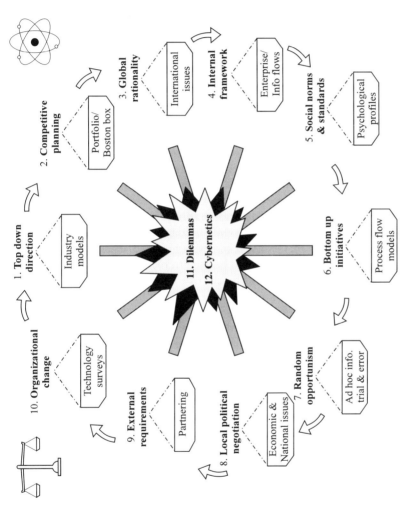

Fig. 7.5 Tools for exploring the details of conflict

future. Somehow, management have to find ways to fulfil international standards and local regulations, to create internationally appealing products which satisfy local cultural tastes and preferences. Corporations today must understand the interests of both foreign and local markets and then find ways to fulfil both if they are to remain operationally viable.

Enterprise models are a good way to work through the detail of how to structure an organization to meet known requirements. The information will highlight the weaknesses that need to be buffered by partnering. Partners will, in turn, increase the information input from the outside world, which will feed back into the enterprise model to change its form. The bidirectional information flow between enterprise and partners will stretch the organization and hone fitness.

Finally, psychological analysis and technology surveys are complementary information sets. The organization needs to understand the impact of technology on people, and the effect of people on technology, if it is to stand any chance of integrating them effectively into a 'bionic' organization, with the flexibility to cope with changing conditions.

This book is not the place to explore any of these tools and techniques in detail. The objective of this section has been simply to show, by way of example, how the wheel can provide guidance on the sort of tools and techniques best suited to the problems; a guide to what information to collect or what intervention could be used to rectify a weak characteristic. Clearly, there are many other choices of tools and techniques (Fig. 6.10 identified some that Xerox used). Over time an organization will develop its own portfolio of suitable remedies.

Part 1 of this book explained why paradoxical management is so important, and why paradox has to become the next strategic dimension. This chapter has outlined the practical steps an organization can take towards implementing paradoxical management for improved performance. The next chapter will consider how the process affects financial results and suggest some technological tools that provide valuable support. Then, and only then, is it possible to comprehend the true nature of process, in what is popularly called Business Process Re-engineering.

The transformation experience

The workers have nothing to lose but their chains.
They have a world to gain. Workers of the world unite.
Karl Marx, *The Communist Manifesto*

8.1 Introduction

It is all very well declaring that transformation has occurred when every-one's behaviour has changed, but if changed behaviour does not improve financial performance, who cares? No-one is even going to embark on a voyage of transformation if there isn't a promise of a better bottom line at the end of it. The transformation experience must have more than altruistic objectives. Fortunately it does; successful paradox resolution corresponds to greater bottom line returns. The first section of this chapter presents the evidence behind the financial aspects of the trans-formation experience.

The next section reviews the technological aspects. Better profits may be the desirable end, but information technology is an important means to achieving it. Parts of the organization are still struggling to work productively with technology; it is not yet fully integrated into everyone's life. If the Bionic Organization is still a long way off, bridging the IT–business divide may be one of the biggest obstacles to getting there. Technology is fairly pervasive below management level but senior man-agers often fight shy of direct contact with technology. They have sec-retaries, accountants, central processing departments and all manner of experts to provide the information they need and to buffer them from direct interaction. Perhaps the time has come to change management processes too, then those in control will have *first hand* experience of technology's benefits. The second section of this chapter introduces some IT-based decision making tools that can substantially increase manage-ment productivity. In fact, together they can actually transform the management process.

The final section of this chapter covers the procedural aspect of the transformation experience. How can we coordinate the various tones and colours in the organizational palette into a harmonious and three-dimensional picture of the Butterfly Effect in action. In other words, how do we integrate corporate character, technology and the various control parameters in order to manage Chaos. The true relevance of process is continuous feedback, so Chapter 8 ends by explaining how to use the paradox wheel to create a self-organizing picture of a united, competitive, viable, agile, and strong corporation.

8.2   How paradox affects financial performance

The framework described in this book is the product of more than two years' research. But it covers much more ground than two years. In fact, it is a synthesis of more than 25 years' experience, accumulated by knowledgeable experts in many fields. The model combines teaching and practice in strategy, organizational behaviour, and information systems management with recent ideas of re-engineering and learning and sets them all in the 1990s context of Chaos. The paradoxes that emerged from this are common to all these areas of knowledge. They occur in both the literature and in practice. One might reasonably expect that such an accumulation of acknowledged expertise and business experience should have some influence on profitability.

Hampden Turner[2] identified a clear connection between successful paradox resolution and financial performance in a study of the white goods, oil and computer industries. Having worked with various organizations in these industries, he found that those who best reconciled their specific industry conflicts outperformed those who did not.

With Hampden Turner's precedent in mind, the author used a personality questionnaire, like the one in Appendix A, to test the connection between balanced personality and better financial performance. The companies which responded spanned a range of industries and included both general managers and specialists. Nearly 100 of the organizations in Appendix B completed the survey (the others listed were either focus group participants, or helped with another survey in the research). In the interests of corporate confidentiality, the following analysis does not attribute results directly to any individual company.

The first step in the analysis was to decide which measure of financial performance would be most meaningful. Clearly, there are many choices. For the sake of consistency, it was necessary to settle on one that was appropriate for all industries, and relevant to what was being tested. Balance sheet ratios were discarded, because the figures there are an accumulation of many years results. The survey was measuring the organization's *current* ability to resolve paradox, so prior year successes and failures would only confuse the issue. Taxation was excluded from the equation, because, again, it can reflect prior year allowances; besides taxes are rarely consistent for companies even within an industry, let alone in different industries. Earnings per share, although ostensibly a reasonable choice, was not an option, because some of the respondents did not have share capital. In the end, the simplest comparable measure of effectiveness was chosen; the ratio of profits before tax to total operating income. This measurement can be applied to any industry and is the most recent outcome from the conditions being tested. It also allows for any difference in size between the organizations being compared.

The survey was conducted in 1994,[69] so the analysis was based on published accounts for 1993. Disparities were eliminated wherever possible. So, for example, where one organization had several lines of business, and the respondent was answering for only one segment of these, the results were taken for the appropriate segment and compared only to those other companies competing in the same segment.

Inter-organization comparisons are only feasible within an industry, because different conditions prevail in each industry sector. Some industries suffer from lower profit margins than others, because they are resource intensive, or sell stable commodities; others make higher margins because they are more capital intensive or they sell luxuries. Responses to the questionnaire provided four industry groups with several suitable respondents.

The goal was to see whether successful paradox resolution combined with the presence of revolutionary characteristics was a reasonable predictor of industry ranking. In other words, would those with the best profit/income record be the best at resolving the paradoxes and have the most revolutionary traits. There is *no* suggestion of correlation here. It is not possible to say that a score of x will give a profit of y. The Butterfly Effect precludes linear relationships. However, it is possible to say that when the paradoxes are more nearly in balance and the organization has some revolutionary attitudes, results are better. Of course, the managers of the superior performing organizations were not explicitly following the rules of paradoxical management, but it is possible that there was some implicit understanding.

A ranking index score was calculated from the responses for the three groups of variables. This summarized the overall effect of strategic paradoxes, performance inhibitors and revolutionary characteristics. Since good performance on the dilemmas is reflected by low scores (cf. Chapter 7), but good performance on the characteristics produces high scores, a consolidated performance score needs to correct for the inverse polarity. A dilemma score actually indicates how much is left to achieve; it can be converted to a score that shows how much has already been achieved by deducting it from 100.*

Fig. 8.1 shows how the index was calculated for each organization. In cases where more than one person from the organization responded, the results were averaged. If the questionnaire was being used inside an organization where the differences could be explored in detail, averaging would be wrong. In the context of planning, differences bring enlightenment and

---

*Theoretically this should be 212.5 (i.e. 15 times the length of the diagonal from 0 to 10/10, but this only makes a larger index and does not change the rank order, so 100 was used for convenience.

	(100–total top level dilemma scores) (A1.1a–e)	(100–total sub dilemma scores) (A1.2a–j)	Sum of scores on qualities (A1.3)	TOTAL	Rank
Industry 1					
Respondent A	67.5	41.3	60	168.8	1
Respondent B	65.1	43.2	55	163.3	2
Respondent C	66.2	44.3	45	155.5	3
Respondent D	68.9	40.8	39	148.7	4
Industry 2					
Respondent A	60.2	42.5	53	155.7	1
Respondent B	65.8	44.3	37	147.1	2
Respondent C	62.4	36.9	38	137.3	3
Industry 3					
Respondent A	74.5	48.8	70	193.3	1
Respondent B	79.1	55.7	58	192.8	2
Respondent C	61.9	29.0	41	131.9	3
Industry 4					
Respondent A	79.6	57.8	73	210.4	1
Respondent B	77.9	46.5	72	196.4	2

Fig. 8.1 Ranking index of the selected organizations

show where action is required. In this case, the objectives were different. This was a general survey, to test the association between profit and paradox resolution. No practical interference in the affairs of each company was intended and details were unavailable. Averaging was an obvious way to accommodate both perspectives, and still reflect the reality that both viewpoints would have influenced financial results.

Fig. 8.2 shows the final results for the four industries. The higher the score, the more dilemmas are being reconciled, and the more revolutionary characteristics are present. Clearly, a balanced personality and revolutionary tendencies have a positive effect on financial performance. The less these qualities are present, the weaker the performance. The single anomaly in the ordering was the result of a one-off event that severely distorted the 1993 trading results. Without this unusual occurrence, which was connected to restructuring, the ranking would have been completely in line with each organization's ability to reconcile paradox and act in the desired revolutionary fashion.

It is not surprising that there is a correspondence between profit and paradox. Dilemmas are just a way of looking at a complex reality from various angles. In the end, a group of paradoxes are simply measuring different aspects of a larger whole. Fifteen paradoxes capture a good proportion of the corporate attitude. The profit calculation is the end result of the whole attitude to business. The cumulative effect of good performance on several dilemmas will work like the Butterfly Effect. Virtuous circles will accumulate to produce more than the sum of their

	TOTAL	Rank	Profit before tax (£M)	Revenue (£M)	PBT/ Revenue %	Rank
Industry 1						
Respondent A	168.8	1	844.0	3602.0	23.4	1
Respondent B	163.3	2	664.0	7392.0	8.9	4*
Respondent C	155.5	3	301.0	1999.0	15.1	2
Respondent D	148.7	4	989.0	6995.0	14.1	3
Industry 2						
Respondent A	155.7	1	865.8	1883.1	46.0	1
Respondent B	147.1	2	216.5	669.0	32.4	2
Respondent C	137.3	3	205.1	980.7	22.0	3
Industry 3						
Respondent A	193.3	1	3506.0	5038.4	69.5	1
Respondent B	192.8	2	1339.3	2013.3	66.5	2
Respondent C	131.9	3	2041.9	4944.4	41.3	3
Industry 4						
Respondent A	210.4	1	37.1	1587.4	2.4	1
Respondent B	196.4	2	16.5	1143.1	1.4	2

*The 1993 results for respondent 1B were halved by an item called USA transition.
Without this item their PBT to revenue would have been 18.1% and in line with ranking.

Fig. 8.2 Paradox resolution predicts profit ranking

parts. In fact, the survey also showed that organizations who best reconcile dilemmas got more benefits from their investments in IT (the average
of the 10 questions on Benefits Accrual in Appendix A, Fig. A1.4) and
were most satisfied with the overall effectiveness of information technology in their business. These positive attitudes no doubt fed back
into the improvement of competitive acuity. Unlike many other analysis
techniques, working within a paradoxical framework makes it possible
to break down complex situations into manageable parts, without
destroying the relationship between them.

Whatever the rationale behind the connections, one thing is clear.
Transforming behaviour by paradoxical management has a demon-
strably positive effect on bottom line profitability.

8.3 The value of technological support

By using a computer model we learn what constitutes relevant information.
When people play with the models, they are actually creating a new language
among themselves, that expresses the knowledge that they have acquired.

De Geus, 1988[27]

When businesses get interested in transformation, the management process is not the first thing that they think to change. Managers immediately

call meetings, organize agendas, and start talking and planning. They acknowledge that IT can change the way business operates, but its contribution is often abstracted from their own work. Yet, IT can improve the meeting, organizing, talking and planning process too.

Fig. 8.3 shows a selection of recent technological developments designed to do just that. Each can improve management productivity along various strategic dimensions of the wheel.

Today's manager needs new ways to handle information. The volume of information to be managed is increasing, as is the number of people with whom to share it. More information and more people mean more connections, and less time. Clearly, anything that will help make sense of the information Chaos should be a first consideration.

Fig. 8.4 summarizes some quantifiable benefits in terms of management productivity.

Introducing IT into the softer areas of a manager's job has other less tangible benefits too. When managers allow IT to change the way they work, they send a subtle message that reinforces the perceived value of IT (Underlying paradox 2) across the organization. The action has symbolic value. Often symbolic actions are more powerful than words. Other parts of the business may be much more ready to accept change, when they are following the example of senior management. By the use of IT, managers erect a pillar of support for the bridge across the IT–business divide.

Fig. 8.5 puts the benefits in the context of paradoxical management. The following sections will look briefly at the experience of using these technologies, starting from the top of the circle and working clockwise. Readers may wish simply to sample the parts that can remedy their identified weak spots, rather than read all of the subsections of Sec. 8.3.

Executive Information Systems (EIS) and Executive Support Systems (ESS). (Refining Top down direction)

> Too many information systems have been designed for everything and everybody in the company except high level decision makers, who tend to find them 'data rich and insight poor'. . . an ESS is designed with the needs of the leader in mind.
>
> Sprague and Watson, 1993[70]

There is an obvious and intuitive connection between the function of an Executive Information System (EIS) and the requirement to create a leaders vision. An EIS is a:

> . . . computerized system that provides executives with easy access to internal and external information that is relevant to their critical success factors.
>
> Sprague and Watson, 1993[70]

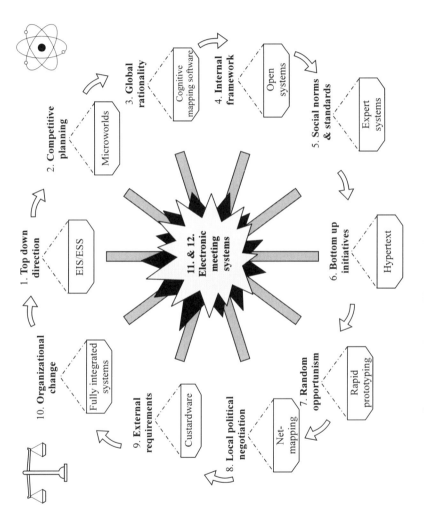

Fig. 8.3 IT tools to assist the would-be revolutionary

Over the nine month life of a specific project at Boeing 64 groups made up of, on average, 10 people, registered the following savings using groupware for planning employee surveys, IS requirements definition, Re-engineering and general problem definition.

	Mean saving per meeting	Total saving	Percent saving
Labour hours	182 hrs	11,678 hrs	71
Labour cost $	6,754	432,260	71
Flowtime	28 days	1,773 days	91

Participants registered the following mean satisfaction levels out of maximum score of 6.

Decisions reached by group consensus	4.77
Improved information gathering and decision making	5.04
Organization made use of session output/product	4.83
Would use groupware again	5.38

Fig. 8.4 Benefits of groupware (adapted from Quinn, 1992)[71]

The concept is a relatively recent development and the technology to support it is changing so rapidly, that any attempt to define the nature of such systems is likely to be out of date before it is published. However, it is the principles underpinning the use of an EIS that are of particular interest.

Generally, most systems are customized for a small group of users, who have direct on-line access to a wide range of data from both internal and external sources. The user generally has the ability to integrate various elements of the data, as well to 'drill down' below the summarized trends to look more closely at the supporting detail. The presentation is typically graphical or tabular but it can also be textual. Most systems use colour to create impact.

The objective is to give senior executives the ability to filter, compress and track data which is critical to organizational success, *in their own preferred format*. An EIS gives direct access to information, uncoloured by the interpretations of others. When combined with electronic communication systems, data analysis tools and organizing tools, an EIS becomes a powerful tool for exploring both sides of an argument. Then it provides balanced input to strategic direction.

To date there have been only a few successful EIS developments. The fragmented nature of executive work, the hesitation of some executives to develop the necessary keyboard skills, inadequate data availability and the user unfriendliness of the technology have often undermined the

Software tool	Application advantages
Executive information systems (Top down)	Successful systems build top level commitment to IT solutions. Refine information to manageable proportions without losing access to detail.
Microworlds (Competitive planning)	Allow users to safely explore far-reaching and uncertain strategic scenarios. Opens up new perspectives.
Cognitive mapping software (Global rationality)	Emphasizes the feedback loops. Provides a manageable information structure where cause and effect are dissociated.
Open systems (Internal framework)	Facilitates free flow of information. Interconnectivity stimulates interaction.
Expert systems (Social norms & standards)	Standardize the communication of expensive expert knowledge. Overcomes time and availability restrictions.
Hypertext (Bottoms up)	Open-ended information exploration aids creativity. Semantic net of information supports flexible team working.
Rapid prototyping (Random opportunism)	Allows trial and error to minimize large-scale risk. Flexible and responsive approach to changing strategy.
Netmapping (Local political negotiation)	Shows where political influence is misaligned with strategic objectives. Identifies key players in new processes.
Custardware (External requirements)	Makes systems responsive to changes in environment without major expense. Provides prompt and accurate response using existing data.
Fully integrated systems (Organizational change)	The necessary foundation for knowledge sharing. Integrated organizational memory boosts performance.

Fig. 8.5   Groupware opportunities in the context of revolution

success of the implementation. However, a good system, well implemented, can provide invaluable support for top management direction. Paul Allaire, CEO of Xerox, William Smithburg, CEO of Quaker Oats and Finn Caspersen, CEO of Beneficial, are three keen ESS users.

The benefits are substantial:

- An improvement in the quality of strategic plans.
- Greater creativity.
- Flatter lines of communication and control.
- Greater responsiveness.
- Better environmental scanning.
- Less meddling and more time for the leader to do diagnostic work, which leads to greater productivity.
- More effective communication because the message is compressed (summarized) and the data is fresh.

- Senior executives know more about the trends hidden in the chaos and can explore their effect more easily.
- Greater potential to recognize the need for change and respond more rapidly.

Clearly, these are all desirable attributes for the development of a learning environment.

Microworlds (enhancing competitive planning)

Microworlds are computerized simulations used in the competitive planning process. Users can model conflicts, experiment with the variables and develop outcomes based on their own personal criteria, without the risk of live action. The simulations are dynamic and interactive and provide an uninhibiting structure during the process of competitive analysis.

We know that there are two elements of learning: learning through teaching and learning through doing. There is a tendency to view learning as predominantly a classroom exercise, in which knowledge is handed down by the teacher; such learning is incomplete. Learning by doing is equally important. It is the last stage in the challenge, change, crystallize cycle. People claim to learn from experience, but, as Senge points out all too often, 'we never experience the consequences of many of our most important decisions'.[51] Cause and effect are dissociated because jobs change, events interfere and time gets in the way. Feedback loops are non-linear in chaotic systems, so we cannot really learn as much as we ought to from experience. Microworlds are a way to 'compress time and space'[51] and so help linearize the feedback loop and retrieve the lost learning potential.

The experience at Royal Dutch Shell[27] identified the following benefits:

- Electronic data management enables users to handle more complexity than the human mind can do unaided

> most people deal with only 3 or 4 variables at a time and do so through only one or two iterations.
>
> Etzioni, 1989[72]

- Microworlds provide hands-on experience of the consequences of changing rules, without the risk of implementation.
- Successful examples provide a ready-made model for implementation.
- Exploring consequences helps to generate commitment before action is taken.
- Users start to develop a common language based on the knowledge acquired.

- Each side can make theoretical concessions without commitment. Users then find out whether a change is truly detrimental to their interests. Often, the feared consequences never actually materialize.
- Users can surface hidden assumptions and constraints on a solution.
- The models capture the essence of the organizational memory for future learning.
- People come to terms with the separation of cause and effect in complex systems.
- Hands on involvement teaches the user what information is really valuable, and what is superfluous.
- Usage helps develop confidence in the value of the intuitive response, in a safe environment.

Cognitive mapping software (exploring global rationality)

When organizations appear static and solid, they are actually dynamically maintaining a steady state through their loops.

Sigismund Huff, 1990[73]

Cognitive mapping is just a grand name for mind mapping. It is simply a process of drawing the complex relationship between events and facts as a series of interconnected loops. In other words, it is a way to get information Chaos down on paper and explore the consequences.

Cognitive mapping software essentially computerizes this way of exploring and managing ideas. Employees work in groups to model the interrelationship between their ideas with the aid of a piece of software that manages the links. Various packages are available, Appendix C contains details of two worth considering. Mapping the connections helps a group to explore and agree upon the interconnected consequences of change by collectively assembling a map. As an example, Fig. 8.6 maps the potential interrelationships between the strategic dimensions in this book.

By looking at a business as a series of loops, the user is freed from some of the more common preconceptions about the organization. Connecting ideas in loops cuts across artificial boundaries, such as departments, corporate entities or markets. This makes it easier to explore the full dynamics of a situation, without the method introducing implicit prejudice.

Interactions between various parts of the map can be classified as either 'deviation amplifying' or 'deviation countering loops'.[73] Deviation amplifying loops produce either positive or negative effect, but, whichever it is, the loop magnifies the effect of an action. This is where unpredictability

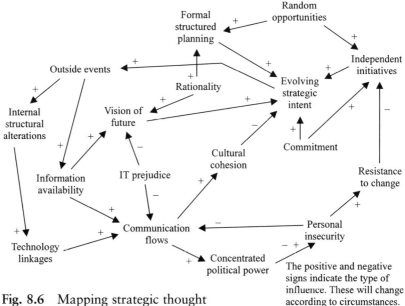

Fig. 8.6   Mapping strategic thought

The positive and negative signs indicate the type of influence. These will change according to circumstances.

comes from. Remember the strange attractors in Chapter 1. Deviation countering loops are the source of stability in the system, the chaotic limit cycles; small changes at one node work antagonistically on other nodes in the loop to slow the effect (Fig. 8.7). The rate of transformation will depend on the number and mix of each of the two types of loop.

Mapping the loops, at least, improves a manager's ability to analyse the chaotic activity in the corporate environment; it becomes possible to track an action through the obstacles between cause and desired effect. For example, the software allows users to zoom in on related concepts so as to extract themes. Lower level maps can be merged and cross referenced to synthesize key activities. Greater understanding will produce more informed and more effective planning. Once the analysis is complete the nodes on the map can be translated into a report that provides powerful and highly concentrated argument for decisions, because it concentrates on the most influential variables. In other words this is not only a valuable ideas exploration tool, it is also a potent political force.

The benefits of such an unusual descriptive format are many:

- It provides a manageable IT-based structure within which to explore ideas.
- Organizational memory is held in a compact form.
- It increases people's capacity to understand complex situations.

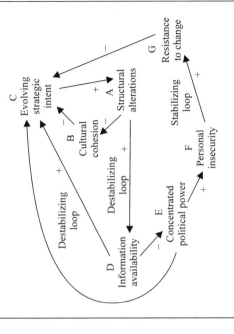

A naturally balanced system

The growth coming from loop A,B,C,D,E is automatically limited by loop A,E

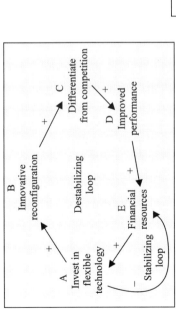

A more complex system poised for growth

The loop C,A,D,E,F,G limits the effect of both destabilizing loops A,B,C and A,D,E,C

It is important to watch for the cumulative effects of the signs. They may not be the same all the way round the loop.
For example, increased information availability (D) reduces political power, which can increase personal insecurity. This increases resistance to change and limits the speed at which strategic intents can evolve.

If structural alterations (A) increase cultural cohesion (B) then the signs on A-B and B-C would both become positive, and loop A,B,C would tend to counteract the positive effect of A,D,C

Fig. 8.7 Analysing the consequences of loops

157

- Maps of all the interdependencies provide a readily accessible reference against which anyone can evaluate their information responsibility.
- Explicit pictures of the interdependencies pinpoint where intervention and control are needed.
- Cosy compartments are eliminated.
- The tool is dynamic, and flexible.
- Maps provide a clear indication of how future changes will impact the social system as a whole (Fig. 8.8). Updated maps show where corrective action is needed to maintain the balance of the whole, and where intervention could be damaging; for instance, if an important deviation countering loop was suddenly disrupted.
- The process of developing the maps helps build team consensus.
- The structure of the process assists innovation and intuitive reasoning by making the patterns between ideas explicit.
- Examining the loops will suggest routes for conflict resolution.
- The maps offer a means of pinpointing where the barriers and incentives to change exist.

In summary, this is an important weather forecasting tool that will actually help managers avoid tornadoes of the Butterfly Effect.

Open systems (developing the internal framework)

The concept of a flexible architecture is an ideal that has been around for over a decade. Industry has been calling for communication standards that will allow one set of hardware to talk to another with complete freedom. Open systems are similar to the concept of children's Lego blocks. In theory, an organization should be able to use every element of its computer technology (the electronic architecture) as an interchangeable building block, and reconstruct them into different shapes according to changing business needs. Up until recently this was little more than a pipe dream, because hardware manufacturers had done little to make it a viable proposition.

In the 1990s, the decade of burgeoning knowledge power, the question of open systems is not so much one of 'whether an organization should migrate but when and how'.[74] Yet there is still resistance. Most business managers are more interested in applications because they see direct benefits from them. Part of the difficulty lies in the massive investments in existing systems that are not easily connected. The rest of the problem lies in the fact that architecture is a dry subject which is often left to 'techies'. Nonetheless, getting the underlying structure right does have definite corporate fitness benefits.

Vernon's Pools moved to an open systems platform. The company believed that doing so made a crucial contribution to the success of its tele sales services. Open systems allowed Vernon's to deal with

Strategic intervention cuts the loop

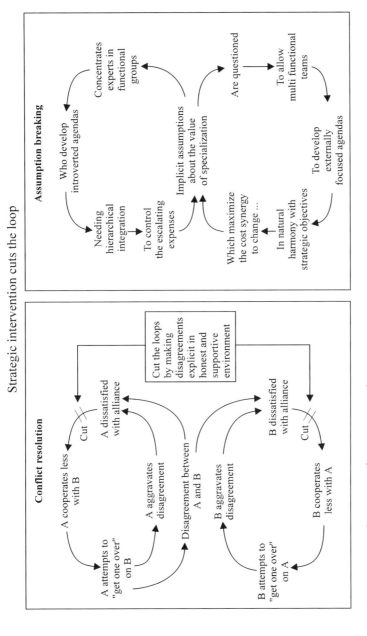

Fig. 8.8   Breaking out of vicious spirals

fluctuations in demand incrementally rather than by large expensive systems upgrades. Easy scalability opened the door to other new projects that would otherwise have been rejected, because they were burdened with the cost of a large upgrade. Churchill Insurance also identified scalability as a major benefit. When the company experienced sudden large increases in the number of on-line operatives, the system response time declined rapidly. Because of the modular nature of open systems they were able to restore performance level within 24 hours, by a single phone call. Scalable open systems allow an organization to quickly and cheaply match capacity to the changing demands of customers.

Wandsworth Borough Council found different benefits. With open systems it was able to complete a wider variety of technology projects, in shorter lead time and with better levels of user satisfaction. IT staff tended to become enablers who were an integral part of new application developments in business units. The change to open systems both increased the number of new applications and encouraged a more positive attitude to IT as an important contributor to new developments.

Clearly, an open systems architecture has a crucial role to play in the more flexible fractal structure of a transformed organization.

Expert systems (extending social norms and standards)

Expert systems, or artificial intelligence (AI) as it is often called, is a way of handling information that is not dependent on traditional algorithmic processing. A sort of 'intuitive computer'. Expert systems can handle qualitative data, 'fuzzy logic' and ambiguity, which means they can still make recommendations even when problems are too complicated for there to be one solution. Clearly a necessary tool for Chaos management.

Expert systems can either be used on their own, or in conjunction with people, as a supplement to human knowledge and reasoning capability.

There are currently few such systems in practical use, but all the ones that are have one thing in common. They 'preserve and disseminate scarce expertise'.[71] The interpretive abilities of a core of expensive experts can be encoded into a system and then shared throughout an organization. More people get access to expert advice in a consistent format.

The applications are varied. The Schlumberger Corporation assembled the accumulated expertise of its best troubleshooting geologists into a system called Dipmeter Advisor, which now supports a distributed network of field geologists. Thus, the most expensive knowledge was 'standardized' into a format accessible to others. Digital Equipment Corporation (DEC) use an expert system to help to configure the detailed components of VAX systems to satisfy customer requirements. MYCIN is a medical diagnosis program that is used to validate the diagnoses of overstressed doctors. By acting as a secondary failsafe adviser it saves lives. Steamer Program is an expert system that teaches people how to operate a steam plant and provide corrective input to help them avoid mistakes in the future. Shell has found significant savings in drilling costs, as a result of its geological expert system; it can identify the best places to find oil more precisely than a human because it is consistent.

The major benefit of such systems lies in their ability to communicate complex knowledge effectively, in an accessible way. The ability to share expertise with others in the organization directly improves the elasticity of organizational resources, by diffusing knowledge principles more widely to change behaviour.

Hypertext (encouraging bottom up initiatives)

Hypertext gives flexible access to information and encourages exploration, without introducing the constraints of a preconceived framework. Appropriately described as 'non-linear text', a Hypertext database allows users to follow a random trail through the data according to their interest. The system is basically a three-dimensional network of information nodes and connectors between the nodes. Nodes can contain textual, graphical, video or audio images and sound; connectors are usually labels, icons or 'hot spots' on which users click a mouse. A kind of flexible 'help' system.

Hypertext has traditionally been used as a means of browsing through an information library, but it can be used in other ways. Businesses can generate customized documents and presentations, for example, reference books, training manuals and product demonstrations, which can be followed according to the users' interests rather than in a prescribed sequence. A Hypertext database of corporate initiatives would make it easy to find the synergy between vision and action.

Hypertext can increase creativity, in any of the following ways:

- No one reader will follow the same trail through the information. Each will make different connections and so reach a different conclusion. If members of a team used a Hypertext system to explore the same question, the different answers they generated would provide a more comprehensive and accurate picture of reality than any one person alone.
- By giving information a fractal structure that mimics the desired organizational form, users can create infinite knowledge from a finite amount of information.
- Interaction is not restricted by rigidly structured information patterns that automatically channel thinking down well worn tracks.
- The database provides a ready access to important aspects of the developing organizational memory. This improves the quality of the linkages between all the participants with strategic responsibility.

Rapid prototyping (validating random opportunism)

Building a mock up of proposed information systems is a quick and easy way to see if it will work. As one senior manager pointed out to the author:

> No one knows what they want. But when they see what you have produced, they suddenly know what it is they don't want. [Focus Group]

Hands on assessment of a redesigned process is a better evaluation mechanism than reading a wish list of benefits that may have many unforeseen pitfalls. Practical involvement is a profitable way to refine wish lists into good practice. Wishes are often too broadly defined to elicit a critique of specifics. For example, ask someone how to improve customer service and they will give you vague answers. Refine your question and ask them what they would do about improving document handling in customer order processing and they will be able to give you more useful answers. Give them a prototype to handle and their suggestions become even more refined and apposite. Experimentation clarifies and reduces risk aversion.

In this context the IT department has a valuable support role to play during the transformation process. Before any major development expenditure is incurred, it needs to build simple prototypes. The use of prototypes in exploratory sessions allow users to walk through the system and find whether ideas produce the expected outcomes. This irons out the 'glitches' before the serious work of programming and building a new system begins.

It may seem an unnecessary expense to build IT system prototypes, but as Tom Heldman, Chief Finance Officer of South West Ohio Steel, clearly articulated:

> We are not just talking about monetary risk here, although it is certainly a factor. Managers at all levels are also concerned about the risk in the development of a non-viable system to which the company is committed because of the expenditure. For some, it is only when they realize that they can get their hands on the prototype at an early stage and assess its utility before going forward, that they can relax.
>
> Rockart and Crescenzi, 1984[75]

So, if that small upfront investment improves commitment and saves you wasting $15 million on the development of a useless system, or even $5 million on post-introduction modifications, it is worth it. The ability to make risk concrete in isolated areas, but protect the organization as a whole improves competitive manoeuvrability by preventing unnecessary waste of resources. It also makes individuals more comfortable because they can get a clearer picture of the end result and so reduce the degree of ambiguity.

Network mapping (understanding local political negotiations)

Contention only occurs when political constituencies interact. Any way to map the effectiveness of these interactions must be a useful adjunct to the learning process. If we can understand how the current informal structure operates, and how that influences the seats of political power, we are in a much better position to design a transformation program that aligns these forces with the strategic direction of the organization as a whole.

Netmapping is a computer-based analysis tool that tracks the interactions between various constituencies Essentially, the technique is simple. Companies collect data about the informal communications surrounding a process, by means of a questionnaire. The questionnaire covers factors such as the frequency of interaction, who initiates the conversation, the means of communication, the perceived importance of the connection, and the topic and quality of the discussion. The data is entered into the software which produces an analysis emphasizing the reciprocal links; in other words, it maps those interactions which both parties acknowledge as regular and of relative importance. The result is a picture (Fig. 8.9) of the strength and weaknesses of the communication channels. Knowing where the information energy is flowing immediately shows where power lies and who is isolated from the community action.

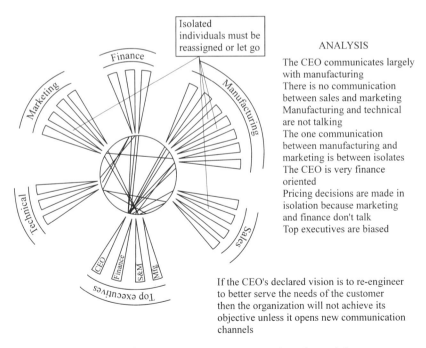

Isolated individuals must be reassigned or let go

ANALYSIS

The CEO communicates largely with manufacturing
There is no communication between sales and marketing
Manufacturing and technical are not talking
The one communication between manufacturing and marketing is between isolates
The CEO is very finance oriented
Pricing decisions are made in isolation because marketing and finance don't talk
Top executives are biased

If the CEO's declared vision is to re-engineer to better serve the needs of the customer then the organization will not achieve its objective unless it opens new communication channels

Fig. 8.9 Analysing the communication network (adapted from Livingston and Berkes, 1993)[76]

Making such factors explicit is important for effective planning. Managers can see whether the political network is aligned with defined strategic objectives. For example, if the CEO spends most of his time communicating with manufacturing and only talks to one isolated person in IT and one in marketing, his declared vision to develop a more customer oriented enterprise through technology would start to look somewhat implausible.

Secondly, in those places where communication is insufficient, managers can design new training programmes, new physical structures, and redirect information flows to correct the insufficiencies. Deliberate action can be taken to overcome the 'information is power' bottlenecks which will inhibit change. Mapping existing patterns of communication will highlight where to restructure relationships with outside agencies in order to improve performance, and where to break down excessively strong cultural centres that may hold back change.

Thirdly, the maps pinpoint the vital players in any process that is under redesign. Identifying information owners helps build effective teams, that possess the necessary knowledge to do their job; identification of non-communicators shows up who will not easily fit into the new interactive organization. Such an analysis can prevent wastage of valuable human resources during the change process. The knowledge lynch pins are not lost in the haste to cut back costs and organizational memory is preserved. Those with the least knowledge are no great loss.

Network mapping is a valuable diagnostic tool that identifies the strengths and weaknesses in the fundamental raw material of the organization—it's people. An understanding of how their interactions are working provides information that will improve the operational viability of any plans.

Custardware (satisfying external requirements)

'Custardware' is a proprietary consultants' term that is supposed to be 'sexy,'[77] but the idea is generalizable. Custardware is the sort of software that you might 'pour' over your existing applications in order to provide a better service to the end user. Remember the user is external to the mysteries of the IT department, so any way of providing better access to data using a responsive and customizable process is desirable.

The whole idea of transformation is to break down the barriers currently limiting the organization. Looking outside the functional blinkers means end users need different information. Often, it would require huge investments to build new data architectures. Much of the data is already available, but it is just not accessible. Custardware is a cheaper and simpler way to supplement the missing information and introduce new ways to access it.

Custardware has the following five characteristics:

1. *Front end*—It is a sophisticated front end that leaves existing systems unchanged, but allows end users to work in a manner more appropriate to the reconfigured business.
2. *Fast track*—Time is a critical success factor for most organizations and custardware gives the organization a fast track solution which removes the technological barriers to change.
3. *Federated*—Cross-functional interaction requires cross-system operation in many organizations. Custardware is non-proprietary software that will connect many systems in a loose federal structure.
4. *Friendly*—The user interface is friendly and easily accepted, which helps reduce a person's initial resistance to new working conditions.
5. *Flexible*—Inbuilt into the custardware solutions will be the facility to amend and update the software to accommodate continuous environmental change.

Graphical user interfaces, client–server architectures and open systems all assist in the sort of rapid applications development pioneered by custardware.

The benefits are as varied as the customer requirements. However, a few examples will give readers an idea of what can be achieved.

■ British Aerospace plc (BAe) changed its entire manufacturing philosophy in a bid to reduce costs by a swingeing 30 per cent. The organization was divided into cells which were the equivalent of mini businesses. The IT support needed to move fast to keep pace with the massive turbulence this created in the data flows. A custardware solution was able to combine data from various legacy systems so that managers could compare the performance of various cells, as well as track overall manufacturing performance.
■ An insurance company used the idea of custardware to build working prototypes of many of its key processes, without disruption to existing operations.
■ GEC Plessey Semiconductors used custardware to provide flexible but transparent access to data in many plants around the world, despite their differing requirements. This was one way to become 'centrally/decentralized' without major new investment.

The principle advantage of such a tool is that it allows the IT department to provide rapid solutions to customer requirements without huge investment and long response times. This improves customer satisfaction and increases the belief in IT as a valuable strategic resource. Custardware increases the physical fitness of an organization for its external environment.

Fully integrated systems (organizational change)

Just like organizational transformation, transforming information processes is also a progressive programme. All of the foregoing systems are incremental ways to improve the information flows relevant to the management process. The full value will erupt spontaneously when all of these new technologies work together to provide an uninterruptable power supply of information to improve management judgement. As yet this is an ideal, not a practicality, however, technology is moving steadily towards such a future. When it arrives, the consequent knowledge explosion will initiate even more changes within our organizations and start a further phase in the evolution of this information revolution. Naturally, this is key to organizational elasticity.

Electronic meeting systems (EMS) (paradox reconciliation and organizational learning)

Electronic meeting systems (EMS) sit at the centre of the circle because they are useful for all 10 dimensions. An EMS is a way for people to gather, talk, deal with conflict and reach consensus through the medium of computers. It also provides a more comprehensive level of support than any of the other groupware offerings described in this section, because it has multiplexed interactive capability.

There are various systems on the market (see Appendix C). The more sophisticated versions offer an integrated set of software tools, many of which have distinct advantages for every aspect of the cycle of strategy development (Fig. 8.10).

Participation in the use of such systems can be simultaneous, staggered or ad hoc, and participants can be widely distributed or collected together in one place. System configurations can be in-house installed systems, rented on an on-call basis, or accessed remotely from the vendor's site (Fig. 8.11).

Whatever the layout, each meeting participant receives the input of every other group member via the computer screen. Sessions can be 'chauffeured', by a facilitator, or led by a group member.

How does an EMS help resolve dilemmas to produce more learning? Simply by removing many of the logistical and emotional obstacles that stand in the way.

Sharing strategic responsibility requires unimpeded conversation between the few at the top and the many at the bottom.

Historically this cycle of uninhibited interaction has been difficult to implement for several reasons:

- Meetings large enough to communicate with everyone are generally unproductive, restricting meeting size usually according

Tool	Function	Use for strategic aspect
Ideas generation		
Brainstorming	Anonymous ideas entry	1&6
Topic commenter	Electronic index cards for topical discussion	1,2,3,6
Group outliner	Organizing ideas in outline	2&3
Ideas organization		
Ideas organizer	Categorizing ideas generated	1&6
Idea analyser	Consolidating comments	1,2,3
Group writer	Joint document authoring	5,6,8
Prioritizing		
Vote selection	Various voting methods	8,11
Alternative evaluation	Ranking against criteria	6,7,9
Questionnaire	Electronic surveys	any
Group matrix	Rating on 2 × 2 matrix	11
Policy development		
Policy formulation	Structured consensus building	8
Stakeholder ID	Surface key stakeholders	4,5,8,9
Organizational memory		
Enterprise analyser	Analyses group data in semantic net	1,2,3,4,12
Graphical browser	Zoom in and out net	1,2,3,4,6,12
Group dictionary	Develop common definitions	1,5,6
Brief case	Read only access to stored text	
Session management	Pre-session planning, in-session control and post-session analysis	12

Fig. 8.10 Contents of a sophisticated EMS toolbox (Group Systems by Ventana Corporation)

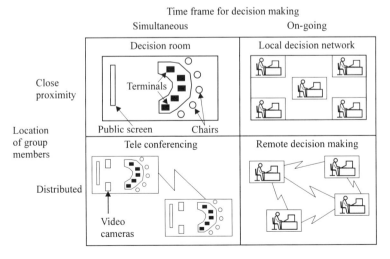

Fig. 8.11 Alternative space/time EMS configurations (from Sprague and Watson, 1993)[70]

to hierarchical status, creates too many meetings and inaccurate message translation.

- Hierarchical relationships tend to inhibit honesty, particularly when managers resent or reject questioning from subordinates.
- The logistics of gathering a wide span of opinions was problematic, in that it was time consuming, hard to handle in terms of physical space for a meeting and hard to analyse afterwards.
- People at lower levels were not always comfortable speaking out in person.
- Functional disputes and power plays often sidetracked the strategic discussion in open venues.

Electronic meetings circumvent many of these problems:

- Participant anonymity in an electronic meeting encourages people to comment freely, in the knowledge that their input is not attributable to them. This eliminates many of the political and emotional barriers to open participation. Honesty becomes much easier in the circumstances.
- The process naturally balances the contributions of top and bottom, because it supports communication between all levels *on equal terms*.
- The work of moulding the content into a form appropriate to the organizational context can run in parallel with the ideas development phase, which saves time and helps prevent many misunderstandings and mistakes.
- Everyone can speak simultaneously, which both increases the number of ideas generated and makes issues more immediate and unavoidable.
- Hard copy of the discussion is available for later use, which immediately confirms, in writing, the commitments made.
- The method of working reduces the tendency for people to forget to make those small but vital points on which a solution often depends, simply because the discussion moved on too rapidly for them to contribute.

Use of an EMS in any strategic review process electronically expands the number of people involved, which overcomes all the disadvantages of group dynamics listed above while adding value to the review. Scheduling regular strategy review sessions between a mixed group of senior and junior staff—perhaps as a precursor to quarterly forecasting exercises—would create a valuable opportunity to spread learning, explore suggestions and build an unbiased consensus for action:

- A wider audience will generate more ideas.

- Involvement at an early stage will improve morale and support for the strategy.
- Continuous participation in reviewing a strategic agenda for change builds an environment where change is accepted as the norm.
- Greater input can be gathered in less time and analysed in more detail, with the result that small points are less likely to be missed.
- The process offers an opportunity to evaluate and develop the quality of strategic thinking lower in the organization.
- It is an immediate positive demonstration of the benefits to be achieved through innovative use of information technology. Such early positive feedback should improve the perspective on information value.

Regular, electronically facilitated meetings also offer many opportunities to open up the communication channels, so that we can integrate the random response into the more formal planning system. The advantage of all electronic analysis is that it can handle larger volumes of soft data more conveniently than the human brain, which improves the quality of rational decision making.

Some of the tools, such as brainstorming and categorizing, promote conflict. However, negotiation can be more honest and productive because people do not have to struggle with status inequalities and the fear of offending a superior. 'Human Parallel Processing' (in other words, the ability to interact simultaneously) also stops certain personalities dominating a discussion. Then we get equitable participation. Consensus building is built into the software to resolve the conflict generated. The prioritizing and policy development elements of the groupware can then be used to define a plan of action. Overall, the viability of strategic plans can be better tested, because more people have had uninhibited involvement. Generally, the whole process promotes the sort of positive political interaction that Stacey sees as the best means of organizational control amidst Chaos.

Electronic support for group consensus is particularly useful in the context of the internal/external tension. Technology can cross the borders without some of the inherent prejudices that might hinder a human intermediary. Decisions between organizational partners, joint venture negotiations could all be conducted by EMS. The particular benefit in this case lies in the common *inter*-organizational memory that is automatically accumulated. The detail of the discussions are preserved electronically, and reference back to them can prevent many future misunderstandings and disagreements on both sides, because the content of important conversations cannot be skewed by selective memory. Thus we can effortlessly support the total honesty requirement.

In summary, users have found that when used for planning Re-engineering projects:

- 50 per cent less man hours are required at the Re-engineering design stage.[78]
- With continued usage, calendar time for the entire programme is cut by about 80 per cent.[78]

This review has considered a selection of emerging technologies. Each has an impact on the way management deals with the various aspects of business, because it changes the information available. Altering information processes at this higher level can make a significant contribution to behavioural transformation. The field is very fluid and new technologies are emerging all the time, the key is to keep the organization open to new methods of managing people and information in combination.

8.4   The true relevance of process

The time has come for a return to Chaos. Chaos is Nature's revolutionary management system. Transformation occurs in Nature when many small disturbances are amplified to produce step change, but the process is not uniform. Think of heating a pan of water. Initially, the energy input produces very little obvious effect. The water looks the same. Put your finger in it and parts of it will be cold, some a little warmer and others warmer still. The energy is not evenly distributed. Gradually, as more heat is applied, the surface starts to swirl. When the temperature reaches boiling point, there is sudden intense activity. Yet even then it is not homogeneous. The surface of the water is bubbling furiously, but some of the water is completely changing its characteristics; it is vaporizing into steam. Clearly, some of the water molecules have more energy than others. In fact, if we could look more closely at the remaining water in the pan, the same would be true. Some of the molecules in the liquid would have more energy than others. There would be eddies and smooth sections, and some where transformation is about to take place. The energy input has been constant, but the result is not.

This is what organizational transformation will be like. Not smooth but turbulent. It is no good embarking on this process and expecting consistent results. Parts of the organization will gather enough energy to make that leap from water to steam, and parts will remain stubbornly as plain old water right until the pan is almost dry.

Taking the analogy one step further, steam does not stay steam for long without more energy input. After a while it makes the sudden transition back from a gas to a liquid—and not even a boiling liquid either. Organizational behaviour will crystallize, without further energy input.

Of course, that is not a bad thing. Always floating around in a cloud of steam is not healthy. The objective of the whole exercise is to distil the water, purify the organization and then use the result. Eventually, of course, we will need to repeat the distillation process, to challenge, change and recrystallize again.

The point of this analogy is to emphasize the continuity of process. Process is often seen as a means to an end. There is no end! Life is a never ending cycle of wheels, within wheels, within wheels. So is business. All that is possible is to change the rate at which the wheels turn, by turning the heat up or down. Indeed, the only difference between evolution and revolution is the letter R, which could well stand for rate of change. So how can we turn the heat up so that revolution occurs quickly? Simply by increasing the energy input. In the case of organizations that input is learning.*

The framework in this book is designed to stimulate learning through the conflict present in paradox. The more often decisions are made in the context of paradox, the more learning will occur. (The next chapter will test this assertion by examining the case of two car manufacturers, Volvo and NUMMI.) Consequently, if a business uses the model independently in different parts of the organization, to answer different questions, energy levels will increase, and change will happen more quickly.

Fig. 8.12 shows how this would work as a successive progression of paradox wheels.

The questions on the left of the graph are six implementation issues relating to Re-engineering that emerged from the first European

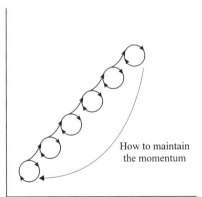

How to learn from other organizations

How to affect skills, structures & cultures

How to measure success

How to make changes

How to generate ideas for redesign

How to model & understand existing processes

How to maintain the momentum

Fig. 8.12 Repetitions of the paradox wheel instil challenge at every level of BPR

*It is interesting to note that learning itself follows the same process that has been described—lots of small steps and then a sudden 'Eureka!' The whole process of change is truly fractal!

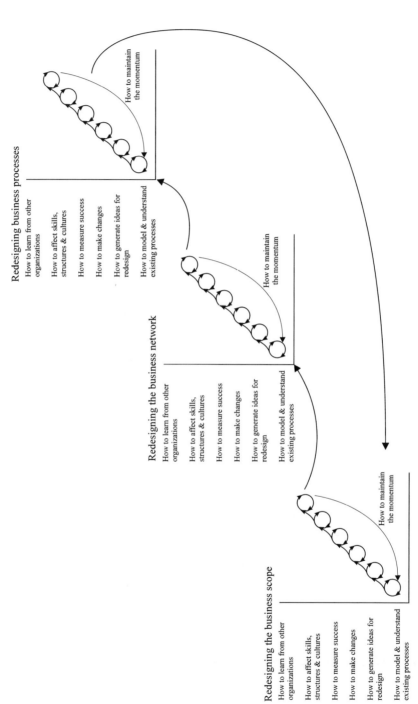

Redesigning business processes

How to learn from other
organizations

How to affect skills,
structures & cultures

How to measure success

How to make changes

How to generate ideas for
redesign

How to model & understand
existing processes

How to maintain
the momentum

Redesigning the business network

How to learn from other
organizations

How to affect skills,
structures & cultures

How to measure success

How to make changes

How to generate ideas for
redesign

How to model & understand
existing processes

How to maintain
the momentum

Redesigning the business scope

How to learn from other
organizations

How to affect skills,
structures & cultures

How to measure success

How to make changes

How to generate ideas for
redesign

How to model & understand
existing processes

How to maintain
the momentum

Fig. 8.13 A self-organizing process that can give order to the Chaos

conference on Re-engineering at Cranfield Business School.[79] The answer to the seventh—how to maintain the momentum?—is the subject of this section.* These questions have been chosen only to give readers a general progression of issues surrounding transformation. In practice, users would customize the questions to their own circumstances. If the framework for evolutionary revolution is used to answer each of these six questions and the results are part of a continuous feedback loop, the process is self-sustaining. The infinite variety of decisions taken to keep the wheel in balance will create rich and interesting results (just like the fractal beauty of the gingerbreadman pictures (Fig. 1.5).

If the pattern is extended as shown in Fig. 8.13 the energy will permeate through all levels of the organization and its environment to provide a self-organizing process that gives order to Chaos.

This may sound a little bizarre, but it is no more than Nature's way to produce revolution. Mother Nature has tested her method over many millennia, which is more than can be said for any business theory! The conflicts in the model are interpretable and relevant at any level of operation, from personal to international. Because the results are dependent on user interpretation, the framework does not constrain the process or box answers into preconceived niches. Then the true relevance of process is clear—to encourage organizations to create infinite variety in finite form by a fractal decision making process.

This chapter has looked at the experience of transformation from three different aspects: financial, technological and procedural. Undoubtedly it is a very complicated experience, with a lot of things to keep in mind. The amount of things to deal with may seem overwhelming, but one piece of encouragement exists. All you really need to do is keep 15 paradoxes in mind. Whether you are dealing with information, management, employees or technology, the framework puts all of them into a constantly ordered format, that can ultimately improve financial performance.

The next chapter will consider the transformation experience from a different perspective, and ask 'does paradoxical management produce more learning?'

---

*There were 10 questions in all. The other three are: What is BPR? Where does it fit with other management disciplines? and What makes it happen? The response to these is, obviously, a continuous and spontaneous process that affects all disciplines driven by learning.

A comparative study across organizational boundaries —the NUMMI/Volvo learning experience

In sailing, good crews maintain meticulous standards and disciplines for sails, halyards, ropes, tools, nautical instruments and safety equipment, in order to concentrate on the creative part of the adventure, respond to unpredictable shifts and meet emergencies promptly. The same applies to manufacturing.
Berggren, 1994[80]

9.1 Introduction

Transformation is a continuous process and learning is what keeps the wheels of change turning. That was the conclusion of the last chapter, but is it true in practice? Further, is it really such a disaster if all dimensions of the wheel are not in balance? Organizations have been carrying out radical change programmes without equalizing the tensions around a wheel for a long time; transformation still happens, even when some aspects of strategy are under-utilized. The question is, are the results any better if the tensions are managed? Normally such a question would be extremely difficult to answer. Fortunately, recent experiments in the automotive industry have provided an unusual opportunity for a 'controlled' comparison of different learning approaches in action. As this chapter will show, even with the best intentions, organizational learning does not occur unless all aspects of the paradox wheel are in balance. A selective approach produces inferior results.

NUMMI* and Volvo** are the two organizations in question. Car manufacturing is, in fact, an ideal setting in which to examine the potential for learning. Production is standardized and labour intensive. Standardization simplifies inter-plant comparison; labour intensiveness brings in the human dimension and the setting of a manufacturing plant introduces the human–technology interface.

---

*NUMMI—New United Motor Manufacturing Inc., a joint venture between Toyota and General Motors in the USA.
**The Volvo plant was at Uddevalla in Sweden and, in fact, Volvo has since closed the factory and discontinued the experiment.

NUMMI works to what has been called the 'lean production model'. The method is strong on the hard control elements on the right of the circle (Fig. 9.1)—direction, planning, rationality, structure and social norms. Many people have criticized this model for the pressure that it puts on workers, but the hard aspects of organizational control are supplemented, in near equal proportions, by softer philosophies, such as worker empowerment, opportunity, negotiation, quality and incremental change.

The Volvo alternative, on the other hand, is much more unbalanced. Certainly it is 'human centred', but the harder aspects of management have become completely subservient to the ideal of creating a truly fulfilling working environment. Volvo abandoned the old style regime of production line operation—short cycle times, rigidly controlled and repetitive action—in order to make working conditions more attractive to an employment market where labour was in short supply. Instead, the Swedish car manufacturer started on a much publicized experiment with independent work groups and a return to a craftsman type ethic. The idea was to give employees plenty of opportunities for individual learning, and hence fulfilment. Unfortunately, in the desire to redesign Volvo threw out the baby with the bath water. They introduced self-fulfilment and lost organizational control. In this respect, Uddevalla was a typical example of over-compensation. Overemphasis on the softer aspects on the left of the wheel improved the quality of working life but produced disappointing organizational results. As will become clear,

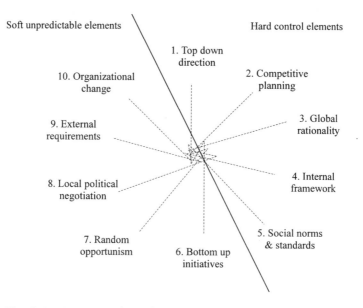

Fig. 9.1 'Power without love becomes brutal, feeling without strength becomes sentimental'

independent action and opportunity produced change, but the learning was confined to pockets which never became institutionalized. In fact, many Volvo executives believed that Uddevalla would not have been built under contemporary circumstances.

The details of these two cases* will show that NUMMI used all the characteristics of learning simultaneously; Volvo did not. In so doing NUMMI achieved outstanding results and overcame many of the traditional US labour relationship problems, whereas Volvo could do little more than match the performance of its other plant at Torslanda.

9.2   The NUMMI/Uddevalla stories

Both organizations started with the same premiss. Managers were 'truly committed to treating employees as their most important assets'[81] (1 N & U). The primary strategic objective was to maximize human resources—undoubtedly a sensible starting point in a world where knowledge is a growing source of power. The words 'truly committed' are important in this context. Many organizations say that their employees are their most important asset, but they are only paying lip service to the notion. NUMMI and Volvo were both committed enough to put their ideas into action. Both organizations set about translating words into action by deliberately laying down the conditions for a learning environment (12 N & U). The guiding principle was to satisfy employees personal aspirations and their higher order needs—self-fulfilment and self-actualization. However, this is where the two organizations part company. Although both corporate visions centred on learning, the reasons for choosing that vision were different. NUMMI viewed it as a means of improving competitive performance, Volvo Uddevalla had more altruistic goals; it was simply seen as a way to increase the quality of working life. This led to substantial differences in the way each company chose to increase the potential to learn.

How NUMMI tackled the process of creating a learning organization

The NUMMI model is based on the philosophy that a system of specialized, well documented work tasks, strongly enforced procedures and

---

*The notes in brackets highlight the way that strategic dimensions of the wheel have been interpreted in the context of car manufacture. An italicized letter N and/or U identifies when a characteristic is present in either the NUMMI or Uddevalla case, respectively. The number next to the letter indicates the relevant aspect on the paradox wheel. Some points have (N & U) others only (N) or (U). Figures 9.2 and 9.3 show how these points work together to produce a different end result for each plant.

job rotation will maximize the potential for learning. The Uddevalla model, on the other hand, starts from the premiss that:

> organizational adaptability and learning is best served by lengthened work cycles and a return to craft like work forms that give the teams substantial latitude in how they perform their tasks and authority over what have traditionally been higher level management decisions.
>
> Adler and Cole, 1993[81]

This difference in interpretation completely altered the outlook on competitive planning at each plant, and this illustrates the importance of considering the interactive effect of the paradoxes. In the context of production, competitive planning has to be interpreted as modelling operational procedures and designing strategies to remedy the weaknesses and capitalize on the strengths. It may seem strange to call this competitive planning, but it is not illogical. Production superiority, in terms of quality and timeliness, is a major source of competitive advantage, so improving manufacturing productivity is an integral part of the whole organization's competitive plan.

Car manufacturing is a repetitive job. The ability to standardize procedures gives car manufacturers a natural learning advantage because knowledge transmission becomes easier. NUMMI recognized this and capitalized on it. Operational procedures and work methods were planned tightly, down to the last detail, (2 N) but in doing so, the company did not fall into the trap of 'despotic Taylorism'. The standards were not arbitrary targets designed to pressurize a recalcitrant workforce into greater productivity. Instead, the work teams themselves were continually defining their own objectives. Workers were taught the principles of time and motion study, so that they could time their own work, compare it with new alternatives and identify which was the most efficient. Of course, the danger of standardization is stultification. Too much orthodoxy obscures opportunity. To keep people thinking and balance the emphasis on formal advance planning, NUMMI used job rotation within teams. Changing jobs brings a new perspective to the task at hand, which increases the chance of spotting a particularly advantageous combination of circumstances (7 N). This process integrates the unplanned response to random opportunity into the formally planned work methods.

NUMMI gained six advantages[82] from allowing line workers to strictly define the factors affecting competitiveness. Firstly, precise instructions reduced set up time. Set up time is a crucial factor in efficient production, particularly when there is a variety of products to be made. Secondly, the best procedure on every job is codified, which allows workers to rotate jobs with minimum efficiency loss. Thirdly, the quality standard provides a convenient target to be challenged. Fourthly, workers could be empowered to act, but still within a framework that fitted with top level objectives. Fifthly, those immersed in the details of Chaos feed the knowledge back into the formal planning loop to refine the forecasting process. Finally, the process produces a commonly understood language for shared learning.

NUMMI, also, laid down simple rules so that the whole organization could benefit from the successful resolution of the planned/opportunistic (2/7) paradox. Management screened suggestions. Those that were implementable in an identical format across all work teams became the ideal for the whole plant. They were immediately written into the standard operating practice (3 N). In this way NUMMI constantly raised the ideals and simultaneously achieved a high degree of rationality throughout production operations. However, the pursuit of ideals in the extreme is dangerous. The pressure on the workers to perform is constantly being intensified. The danger of a system that expects continuous improvement is that workers are driven like machines and eventually will be pushed to the point of collapse. NUMMI recognized and dealt with that danger too. Union participation in a broad range of policy decisions was deliberately strong at NUMMI. All major problems were investigated jointly by the management and the union. Many of the decisions that were previously the sole prerogative of management were made open to negotiation. For example, management committed in advance to consultation before acting on questions of lay-offs, schedule changes and major investments (8 N). Giving power to the voice of the workers sustains equity. Management can pursue ideals in the full knowledge that organizational excesses will be curbed by conflict with the unions.

The structure of NUMMI's production operation was quite fragmented. NUMMI teams comprised four or five workers and a team leader. All team members were paid hourly, and their work cycle was rarely more that about 60 seconds. The teams in final assembly were highly interdependent; groups, linked in series, worked to just-in-time (JIT) methods (4 N). Team leaders were jointly selected by union representatives and management, by use of formal objective tests. Democratic processes were important to the continuing success of the fragmented structure because the method of working exerted intense pressure on workers. They needed to feel part of this pressure, not oppressed by it. However, it was important to keep everyone's outlook focused externally. Otherwise the pressure would become dangerously introverted and counterproductive. NUMMI unified team effort by focusing on the customer and then measuring success against that external yardstick of customer satisfaction (9 N). Keeping reward structures consistent with objectives, eliminated confusing and unproductive conflict. The alignment of performance measurement with outward-looking objectives ensured that internal and external forces remained in balance.

The benefit of the NUMMI structure was that developing ideals came from many different sources. Participation in the suggestion programme was phenomenal. By 1991, over 10,000 suggestions per year were made (an average of five per person) of which over 80 per cent were implemented. At this level of involvement, the direction of NUMMI's strategy (1 N) could not help but be influenced by the grassroots initiatives (6 N). Obviously, the more input there was, the more likely that the ultimate rationale was the best for the company (3 N).

NUMMI's emphasis on standardization also made it easier to establish a common language which everyone understood (5 N). The corporation invested considerable time and effort into training the workers; but training was not confined to expanding workers' opportunities. By concentrating on procedural requirements and familiarity with the norms and standards, it enabled everyone to share a common understanding of the corporate mission, and gave them a sense of belonging to a focused community. In some respects this attitude to training is a limitation on the concept of empowerment because it dictates more closely what the worker can learn. However, the limitation is appropriate in that the learning is kept in line with the strategic direction. Because all NUMMI actions were consistent with organizational goals as well as individual aspirations, training investment produced results in terms of shared outlook. Common goals help to provide stability in the face of change. Strategies for skill development are an important stimulus to the process of incremental improvement (10 N) but when they are focused on a single common purpose, the investment brings more returns to the organization.

The Volvo interpretation

Volvo, Uddevalla, made little of any of the natural advantages in car manufacture. When Uddevalla was first opened the workers were given the procedures from another Volvo plant, but since these were not well designed, they soon fell into disuse. In fact, there was no predetermined corporate strategy for effective strategy (2 U). Everything was guided by the fuzzy notion that the worker must be kept happy. Any notion of detailed methods and defined standards was quickly discarded, because it seemed to be an affront to the craftsmen ethic. Pride in the job was expected to contribute enough improvements (7 U). However, without standards against which to evaluate the improvements, Volvo had no mechanism for identifying, measuring or spreading the value of new ideas generated by individuals or autonomous work teams. This immediately created an obstacle to rationalizing the dispersed activities of the independent teams (3 U). Although the engineering staff from different areas held regular meetings to share ideas, against a non-standard background it was hard enough to pick out the valuable opportunities for global improvement, let alone find the synergy for the organization as a whole.

Uddevalla also deliberately avoided the conflict necessary to refine the organizational rationale. Like NUMMI, there was a strong union presence at Uddevalla, but Volvo's objective was high worker satisfaction, so the union was allowed to play a disproportionately strong role in the design and governance of the plant (8 U). This gave it too much power. By abdicating power Volvo avoided the conflict that could have enabled it to pursue the ideal.

There is no comparative data for employee participation in suggestion programmes at Uddevalla. However if absenteeism and worker satisfaction (as evidenced in Fig. 9.2) are any indication of participation, the results are unlikely to have been outstanding. Structural mechanisms for collecting and spreading the good suggestions were absent anyway. In addition, there were no standards against which to evaluate the improvement a suggestion could make.

At Uddevalla, the structure was driven by radically different ideals to those of Taylor and rationalism. In the mid 1980s Volvo had hit a capacity bottleneck. Production could not keep pace with sales in Sweden, a protected market unthreatened by the spur of Japanese competition. Labour shortages were the driving external criteria, so the main strategic objective was to make conditions in the plant as attractive as possible for Swedish workers. As a motivating force, this was too introverted (4 U). The structure that Volvo settled upon was eight teams, each of which took total responsibility for building an entire car from subsystems. This gave each team of 10 people a work cycle of about two hours. The responsibilities of the team were much more far-reaching than those at the NUMMI plant. Teams planned their own job rotations, selected new recruits for their team, and scheduled their own overtime. Unlike NUMMI, standardization was ignored in the belief that a craftsman would instinctively 'know' when something was not going right. They had no detailed documentation to describe how each task was performed and work teams were left to their own devices, in the name of empowerment. As Adler and Cole commented so sharply:

> In auto assembly operations, when competitiveness hinges so greatly on efficiency and manufacturing quality, this sounds more like abandonment that empowerment.
>
> Adler and Cole, 1993[81]

In summary, the competitive manoeuvrability of the plant was diminished because of the lack of planned management control (2/7); the operational viability of the organization was compromised by this overemphasis on workers (3/8); the physical fitness of the plant was substandard because too much attention was paid to organizing around the worker, and not enough to building a structure that satisfied customers. Policies tended to be more labour market driven than product market driven. Consequently, internal issues got more attention than the external requirements that could have united everyone behind a common goal (4/9). All because the top level vision was interpreted as enabling workers for their own sakes, rather than for the benefit of the organization's (1/6).

Further, team autonomy and decentralized decision making need excellent communication mechanisms if the individual learning gained in the teams is to be used to greatest effect. Uddevalla did not stint on training. Training was a cultural standard (5 U), but unfortunately there was no organizational focus. Huge sums were invested, but they were designed to provide *individual* employees with a wide range of learning opportunities, some of which were not immediately productive for the company. Each worker took 16 months to complete the basic skills training, and then gradually learned all their teammate's roles so that eventually they could build the complete car on their own. After that a worker was trained in teaching skills, spokesperson skills and offered courses that covered other managerial and engineering expertise. However, because there was no thought for how workgroups could learn from each other, incremental change that built on the learning and advances of others was impossible. Unfortunately, as a plant design project leader later admitted:

> the planning team ignored the need for cross group organizational learning.
> Adler and Cole, 1993[81]

Uddevalla used training as a way of maximizing personal opportunities. Effectively, the workers had supplanted the customer as the pre-eminent focus in strategic thinking. NUMMI, on the other hand, used training to deepen knowledge about things that would improve their capacity to satisfy external customers, for example, specific job methods, production control, statistical control and problem solving. Simply broadening the range of knowledge is not enough.

9.3   Analysing the outcome

The overall differences in operation amount to a difference in the quality of learning achieved in each system. At Uddevalla personal learning was high, but organizational learning was not. This is not a win/win partnership, since eventually the workers will leave for pastures new and the company will be left with an expensive investment and no return on it. At NUMMI, personal learning may have been lower at least in terms of breadth, however, the organizational learning was extremely high. If we compare the N's and the U's we can see why (Figs 9.2 and 9.3). NUMMI

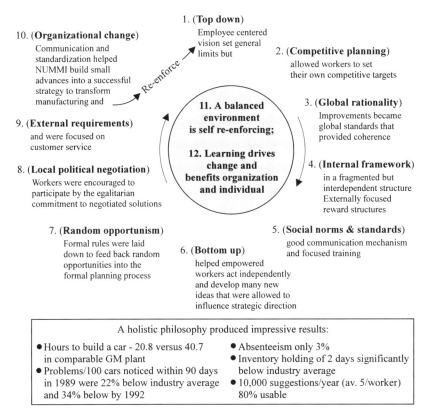

1. (Top down) Employee centered vision set general limits but

2. (Competitive planning) allowed workers to set their own competitive targets

3. (Global rationality) Improvements became global standards that provided coherence

4. (Internal framework) in a fragmented but interdependent structure Externally focused reward structures

5. (Social norms & standards) good communication mechanism and focused training

6. (Bottom up) helped empowered workers act independently and develop many new ideas that were allowed to influence strategic direction

7. (Random opportunism) Formal rules were laid down to feed back random opportunities into the formal planning process

8. (Local political negotiation) Workers were encouraged to participate by the egalitarian commitment to negotiated solutions

9. (External requirements) and were focused on customer service

10. (Organizational change) Communication and standardization helped NUMMI build small advances into a successful strategy to transform manufacturing and

Re-enforce

11. A balanced environment is self re-enforcing;

12. Learning drives change and benefits organization and individual

A holistic philosophy produced impressive results:

- Hours to build a car - 20.8 versus 40.7 in comparable GM plant
- Problems/100 cars noticed within 90 days in 1989 were 22% below industry average and 34% below by 1992
- Absenteeism only 3%
- Inventory holding of 2 days significantly below industry average
- 10,000 suggestions/year (av. 5/worker) 80% usable

Fig. 9.2   A holistic philosophy at NUMMI

shows a more balanced learning personality; Uddevalla has some glaring omissions, which are the root causes of their lesser performance.

It is interesting to compare the reality of NUMMI against Uddevalla's vision of improving quality of life. The evidence at NUMMI seems to suggest that quality of working life was not unpleasant despite the limits upon empowerment. The NUMMI absentee rate was a steady 3 per cent in total, compared to 12 per cent sick leave and 10 per cent long term disability at Uddevalla. Certainly, cultural differences influence these variances. Swedish workers have a long history of poor attendance rates, whereas NUMMI had severe restrictions on absenteeism. But the environment at Uddevalla was obviously not so satisfactory that workers felt inclined to change their patterns of behaviour and, indeed, the results at Uddevalla were no better than in Volvo's conventionally managed Torslanda plant.

The craftsmen model of work adopted at Uddevalla undoubtedly made the Volvo plant a more pleasant place to work. Certainly, every effort was made to satisfy the personal aspirations of the workers, but this was often

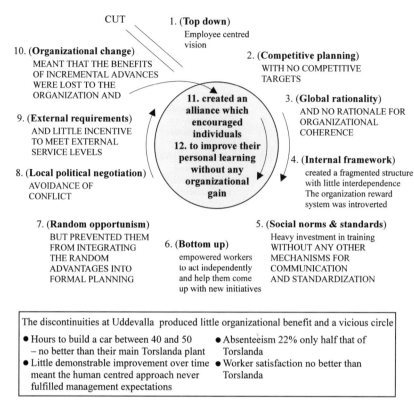

CUT

1. **(Top down)**
Employee centred vision

10. **(Organizational change)**
MEANT THAT THE BENEFITS OF INCREMENTAL ADVANCES WERE LOST TO THE ORGANIZATION AND

2. **(Competitive planning)**
WITH NO COMPETITIVE TARGETS

9. **(External requirements)**
AND LITTLE INCENTIVE TO MEET EXTERNAL SERVICE LEVELS

3. **(Global rationality)**
AND NO RATIONALE FOR ORGANIZATIONAL COHERENCE

8. **(Local political negotiation)**
AVOIDANCE OF CONFLICT

4. **(Internal framework)**
created a fragmented structure with little interdependence The organization reward system was introverted

11. **created an alliance which encouraged individuals**
12. **to improve their personal learning without any organizational gain**

7. **(Random opportunism)**
BUT PREVENTED THEM FROM INTEGRATING THE RANDOM ADVANTAGES INTO FORMAL PLANNING

6. **(Bottom up)**
empowered workers to act independently and help them come up with new initiatives

5. **(Social norms & standards)**
Heavy investment in training WITHOUT ANY OTHER MECHANISMS FOR COMMUNICATION AND STANDARDIZATION

The discontinuities at Uddevalla produced little organizational benefit and a vicious circle

- Hours to build a car between 40 and 50 – no better than their main Torslanda plant
- Little demonstrable improvement over time meant the human centred approach never fulfilled management expectations
- Absenteeism 22% only half that of Torslanda
- Worker satisfaction no better than Torslanda

Fig. 9.3   The discontinuities at Uddevalla

at the expense of organizational benefits. A comparison of man hours to build a car shows that NUMMI outperforms Volvo by a factor of 2:1.

Undoubtedly, in the human centred experiment, employees were well motivated to make use of circumstances and respond to the needs of the situation, but because there was no coordinating mechanism to integrate the learning back into the formal planning process, the tension across this part of the strategy cycle was broken. This demonstrates the effect of mismanaging one of the underlying frictions (organizational benefits versus personal aspirations) that slow the progress of the paradox wheel. It shows clearly the interactive nature of the whole set of 15 dilemmas, and contains an important warning. Moderation in *all* things, not just some! NUMMI, on the other hand, formalized the analysis of process and standardized the results. This enabled them to integrate the worthwhile random responses into the ongoing planning process. Analysts doubt that the continual improvement this produced at NUMMI is sustainable, because workers are likely to get too stressed.[80] This, combined with the fact that NUMMI offers no reward for accumulating new skills, is cited as reason why performance will not last. Certainly, the one danger of this rationally standardized regime is that without a strong political negotiation process, the 'lean production model' risks sliding into a despotic and less productive mode. In the area of management–worker equity, there is arguably room for improvement at NUMMI. This is possibly one area where the company could temper its excesses with the Volvo's humanistic policy of 'pay for knowledge'. Then both parties win, the company's biggest asset increases in value and the employees pay-packet reflects a proportion of that gain.

The NUMMI experiment is a successful re-interpretation of the 'information is power' syndrome. Information and knowledge are not used as tools to control an irresponsible workforce, nor are they used by the workers as a means to subvert the system for their own ends. Instead, information sharing becomes the fuel that powers a strategy of continuous incremental improvements in efficiency and quality, that will ultimately revolutionize the manufacture of cars:

> Continuous improvement does not have to be based on an escalating appro-priation of worker's know how.
>
> Adler and Cole, 1993[81]

Unfortunately, in any country with a historical aversion to union–man-agement cooperation, the effectiveness of the NUMMI model could be under severe strain. Too much unbalanced management power will immediately exert a negative pressure elsewhere in the system. Eventually, this would become a barrier to effective use of the NUMMI model. At Uddevalla the imbalance was totally the opposite. The primary strategic motivation of attracting good people weighted the negotiation process so much in favour of the workers that performance was subjugated.

There are five very important conclusions to be drawn from this par-ticular study:

1. The evidence summarized in Figs 9.2 and 9.3 justifies the contention that a more balanced and inclusive approach to strategy produces better performance. The more an organization balances strategic dimensions of the wheel the more learning can occur.
2. It is obvious from the comparison between the two plants that progressive paradox resolution is interdependent. The various aspects of strategy feed off one another. If one is poorly interpreted, or out of balance, it adversely affects the others. Reciprocal influence will affect the way the revolution evolves just as much as the individual force of each paradox. (Again it is the

Butterfly Effect in action—sensitive dependence on initial conditions.)

3. The textual description shows that even one lower level tension out of balance can have an identifiable influence on all the paradoxes in the upper level learning cycle. Volvo did not balance personal aspirations with organizational benefits. It cost the company dearly in terms of learning, and financial performance.

4. The case shows how important learning is to the end result of any transformation process. The revolution emerges from many small actions, all creating positive energy towards a common objective.

5. Applying the learning cycle to the two assembly plants shows that interpretation of each strategic aspect is very much contingent on context. The generic paradox wheel is applicable not only to every organization, but also to functions within an organization, and processes within processes. In this respect the strategy process mimics the self-similarity of fractals.

Synthesis, creativity and learning

*The test of a first rate intelligence is the ability
to hold two opposed ideas in the mind at the
same time and still retain the ability to function.*
F Scott Fitzgerald

This book started with the statement that management philosophies of the 1970s and 1980s were inadequate for the 1990s and beyond. It began by saying that we need to radically rethink our approach to management. Of course, this is true in one sense, but as the Bible warns us:

That which has been is what will be. That which is done is what will be done, and there is nothing new under the sun.

Ecclesiastes 1:9

So, what is creativity? How does anyone produce anything new? Einstein, Picasso and Mozart were all creative geniuses. What did they have in common? Was it that they magically transformed their fields, by producing something from nothing? No. What lay at the heart of their great abilities was paradox: two existing ideas that did not at first fit together, until they began to consider new combinations. Paradox and synthesis are parallel themes running through the history of business and non-business theory. Physics, psychology and religion each represent a search for seamless integration in the physical, emotional and spiritual domains, respectively. Each field wrestles with its own '*bêtes noires*'. Physicists wrestle with incompatible theories, such as relativity and quantum mechanics, psychologists grapple with the problems of schizophrenia, and ecclesiastics contend with interpretative divisions in religious thought. There is a universal principle common to them all. Whenever there is division the result is havoc; when perspectives come together there is healing. Creativity is a vital healing aid, and learning is the end product.

Synthesis is always a fundamental part of that process. Research shows that breaking the boundaries of any convention, whether it be scientific, artistic or musical, has always been the product of a mind in which 'two or more opposites were conceived simultaneously, existing side by side—as equally valid, operative and true'.[83] The ultimate learning paradox has come to be known as Hegel's dialectic, after Georg Wilhelm Hegel, a nineteenth century German philosopher. He summarized the problem in three words: thesis, antithesis and synthesis. Thesis, from the Greek word 'to place', means an idea or premiss set in a context; antithesis is its opposite; synthesis transforms the two basic elements and moves them into a new dimension. Most cultures contain this notion of 'Yin and Yang'. Eastern cultures also place great weight on the notion of harmony between them; Western cultures, on the other hand, tend to attribute connotations of good or bad to the values and then make either/or choices between them. This judgemental tendency is what interferes with learning. It breaks the feedback loop, and makes reconciliation impossible. We have to learn to suspend judgement and be more open-minded, when we wrestle with dilemmas.

Business theoreticians in some areas are slowly coming round to the idea that synthesis is the route to the future. Strategy experts are beginning to suggest that the more modes of strategic thinking an organization uses, the better it will do.[84] IT gurus [85] have taken the first steps towards integrating the disconnected strands of information systems planning and, in the field of organizational behaviour, researchers and business writers have also embarked on the journey towards unification. This book has been an attempt to take this trend one stage further. To synthesize on the macro scale across business disciplines.

Fig. 10.1 summarizes the recurring parameters in five of these areas. These are the elements that have been combined to form the process of Evolutionary Revolution—the paradox wheel. The ideas and theories in this book are the basic colours available to the creative manager. The framework in this book is just one way of using them to create a new pattern of light and shade and sharpen the focus a bit. The subsidiary levels of the framework are designed to enrich the management paintbox. With it managers can create their own masterpieces by introducing the missing corporate characteristics into what otherwise would be a stark picture, by applying the relevant tools, techniques and technology to deepen the perspective.

Of course, learning itself inevitably has two sides. One is understanding the old, the other is building the new. It is tempting to associate creative learning with the second option only. By association, transformation would then be turning one's back on the old. But it would be wrong to assume that building the new has nothing to do with understanding the old. If we did that, we would not be reconciling the paradox. History and experience are an integral part of our future. It is impossible to dump one's past like a load of excess baggage. Wiping the slate clean and starting again may seem like the easy solution, but the influence of childhood is not so easily disposed of. In the development of a mature personality, every individual has to work through past experience to understand its influence on the future. So, too, must businesses if they want to transform their character. Breaking the boundaries of business convention requires some radical rethinking about how to handle our inheritance.

| | Historical background | | Today's foreground | |
Strategy	Dimensions of organizational effectiveness	IT problems	Requirements for re-engineering	Facets of learning
1. Leadership control from the top	Direction	Little top management involvement	Top level commitment and involvement	Teacher & vision
2. Structured competitive planning in advance	Control	Not aligned with strategy	Model far-reaching strategic intent	Research plan
3. Resources analysis to optimize total added value	Information	Unquantifiable benefits	Set aggressive targets and track them	Resource availability analysis & intuition
4. Creating internal structural fit	Procedures	Inadequate architecture	Reconfigure work systems & IT platform	Internal prejudices and mind set
5. Establishing cultural norms and standards for stability	Standards	Culturally divided from business	Good communication to change culture	Culture and experience
6. Emergent design based on grassroot initiatives	Independent action	Disenfranchised users	Workers participate and make decisions	Student with freedom to act
7. Opportunistic response to random fortuitous circumstances	Flexibility	Inflexible data structures	Pilot and try new ideas	Openness to risk experimentation trial error
8. Political negotiation between local constituencies and conflicting values	Conflicting interests	Politically naïve	Evaluate stakeholders Readiness to negotiate and compromise	Inquiry and advocacy
9. Deliberately manipulating external environment	Customer shareholders	Blinkered to user/customer needs	Recast external relationships	Environmental influences
10. Logically incremental change	Novelty	Restrictive	A systematic process for change before crisis	Translation mechanism from individual to organization

Fig. 10.1 Recurring patterns in different fields of learning

In the context of this book radical rethinking has not been a rejection of the past, rather it is a synthesis of the divisions in the old to produce a new more encompassing way of thinking. It was suggested earlier that a manager needs to keep both the background and the foreground of his picture in focus. In one sense, the framework in this book allows him to do that. Paradox and business Chaos provide the structure on which to hang the background of strategy, information and technology and organizational behaviour. These are then used to enhance the foreground of re-engineering, learning and ideas management technology, such as Group Decision Support Systems. The end result is a more three-dimensional picture of transformation (Fig. 10.2). By amalgamating knowledge accumulated over many decades and highlighting the divisions, the paradox wheel provides a different lens through which the thinking manager can view operations and look for unique ways to combine the values and heal the wounds in his own organization. Then learning will make transformation occur spontaneously.

In principle, the puzzle is easy to assemble. It simply requires exploiting opposition to give depth to the picture; to view conflict not as an obstacle to getting our own way, but as a springboard to a better way. In practice this is never easy. Differences of opinion can seem to undermine authority or status. Frequently, they create emotional reactions of insecurity. Most people respond by erecting a stronger facade of confidence, in an attempt to convince their opponent and themselves. Even though, subconsciously we might acknowledge the element of truth in our opponent's argument,

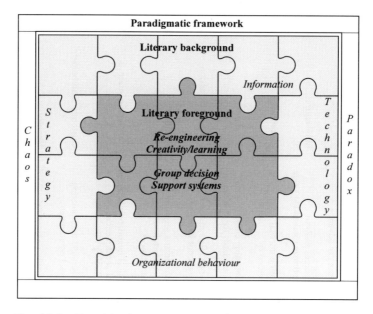

Fig. 10.2   Keeping the components of transformation in focus

it is often difficult to admit it. After all, incomplete knowledge might be seen as a sign of weakness. When power is added to this fatal combination of pride and insecurity, the power holder simply overrules the opposition, but no learning is achieved. Eventually, the balance of power changes, and the opponent gains the upper hand. Then he is poised to come back and knock you sideways with your own success. It is rather like one of those executive toys of the 1970s. Remember the 'Newton's Cradle' (Fig. 10.3) a framework of clashing metallic balls, in which hard, unresisting forces bounce back and forward off one another, exchanging energy and eventually dissipating it in fruitless pendulum-like activity. In fact, this sort of conflict is a limit cycle that creates local turbulence, with no positive effect on the outside world. All rather counterproductive, but it is what we are used to.

So, how do we stop these wasteful clashes. One of the managers, interviewed during the course of this work, made a very telling comment:

> All academics and all consultants, take what is essentially a very rich and complex business problem and slowly take out dimensions, until they are left with a problem that they can solve. The problem is not worth solving, because it contains none of the richness of reality.

Reduce Newton's cradle to two balls, and then disable one of them through the facility of choice! Simple, but *not* effective. In general, the business world has had a rough deal from the purveyors of learning too.

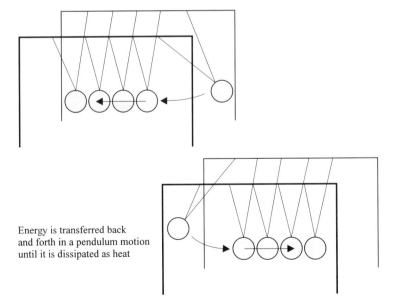

Energy is transferred back and forth in a pendulum motion until it is dissipated as heat

Fig. 10.3   Newton's cradle

Over the past two decades, a whole range of contradictory advice has been introduced to business in the form of management education, but no-one has taught managers how to deal with the conflicts productively. Instead, opposing theories have been left to reverberate around organizations to produce a kind of strategically unplanned Chaos. The time has come to put this right. Instead of breaking down the problem and turning each facet into an autonomous department, a specialist function, or a separate strategic activity, we must take a long hard look at how to integrate disparate dimensions into a seamless and well rounded whole.

Imagine that the metal balls on Newton's cradle are made of plasticine. As soon as they collide they stick together. This eliminates the turbulence, and two balls together become more weighty and influential against outside forces. As soon as we admit that we don't know it all, we have the opportunity to join forces with all the other people who also don't know it all. United, we know more than alone. Eventually, when we merge all the elements of truth, we get a much more complex and accurate picture of reality. Opening the mind to the power of paradox and learning is a question of humility. A requirement to soften the arrogant exterior and see that strength comes from weakness.

We can, of course, temporarily tone down the conflict by separating the horns of the dilemma in time or space. This has been a tolerable solution for many of the organizations mentioned in this book. However, the full benefits of paradoxical management come when we look for synthesis. Synthesis merges two propositions into a logical but superior whole. Of course, having synthesized two dimensions the outcome immediately becomes part of a new paradox to be managed. But that is a benefit not a problem. Learning never stops.

In fact, the interactive combinations cannot be confined within the boundaries of the firm. Even if the paradoxes are resolved for the organization, there are still the idiosyncrasies of society to take into account, as we saw in Chapter 1. Indeed, the factors in Fig. 10.1 and in the paradox wheel are also tensions that have never been satisfactorily resolved with respect to the place of an organization in society.

As Drucker says:

> We already know the central tensions and issues that confront the society of organizations. The tensions created by the community's need for stability and the organization's need to destabilize; the relationship between the individual and the organization, and the responsibilities of one to another; the tension that arises from the organization's need for autonomy and society's stake in the Common Good; the rising demand for socially responsible organizations; the tensions between specialists with specialized knowledge and performance as a team. All of these will be central concerns. They will not be resolved by pronunciamento, philosophy or legislation. They will be resolved where they originate; in the individual organization and in the managers office.
>
> Drucker, 1992[20]

Drucker's tensions (Fig. 10.4) have the same components as Fig. 10.1 and the paradox wheel; it is just that the conflict exists between organizations and the rest of the community.

Most business management books would round off with a concluding section that outlines 'what next'. For a book of this sort, there is no way of predicting 'what next'. The very nature of Chaos makes it impossible. Society's fate depends to a large extent on how well organizations unite values in creative combinations and learn from that experience, both for their own benefit and the benefit of others in the community. Every organization will find its own interpretation of synthesis, and in so doing will create its own unique strategic advantage. For maximum benefit, corporate strategic action should be in the interests of society. This may sound altruistic, but the opposite side of the coin is that the fate of organizations depends upon how well society synthesizes the products of business learning into a fabric that supports ongoing activity. In the end, companies and society must have a symbiotic relationship; people and technology working in harmony, through business, to create a better future for all.

Anyone who has read James Burke's[86] book or seen his television series called simply 'Connections', will know how true this is. Both the book and the TV programme trace the development of some of the technological inventions that have become the mainstays of our society today. Electricity, nuclear fusion, polymers and computers are all the result of

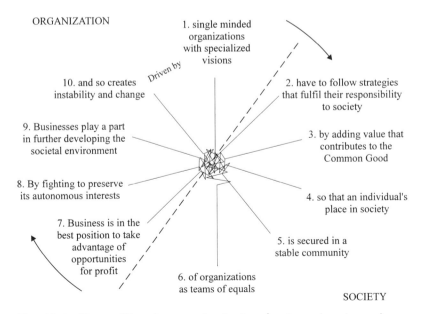

Fig. 10.4   Reconciling the organization's value in society (mapping Drucker's pluralist tensions)

information connections. Information connections brought us to our present and will completely change our future. The pattern of two old facts combining into one new idea has gone on for centuries and will continue for many more. The rate at which paradox and synthesis can work depends on two things—how easily information can be disseminated, and how well people make the necessary connections. This is where technology has made its contribution. Unfortunately, even this creates a terrible paradox. TV, radio, newspapers, and books are all bombarding us with information. There is so much around, and so many ways to distribute it, but only a limited amount of time to absorb it all.

Inevitably, the media invented sound bites. TV presenters, radio announcers, newspaper editors, even book publishers try to simplify the message, compress it and churn it out in digestible chunks. The problem is that sound bites don't fulfil their role. They never really inform. Sometimes they distort, often they frustrate, and always they leave more unsaid than is communicated. Eventually, sound bite communication produces a society of people unable to concentrate for more than 30 seconds without some sort of extra stimulation. Naturally, people react emotionally to issues of child abuse, war, poverty, and violence. Eventually, they either become militant or desensitized, but they never really know the full story behind events, so reactions are misguided and prejudiced, because connections are made based on accurate perceptions. The very medium that is supposed to develop understanding and encourage people to reason, stimulates misunderstanding, emotional reflexes and weakens the ability to reason.

The same happens in organizations. Overburdened senior executives refuse to read memos of more than one page in length, managers make decisions on half the information, constant change becomes desirable because it is a stimulating new challenge that wipes out the old problems. Transforming the organization by improving the information flows speeds up the rate of change, but makes it more difficult to cope with change. Therein lies the paradox of this book. To change or not to change, that is the real question?

Technology has an unbalancing influence on people; development is unsettling. Objectively, this is neither good nor bad. It all depends how the innovations are put into service. In the end, society and organizations have to work it out together. To do this effectively and stimulate further learning, we must explore the paradoxes that shape society, organizations and individual personalities, and find a synthesis that helps us to live in harmony with the science and technology that we have created.

A diagnostic questionnaire for profiling the corporate personality

Profiling your organizational personality

Planning ultimately comes down to one simple task—making choices, contrasting values and ideas in the hope of deciding which will be the most beneficial. Decision makers often instinctively prefer one proposition over another, which inevitably prejudices choice. This questionnaire will tell you just how prejudiced your enterprise is.

Consciously choosing to merge the benefits of two apparently contradictory ideas, increases the chance of developing successful decisions. Further, the more paradoxes an organization reconciles, the more capable of learning it will be. This questionnaire measures the corporate learning capacity, and shows where the mental blockages are.

What you need to do

To complete this questionnaire, all you need to do is circle where, on balance, you believe your enterprise is positioned on *both* scales of 0–10. Remember, the alternatives are not mutually exclusive; it is possible to rate both alternatives simultaneously high or low on the scales.

Below the question, you will find a graph, in which each segment of the question becomes an axis. Use each score as a coordinate on the appropriate axis, and then you can position your enterprise with respect to how well it resolves the paradox. The epithets and metaphors on the face of the graph are there to show the dangers at the extremes, and the goal of reconciliation at point 10/10. Your performance score can be derived by calculating the diagonal distance between your position and point 10/10, by use of Pythagoras' theorem. The lower the score, the better your performance.

Following the five strategic indicators (Fig. A1.1) and the 10 performance inhibitors (Fig. A1.2), you will find 10 questions about the sort of characteristics that will help transformation. These qualities help resolve the paradoxes. Finally, there are 10 questions relating to the track record of information technology investments in your organization, and some demographic data (see Figs. A1.3, A1.4, A1.5). Taken as a whole, the questionnaire will provide a diagnosis of the personality of the company and will act as a benchmark against which to measure ongoing improvement.

It is possible to complete this questionnaire through group discussion, to produce one set of answers that everyone buys into. Alternatively, the questionnaire can be distributed anonymously, and the data can be averaged by group (i.e. department, board, project team) to provide a multi-level picture of what is going on within your enterprise. Computer facilitated completion of the questionnaire is greatly recommended. The use of an electronic meeting system provides the anonymity that will allow honesty and the ability to reach consensus through open discussion, as well as a permanent organizational memory of the path taken.

Ways to use this questionnaire

- To identify which strategic drivers need most attention at the outset of a change programme, by profiling the strengths and weaknesses in the organizational character.
- To stimulate creative thinking on how to change, by considering it in conjunction with the associated analogies and metaphors in Chapters 2 and 4, in the search for solutions to each paradox.
- To identify the missing corporate qualities that need to be encouraged in the new organizational design.
- To help in the selection of which manual and electronic tools and techniques to use. Select the ones that are associated with low scores on the five strategic performance indicators.
- To give a finite structure to the decision making process across all levels of the organization, without inhibiting variety.
- To monitor and measure progress along the most important strategic dimensions, during the change process.
- To help maintain the momentum of change initiatives, by using it to provide quarterly feedback, so that adjustments can be made to the focus of the change initiatives.
- As a specific learning target.
- As a forward looking indicator that has a demonstrable and tangible association with ultimate bottom line performance.

1/6 STRATEGIC PLAYERS   *- Sharing strategic responsibility*

Effective strategy requires two types of input
- a) top level direction to provide coherent
  guidance and control
- b) an abundance of grass root innovations
  in response to chaotic business
  conditions

In the context of strategic responses, please rate your organization,
on BOTH 0 to 10 scales, with respect to how well it

a) provides top level direction
   guidance

LOW	HIGH
0 1 2 3 4 5 6 7 8 9 10

and

b) generates grassroots
   innovations

0 1 2 3 4 5 6 7 8 9 10

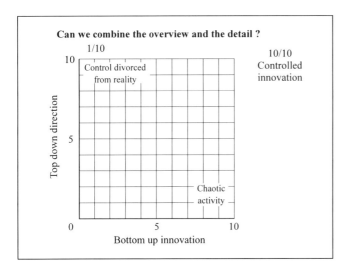

Can we combine the overview and the detail ?

Fig. A1.1(a)   Five strategic performance indicators: strategic players

2/7 COMPETITIVE MANOEUVRABILITY   *- Planning for the unknown*

There are two components of a successful competitive strategy

    a) careful planning and provisioning
       to martial resources for foreseeable events
    b) the opportunistic response to unforeseen
       circumstances occurring at random

In the context of competitive manoeuvring, please rate your
organization, on BOTH 0 to 10 scales, as to how effectively it

LOW	HIGH

a) plans and provisions for
   foreseeable events

0 1 2 3 4 5 6 7 8 9 10

and

b) makes the most of unforeseen
   circumstances

0 1 2 3 4 5 6 7 8 9 10

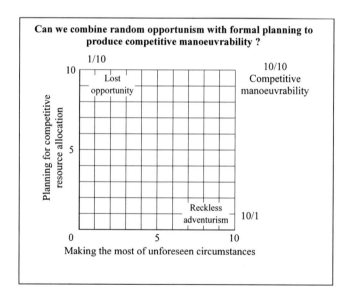

Can we combine random opportunism with formal planning to produce competitive manoeuvrability ?

Fig. A1.1(b)   Five strategic performance indicators: competitive manoeuvrability

3/8 OPERATIONAL VIABILITY   *- Putting ideas into practice*

The most viable strategies for change satisfy two requirements. They

    a) challenge the community to pursue rational ideals
       of excellence

    b) are politically acceptable and realistic
       for member's individual circumstances

In the context of strategic operability, please rate your
organization, on BOTH 0 to 10 scales, as to how effectively it

LOW   HIGH
a) adds value by pushing for theoretical excellence → 0 1 2 3 4 5 6 7 8 9 10
and
b) accommodates political practicalities → 0 1 2 3 4 5 6 7 8 9 10

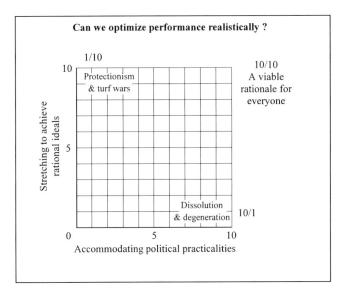

Can we optimize performance realistically ?

1/10 ... Protectionism & turf wars
10/10 A viable rationale for everyone
Stretching to achieve rational ideals
Dissolution & degeneration — 10/1
Accommodating political practicalities

Fig. A1.1(c)   Five strategic performance indicators: operational viability

4/9 ENVIRONMENTAL FITNESS   *- Looking out for internal structure*

A business organizes in order to

    a) have internal support for coping with current
       market conditions
    b) change outside conditions for its own
       competitive advantage

In the context of physical fitness, please rate your organization,
on BOTH 0 to 10 scales, with respect to how effectively

LOW	HIGH
a) its internal structure services external requirements	0 1 2 3 4 5 6 7 8 9 10
	and
b) it uses structure to create a new competitive environment	0 1 2 3 4 5 6 7 8 9 10

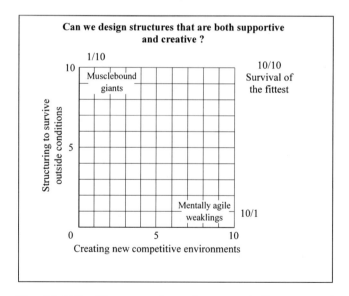

Can we design structures that are both supportive and creative ?

1/10 — Musclebound giants

10/10 Survival of the fittest

Structuring to survive outside conditions

10/1 — Mentally agile weaklings

Creating new competitive environments

Fig. A1.1(d)   Five strategic performance indicators: environmental fitness

5/10 ORGANIZATIONAL ELASTICITY   *- Building unity from diversity*

Resilient organizations develop a supple strength that is made up of two complementary forces

    a) the stabilizing mechanisms that hold everything together but suppress change

    b) the destabilizing activities that encourage change

In the context of strategic elasticity, please rate your organization, on BOTH 0 to 10 scales, with respect to the strength of the

	LOW HIGH
a) stabilizing mechanisms	0 1 2 3 4 5 6 7 8 9 10
	and
b) destabilizing activities	0 1 2 3 4 5 6 7 8 9 10

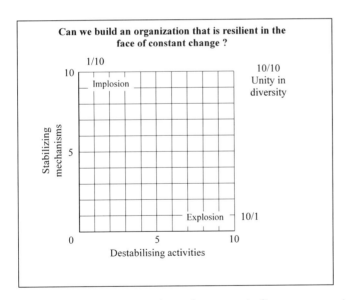

Can we build an organization that is resilient in the face of constant change ?

Stabilizing mechanisms (vertical axis, 0 to 10)
Destabilising activities (horizontal axis, 0 to 10)

1/10 Implosion
10/10 Unity in diversity
10/1 Explosion

Fig. A1.1(e)   Five strategic performance indicators: organizational elasticity

1. TOP DOWN DIRECTION   *- Depth of vision*

    Change must fulfil two objectives

        a) improving short term financial results

        b) improving long term 'ethical' values
           such as quality, trust and social responsibility

    Please rate your organization, on BOTH 0 to 10 scales,
    with respect to the importance attached to

LOW   HIGH
0 1 2 3 4 5 6 7 8 9 10
and
0 1 2 3 4 5 6 7 8 9 10

a) improving short term results

b) improving long term 'ethical'
   values

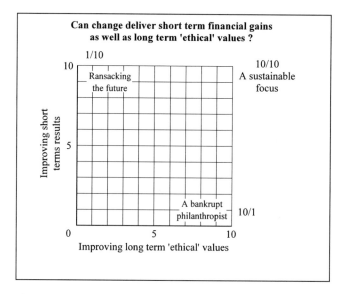

Fig. A1.2(a)   Ten strategic performance inhibitors: top down direction

2. COMPETITIVE PLANNING   *- Competitive acuity*

Incisive strategy allocates scarce cash resources to investments with
the most returns. Information management proposals must compete for
funds against other business activities. Experience tends to make the
benefits of non-IT investments more quantifiable.
Management must prioritize investments on

   a) explicitly quantifiable benefits

   b) a belief that information and technology have an intrinsic,
      but unquantifiable, value as catalyst for profitability

Please rate your organization, on BOTH 0 to 10 scales,
as to the priority management attaches to

   a) explicitly quantifiable benefits
      in investment proposals

LOW	HIGH
0 1 2 3 4 5 6 7 8 9 10	
and	
0 1 2 3 4 5 6 7 8 9 10	

   b) the intrinsic value of information
      management as a catalyst to
      profitability

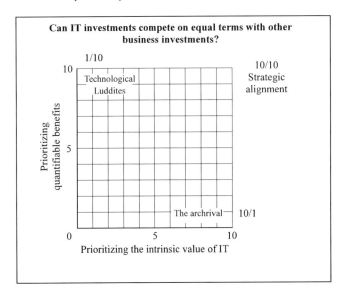

Fig. A1.2(b)   Ten strategic performance inhibitors: competitive
planning

3. GLOBAL RATIONALITY   *- Complete rationality*

In today's chaotic business environment, effective decision makers
need two skills to judge the implications of IT induced business change

　　a) analysis to break down an issue and logically test the
　　　 reasoning behind its changes
　　b) intuition to 'see' the broader implications of
　　　 interacting variables

Please rate your organization, on BOTH 0 to 10 scales,
with respect to the weight attributed to

	LOW　　　　　　HIGH
a) analysis and logical testing of a situation	0 1 2 3 4 5 6 7 8 9 10
	and
b) intuitive judgement of the broader implications	0 1 2 3 4 5 6 7 8 9 10

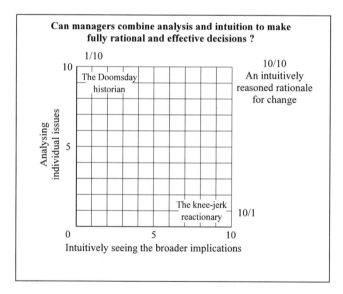

Fig. A1.2(c)　Ten strategic performance inhibitors: global rationality

4. AN INTERNAL FRAMEWORK   *- Structural flexibility*

Organizations have two ways to get value from their information
resources and the supporting technology

  a) centralize for economies of
     scale and integration
  b) decentralize and diversify for variety
     and responsiveness

Please rate your organization, on BOTH 0 to 10 scales,
as to the importance they attach to

a) centralizing authority for economies of scale and integration	LOW HIGH
	0 1 2 3 4 5 6 7 8 9 10
	and
b) decentralizing authority for variety and responsiveness	0 1 2 3 4 5 6 7 8 9 10

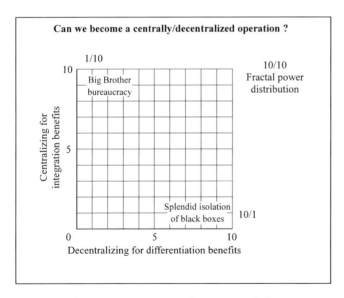

Can we become a centrally/decentralized operation ?

1/10

10/10
Fractal power
distribution

Big Brother
bureaucracy

Centralizing for integration benefits

Splendid isolation
of black boxes   10/1

Decentralizing for differentiation benefits

Fig. A1.2(d) Ten strategic performance inhibitors: an internal
framework

5. SOCIAL NORMS & STANDARDS   *- Communication quality*

Sustaining a coherent response to rapid change in complex
situations requires efficient communication.
There are two components of effective communication

    a) elaborating to avoid ambiguity

    b) abbreviating for the sake of speed

Please rate your organization, on BOTH 0 to 10 scales,
on the level of

	LOW HIGH
a) elaboration to avoid ambiguity	0 1 2 3 4 5 6 7 8 9 10
	and
b) abbreviation to speed up communications	0 1 2 3 4 5 6 7 8 9 10

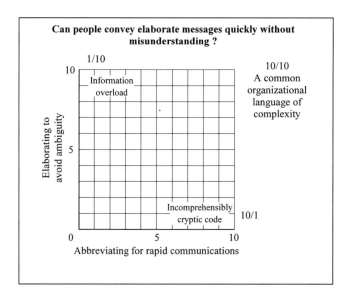

Fig. A1.2(e)   Ten strategic performance inhibitors: social norms and standards

6. BOTTOM UP INITIATIVES   *- Participative scope*

Productive participation requires two qualities

a) timely decision making to keep alternatives to
   manageable proportions
b) widespread discussion to expand input

Please rate your organization, on BOTH 0 to 10 scales,
with respect to the importance attributed to

LOW	HIGH

a) decisiveness to reduce alternatives
   to manageable proportions

0 1 2 3 4 5 6 7 8 9 10

and

b) widespread discussion to expand
   input

0 1 2 3 4 5 6 7 8 9 10

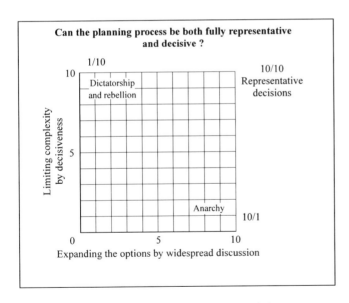

Fig. A1.2(f)   Ten strategic performance inhibitors: Bottom-up
initiatives

7. RANDOM OPPORTUNISM   *- Goal sharing*

Continued support for the uncertainty of ongoing change requires those involved to keep believing that the quest for benefits is worthwhile. In any change there are two stakeholders

   a) those who are fighting for organizational benefits

   b) those who are fighting for their own needs and aspirations

Please rate your organization, on BOTH 0 to 10 scales, as to the priority given to

	LOW										HIGH
a) getting organizational benefits	0	1 2 3 4 5 6 7 8 9 10									
	and										
b) fulfilling personal needs and aspirations	0	1 2 3 4 5 6 7 8 9 10									

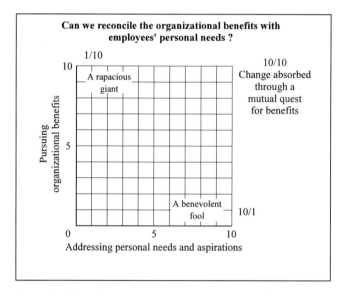

Can we reconcile the organizational benefits with employees' personal needs ?

1/10

10 — A rapacious giant

10/10
Change absorbed through a mutual quest for benefits

Pursuing organizational benefits

5

A benevolent fool — 10/1

0   5   10

Addressing personal needs and aspirations

Fig. A1.2(g)   Ten strategic performance inhibitors: random opportunism

8. LOCAL POLITICAL NEGOTIATION   *- Arbitration skills*

Transformation change requires experts to re-evaluate many of
the fundamental principles of operation. When this happens,
specialists face two challenges

    a) defending the value of experience and conventional
       principles in resistance to change

    b) acceding that traditional principles are outmoded
       in the interests of learning

Please rate your organization, on BOTH 0 to 10 scales,
as to

LOW	HIGH

a) how strongly specialists defend their
    expertise in resistance to change

    0 1 2 3 4 5 6 7 8 9 10

and

b) how readily specialists accede in
    the interests of learning

    0 1 2 3 4 5 6 7 8 9 10

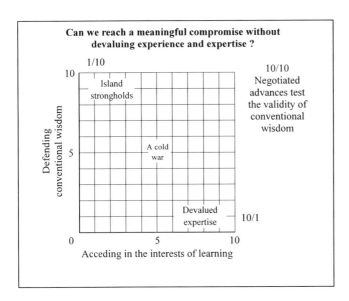

Fig. A1.2(h)   Ten strategic performance inhibitors: local political
negotiation

9. EXTERNAL REQUIREMENTS   *- Service quality*

Satisfying the demands of constantly changing external
conditions requires two qualities

    a) precision and attention to detail

    b) a rapid response

Please rate your organization, on BOTH 0 to 10 scales,
with respect to the importance of

LOW		HIGH

a) precision and attention to detail | 0 1 2 3 4 5 6 7 8 9 10 |

and

b) a speedy response | 0 1 2 3 4 5 6 7 8 9 10 |

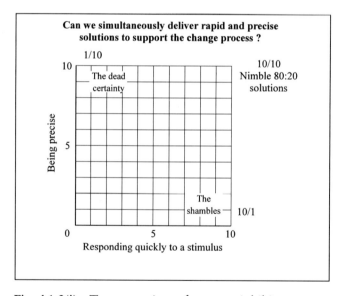

Fig. A1.2(i)   Ten strategic performance inhibitors: external
requirements

10. ORGANIZATIONAL CHANGE   *- Technological utility*

Information and technology developments offer two types of
return on investment

    a) safe returns through greater efficiency and operational
       support
    b) risky returns that differentiate the business

Please rate your organization, on BOTH 0 to 10 scales,
as to the perceived importance of

LOW	HIGH
a) safe support for greater efficiency	0 1 2 3 4 5 6 7 8 9 10
	and
b) taking a risk to transform business operations	0 1 2 3 4 5 6 7 8 9 10

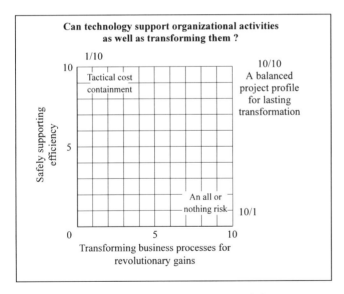

**Can technology support organizational activities
as well as transforming them ?**

Fig. A1.2(j)   Ten strategic performance inhibitors: organizational
change

Please rate the PERFORMANCE of your organization in fulfilling the following criteria by circling the appropriate number on the scale of 0 to 10	Very poor Excellent
1. A commitment to empowerment and openness to criticism	0 1 2 3 4 5 6 7 8 9 10
2. Managing information as a strategic resource	0 1 2 3 4 5 6 7 8 9 10
3. Finding the synergy between apparently unrelated decisions	0 1 2 3 4 5 6 7 8 9 10
4. Building an effective structure for information collection and distribution	0 1 2 3 4 5 6 7 8 9 10
5. Sharing information effectively	0 1 2 3 4 5 6 7 8 9 10
6. Executing change in an environment of trust, integrity and respect	0 1 2 3 4 5 6 7 8 9 10
7. Creating a supportive environment for risk taking	0 1 2 3 4 5 6 7 8 9 10
8. Challenging constraints and prejudices	0 1 2 3 4 5 6 7 8 9 10
9. Discriminating between good and bad ideas	0 1 2 3 4 5 6 7 8 9 10
10. Transforming operations in progressive stages	0 1 2 3 4 5 6 7 8 9 10

Fig. A1.3 Ten desirable qualities for a revolutionary

Please rate the PERFORMANCE of your organization in accruing the following benefits of IT enabled transformation by circling the appropriate number on the scale of 0 to 10	Very poor Excellent
1. Information services enable the fulfilment of strategic organizational objectives	0 1 2 3 4 5 6 7 8 9 10
2. Information technology delivers integrated services to all parts of the business operation	0 1 2 3 4 5 6 7 8 9 10
3. Information technology adds value to our business processes	0 1 2 3 4 5 6 7 8 9 10
4. The internal IT architecture permits rapid and easy adaptation to changes in the environment	0 1 2 3 4 5 6 7 8 9 10
5. Information systems increase the level of effective communication across functional and institutional boundaries	0 1 2 3 4 5 6 7 8 9 10
6. Developing upon localized innovations to give wider corporate value brings significant competitive edge	0 1 2 3 4 5 6 7 8 9 10
7. Broad information sharing stimulates many unplanned but beneficial innovations	0 1 2 3 4 5 6 7 8 9 10
8. Information technology is used to change the way the business operates internally	0 1 2 3 4 5 6 7 8 9 10
9. Information technology improves customer satisfaction with our service	0 1 2 3 4 5 6 7 8 9 10
10. Information technology is used to change the dynamics of the industry	0 1 2 3 4 5 6 7 8 9 10

Fig. A1.4   Ten measures of benefits accrual

Now please give us some general background data

1. From the following general groupings please indicate the position you hold in the enterprise* (*please take enterprise to mean the business entity serviced by the closest Information Service Dept) General Manager/CEO/President/Managing Director Strategic Planning Officer[+] Senior Information Systems or Technology Officer[+] Other functional Officer[+] ([+]where officer can mean director or manager)	Please tick the appropriate box

2. Please indicate the net revenue of the enterprise* for which you work (for public services please use total expenditure)	Million £'s

3. Please state the net profit before tax for revenue in 2	Million £'s

4. Please indicate on the following list how you would classify your enterprise by industry category 1 Financial Services/Investment 2 Retailing 3 Public Service 4 Manufacturing 5 Distribution 6 IT and communications 7 Professional/Consultancy 8 Educational 9 Other, please specify ...	Please tick the appropriate box

5. Please rate your enterprise as to the overall effectiveness of its use of information technology													
Very poor	0	1	2	3	4	5	6	7	8	9	10		Very good

Name _____   Title _____
Company Name _____
Address _____

Town _____   County _____   Postcode _____
Phone No (_____) _____

Fig. A1.5   Background data

Organizations that participated in the research*

AAH Holdings plc
ADT Security Systems
AI Solutions Ltd
All Business Systems
Alliance & Leicester Building Society
Allied Dunbar Assurance plc
Anglia Television Ltd
Armstrong World Industries
Armstrong Europe Sevices
Associated Newspapers
ASW Ltd
AT & T Istel Ltd
BAA plc
Bank of England
Bank of Ireland
Barclays Bank plc
BET plc
Birmingham Midshires Building Society
BMW (GB) Ltd
BP Oil Ltd
Bradford and Bingley Building Society
British Aerospace plc
British Alcan Aluminium plc
British Gas North Eastern
British Steel Corporation
British Telecommunications plc
Bullough plc
BUPA
Canon (UK) Ltd
Caterpillar (UK) Ltd
CCTA
Central Independent Television

Charterhouse Bank Ltd
Christian Salvesen plc
CIN Management Ltd
Clerical & Medical Investment Group
Coats Viyella plc
Coca-Cola & Schweppes Beverages Ltd
Comet Ltd
Continental Can Co UK Ltd
County Natwest Ltd
Credit Lyonnais Capital Markets
Credit Suisse First Boston Ltd
Dairy Crest Foods
Department of Health and Social Services
Dixons Stores Group
Dowty Group
Du Pont UK
DVOIT
East Sussex County Council
Employment Service
Ford Motor Credit Company Ltd
Friends Provident
GA Life
George Wimpey plc
GKN Group Services Ltd
Glaxo Holdings plc
Great Mills (Retail) Ltd
Guinness Brewing Ltd
Guinness Mahon Holdings plc
H & R Johnson Tiles Ltd
Henderson Administration Group plc

*With grateful thanks for their contributions.

Henderson Investment Services
Hewlett Parkard Ltd
Hill Samuel Bank Ltd
Hogg Robinson plc
Honeywell Control Systems
HTV Group plc
IAEA
IBM (UK) Ltd
IPC Magazines Ltd
ITN
ITNET Ltd
J Henry Schroder Wagg & Co
J Wedgewood & Sons Ltd
Jessups plc
John Lewis Partnership
Laura Ashley Group Operations
Laurentian Life plc
Legal & General Group plc
Lehman Brothers
Lex Services plc
London & Edinburgh Trust plc
Lucas Engineering Systems
Marks & Spencer plc
Marley Roof Tiles Co Ltd
Midland Bank Plc
Municipal Mutual Insurance Ltd
National Westminster Bank plc
Newey & Eyre Ltd
Next Computer Services (Grattan plc)
NFC plc
Norwich Winterthur Group
Pergamon Press plc
PHH Europe
Phillips Electronics
Phillips Petroleum Co UK Ltd
Pitney Bowes plc
Port of London Authority
PPC
Prime Computer (UK) Ltd
Provident Financial Group plc
Prudential Corporation plc
Quality Street Ltd
Reed International plc
Reed Regional Newspapers Ltd

Renault UK Ltd
RHM Computing Ltd
Roberts M Douglas Holdings plc
Royal Bank of Scotland plc
Royal London Mutual Insurance Society Ltd
Salisbury Health Authority
Seeboard plc
Sefton Metropolitan Borough Council
SG Warburg Group plc
Short Brothers
Siemens Nixdorf
Skandia Life Assurance Co Ltd
Sketchley Vending
Skipton Building Society
Sony (UK) Ltd
Sphere Drake Insurance Ltd
STC plc
Sterling Winthrop Group Ltd
Superdrug Stores plc
Surrey County Council
Swiss Bank Corporation
Taylor Woodrow Services Ltd
Thames Water Authority
The BOC Group plc
The Littlewoods Organisations plc
The Morgan Crucible Company plc
Top Rank Clubs Ltd
Town & County Building Society
Trafalgar House Information Systems Ltd
TSB Banking and Insurance
Unipart Group Ltd
United Glass Ltd
VAG (UK) Ltd
Vaux Group
WH Smith
W & P Retail Services Ltd
Weir Group Management Systems
Westbury plc
YJ Lovell Group Services Ltd
Yorkshire Building Society
Yorkshire Water Services Ltd

Technological support for the learning organization

Sophisticating electronic meeting systems

Name	Supplier	Function	Operating system
Group Systems V	Ventana Corporation, Tucson Arizona 1 (602) 325 8228	Multiple tools for any time/any place ideas generation and decision support	MS-DOS
Vision Quest	Collaborative Technologies (US), Austin Texas 1 (512) 794 8858		MS-DOS
EIES2	NJ Institute of Technology, New Jersey 1 (201) 596 3388		UNIX
Team Focus	IBM—contact local sales office	Synchronous meeting support	MS-DOS

E-mail type communication organizers

Name	Supplier	Function	Operating System
Lotus Notes	Lotus Development Corporation, Cambridge Mass. 1 (617) 577 8500	Distributed database and agenda management	MS-DOS
Information Lens	Sloan School of Management MIT, Cambridge Mass.	Filtering, sorting and prioritizing messages	Xerox 1100
ForComment	Broderbund Software Direct, San Rafael California 1 (415) 492 3500	Distribution group document authoring	MS-DOS
Higgins	Enable Software Higgins Group, Ballston Lake New York 1 (518) 877 8600	Networked E-mail database	MS-DOS & PS2

E-mail type communication organizers *(continued)*

Name	Supplier	Function	Operating System
The Co-ordinator	Action Technologies, Emeryville California 1 (415) 654 4444	Message intensive work group scheduler	MS-DOS & Novell
Office Express/ Grape VINE	Institute of IT (Australia) 2 389 3800		DEC-VAX

Group prioritizing and consensus

Name	Supplier	Function	Operating System
Option Finder	Option Technologies, Mendota Heights Minnesota 1 (612) 450 1700	Voting and multiple criteria ranking	MS-DOS
Consensus Builder	Magic 7 Software, Los Altos California 1 (415) 941 2616	Group conflict resolution against personal standards	Expert 87
Participate	Eventures Ltd, Allentown PA 1 (215) 770 0650	Facilitates coordination, cooperation, collaboration, conflict management and competitive agreement contact vendor	
Syzygy	Information Research Corp, Charlottesville Virginia 1 (804) 979 8191	Project scheduling and budgeting	contact vendor
Who–What– When enterprise	Chronos Software, San Francisco California 1 (415) 626 4244	Group prioritising and scheduling	contact vendor

Ideas exploration and theme finding

Name	Supplier	Function	Operating System
COPE	University of Strathclyde, Scotland 41 522 4400	Cognitive mapping	MS-DOS, Windows
RESOLVER	The Saunders Consulting Group, PO Box 7014 Station J Ottawa, Ontario Canada Tel: 1 613 592 4767 Fax: 1 613 592 0388	Cognitive mapping	Apple

Ideas exploration and theme finding *(continued)*

Name	Supplier	Function	Operating System
Agenda	Lotus Development Corporation, Cambridge Mass. 1 (617) 577 8500	Concept exploration	MS-DOS
Object Lens	Sloan School of Management MIT	Framing objects into themes	contact vendor
Hypertext	There are various programming languages currently available, such as HyperBase—Cogent Software 1st Class HT (Al Corp.) Knowledge Pro Windows— Knowledge Garden Level 5 Object—Information Builders Nexpert Object—Neuron Data Notecards—Xerox Lisp Hypercard—Clarion Software Visual Basic—Microsoft	All of these allow users to explore connections and intuitive links between ideas and concepts	

EIS/ESS builders

Name	Supplier	Function	Operating System
EIS-Track Executive Decisions	IBM		mainframe main-frame/PC
Focus EIS Level 5	Information Builders 1250 Broadway New York NY 10001 USA	Executive Information Access	PC
Express EIS Express PC	Information Resources 200 Fifth Avenue Waltham MA 02254		mainframe PC
EIS Toolkit	Micro Strategy One Commerce Center Wilmington DE 19811		PC

Bibliography

1. Hamel. G. and Prahalad, C.K. 'Strategic intent'. *Harvard Business Review*, **67**(3), May/June, 1989.
2. Hampden Turner, C. *Charting the Corporate Mind*, Blackwell, Oxford, 1990.
3. Peters, T.J. and Waterman, R.H. *In Search of Excellence; Lessons from America's Best Run Companies*, Harper & Row, New York, 1982.
4. Gleick, J. *Chaos: Making a New Science*, Cardinal/Sphere Books, London, 1987.
5. Percival I. 'Chaos, a science for the real world' in N. Hall (Ed.) *Exploring Chaos*, W.W. Norton & Co., New York, 1991.
6. Lorenz, E. 'Predictability; does the flap of a butterfly wing in Brazil set off a tornado in Texas?' Address to the Annual Meeting of the American Association for the Advancement of Science, 1979.
7. Stewart, I. *Does God Play Dice? The New Mathematics of Chaos*, Penguin Books, London, 1990.
8. Mandelbrot, B.B. *The Fractal Geometry of Nature*, W.H.Freeman & Co., New York, 1977.
9. Casti, J.L. *Complexification: Explaining the Paradoxical World Through the Science of Surprise*, Harper Collins, New York, 1994.
10. Stacey, R.D. *The Chaos Frontier. Creative Strategic Control for Business*, Butterworth-Heinemann Ltd., Oxford, 1991.
11. Stacey, R.D. *Strategic Management and Organisational Dynamics*, Pitman, London, 1993.
12. Hamel, G. and Prahalad, C.K. *Competing for the Future*, Harvard Business Books, Boston, 1994.
13. Pascale, R.T. *Managing on the Edge. How the Smartest Companies Use Conflict to Stay Ahead*, Touchstone Simon & Schuster, New York, 1990.
14. Toffler, A. *Powershift. Knowledge, Wealth & Violence at the Edge of the 21st Century*, Bantam, New York, 1990.
15. Hammer, M.J. 'Re-engineering work: don't automate, obliterate', *Harvard Business Review*, **68**(4), July/August, 1990.
16. Nadler, D., in Thackray, J. 'Fads fixes and fictions', *Management Today*, June, 1993.

17. Scott Morton M.S. (Ed.) *The Corporation of the 1990s. Information Technology and Organisational Transformation*, Oxford University Press, Oxford, 1991.
18. Toffler, A. *Future Shock*, Bantam Books, New York, 1970.
19. Rockart, J.F. and Scott Morton, M.S. 'Implications of changes in information technology for corporate strategy', *Interfaces*, **14**(1), January/February, 1984.
20. Drucker, P. 'The new society of organisations', *Harvard Business Review*, 70(5), September/October, 1992.
21. Drucker, P. 'A turnaround primer', *Wall Street Journal*, 28 July, 1993.
22. Blumenthal, B. and Haspeslagh, P. 'Towards a definition of corporate transformation', *Sloan Management Review*, 35(3), Spring, 1994.
23. Garvin, D.A. 'Building a Learning Organisation', *Harvard Business Review*, 71(4), July/August, 1993.
24. Toffler, A. *The Third Wave*, Pan Books, London, 1980.
25. Argyris, C. 'Double loop learning in organisations', *Harvard Business Review*, 55(5), September/October, 1977.
26. Haeckel, S.H. and Nolan, R.L. 'Managing by wire', *Harvard Business Review*, 71(5), September/October, 1993.
27. De Geus, A. 'Planning as learning', *Harvard Business Review*, 66(2), March/April, 1988.
28. Bartlett, C.A. and Ghoshall, S. 'Managing across borders: new organisational responses', *Sloan Management Review*, 29(1), Fall, 1987.
29. Handy, C. *The Age of Paradox*, Harvard Business School Press, Boston, 1994. (The same book in the UK was published under the thought provoking title of *The Empty Raincoat*.)
30. Von Simpson, E.M. 'The centrally decentralized IS organization: how to centralise the information systems function without losing responsiveness to technology users', *Harvard Business Review*, 68(4), July/August, 1990.
31. Handy, C. *The Age of Unreason*, Business Books Ltd, Century Hutchinson, London, 1989.
32. Hampden Turner, C. and Trompenaars, A. *The Seven Cultures of Capitalism*, Doubleday, New York, 1993.
33. Hampden Turner, C. *Maps of the Mind*, Macmillan Books, New York, 1981.
34. Hampden Turner, C. *Corporate Culture: From Vicious to Virtuous Circles*, Economist Books, London, 1990.
35. Mitroff, I.I. and Featheringham, T.R. 'On systemic problem solving and the error of the third kind', *Behavioural Science*, **19**, 1974.
36. Hampden Turner, C. 'An elusive sense of wholeness', unpublished paper written for Coopers & Lybrand, Henley, December, 1993.

37. Hall, G., Rosenthal, J. and Wade, J. 'How to make Re-engineering really work', *Harvard Business Review*, **71**(6), November–December, 1993.

38. Burton Swanson, E. 'Rationality and politics in information system design and implementation. A juxtaposition of two views', *Accounting Organisations and Society*, 8(2/3), 1983.

39. Quinn Mills, D. and Friesen, B. 'The learning organisation', *European Management Journal*, **10**(2), 1992.

40. Weick, K. and Daft, R.L. 'Towards a model of organisations as interpretation systems', *Academy of Management Review*, **9**(2), 1984.

41. Janis, I. *Victims of Group Think*, Houghton Mifflin, Boston, 1972.

42. Greve, W.H., Starbuck, A. and Hedberg, B.L.T. 'Responding to crisis'. *Journal of Business Administration*, **9**(2), 1978.

43. Weick, K.E. *The Social Psychology of Organising*, Addison Wesley, Reading, MA, 1979.

44. Short, J.E. and Venkatraman, N. 'Beyond business process redesign: redefining Baxter's business network', *Sloan Management Review*, 34(1), 1992.

45. Hamel, G. and Prahalad, C.K. 'Strategic Intent', *Harvard Business Review*, **67**(3), May/June, 1989.

46. Hamel, G. and Prahalad, C.K. 'Strategy as stretch and leverage', *Harvard Business Review*, **71**(3), March/April, 1993.

47. Nonaka, I. 'The knowledge creating company', *Harvard Business Review*, **69**(6), November/December, 1991.

48. Handy, C. 'Balancing corporate power: a new federalist paper', *Harvard Business Review*, **70**(6), November/December, 1992.

49. Argyris, C. *Strategy Change and Defensive Routines*, Ballinger, USA, 1985.

50. Argyris, C. 'Teaching smart people how to learn', *Harvard Business Review*, **69**(3), May/June, 1991.

51. Senge, P.M. *The Fifth Discipline. The Art and Practise of the Learning Organisation*, Century Business Books, London, 1990.

52. Stacey, R.D. *Managing Chaos. Dynamic Business Strategies in an Unpredictable World*, Kogan Page, London, 1992.

53. Miles, R.E. and Snow, C.C. 'Organisational fit' extracted from 'Fit, failure and the Hall of Fame', *California Management Review*, **26**(3), 1984, and republished in *Organisational Theory*, D. Pugh (Ed.), Penguin Books, London, 1990.

54. Byrne, J.A. 'The virtual corporation', *Business Week*, 8 February, 1993.

55. Grindley, K. *Managing IT at Board Level. The Hidden Agenda Exposed*, Pitman, London, 1991.

56. Stacey, R.D. *Dynamic Strategic Management for the 1990s. Balancing Opportunism and Business Planning*, Kogan Page, London, 1990.
57. Rothfeder, J. 'CIO is starting to stand for Career Is Over', *Business Week*, 26 February, 1990.
58. Elbow, P. *Embracing Contraries, Explorations in Learning and Teaching*, Oxford University Press, Oxford, 1986.
59. Simon, H.A. 'Making management decisions—the role of intuition and emotion', *Academy of Management Executive*, February, 1987.
60. Etzioni, A. 'Humble decision making', *Harvard Business Review*, 67(4), July/August, 1989.
61. Davenport, T.H., Eccles, R.G and Prusak, L. 'Information politics', *Sloan Management Review*, 34(1), Fall, 1992.
62. Keen, P.G.W. *Every Manager's Guide to Information Technology—a Glossary of Terms*, Harvard Business School Press, Boston, 1991.
63. Conner, D. 'Building a resilient culture for accelerated technological change', presentation to the annual SIM conference, Los Angeles, 20 October, 1992.
64. Leonard Barton, D. 'The factory as a learning laboratory', *Sloan Management Review*, 34(1), 1992.
65. McKenzie, J. 'Managing for benefits: lessons for the future', Coopers & Lybrand IT Partnership report, 1991.
66. Kearns, D.T. and Adler, D.A. *Prophets in the Dark. How Xerox Reinvented Itself and Beat Back the Japanese*, Harper Collins, New York, 1992.
67. Reichheld, F.F. 'Loyalty based management', *Harvard Business Review*, 71(2), March/April, 1993.
68. Harris, K. 'Productivity, can America win?', speech at SIM annual conference, Los Angeles, 19 October, 1992.
69. McKenzie, J. 'Chaos, paradox and learning—key composites in the revolutionary change process; towards a more holistic, strategic paradigm for transformation', PhD thesis, Henley Management College, November, 1994.
70. Sprague, R.H and Watson, H.J. *Decision Support Systems—Putting Theory into Practise*, Prentice Hall, Englewood Cliffs, 1993.
71. Quinn, Post, B. 'Building the business case for Groupware', Boeing Best Paper Award, summarized in Groupware Report, University of Georgia, 1992.
72. Etzioni, A. 'Humble decision making', *Harvard Business Review*, 67(4), July/August, 1989.
73. Sigismund Huff, A. (Ed.) *Mapping Strategic Thought*, John Wiley, New York, 1990.
74. The IT Partnership Report. *Open Systems—Successful Migration*, Coopers & Lybrand, London, February, 1993.

75. Rockart, J.F. and Crescenzi, A.D. 'Engaging top management in information technology', *Sloan Management Review*, **25**(4), Summer, 1984.
76. Livingston, D.G. and Berkes, L.J. *Netmap—an Innovative Diagnostic Tool*, Brochure, 1993.
77. Coopers & Lybrand. 'Systems building Issue 2—Custardware', IT Partnership bulletin, 1993.
78. Dennis, A. 'Electronic meeting systems and business process modelling', unpublished study, University of Georgia, 1993.
79. Burke, G. and Peppard, J. 'Business process redesign; research directions', *Journal of Corporate Transformation*, 1994.
80. Berggren, C. 'Point/counterpoint: NUMMI vs Uddevalla', *Sloan Management Review*, **35**(2), 1994.
81. Adler, P.S. and Cole, R.E. 'Designed for learning—a tale of two auto plants', *Sloan Management Review*, Spring, 1993.
82. Adler, P.S. 'Time and motion regained', *Harvard Business Review*, **71**(1), January/February, 1993.
83. Rothenburg, A. *The Emerging Goddess*, University of Chicago Press, Chicago, 1979.
84. Hart, S.L. 'An integrative framework for strategy making processes', *Academy of Management Review*, **17**(2), 1992.
85. Earl, M.J. *Management Strategies for Information Technology*, Prentice Hall, London, 1989.
86. Burke, J. *Connections*, Macmillan, London, 1978.

Index